Your Pet Called

YOUR PET CALLED

*More Than 70 Stories Your Pets Told Me
to Heal Your Soul and Mend Your Heart*

DR. MONICA DIEDRICH

Published By Two Paws Up Press
Anaheim, California, USA • 2020

FIRST EDITION

Your Pet Called: More Than 70 Stories Your Pets Told Me to Heal Your Soul and Mend Your Heart

Copyright © 2020 by Dr. Monica Diedrich

PUBLISHED BY TWO PAWS UP PRESS

Website: PetCommunicator.com
Phone: (714) 772-2207 (does not accept text messages)
Email: drmonica@petcommunicator.com
MSN Messenger: drmonicadiedrich
Skype: drmonicadiedrich1
Facebook chat: Dra Monica Dulman Diedrich

All photographs used with permission from pet parents.

Back cover & book interior design by Yolie Hernandez (MultimediaPublishingProject.com | Phone: 480-939-9689)

Paperback ISBN 13: 978-0-9794486-4-5
E-book ISBN 13: 978-0-9794486-5-2

All rights reserved, including the right of reproduction in whole or in part in any form.

Printed in the United States of America.

Dedication

This book is dedicated to two people whom I love and want to honor: my husband, Albert Diedrich, and my ghostwriter/editor, Colleen Fox.

Colleen has known me for 20 years. She knows me so well that she can take anything I write in draft form and finesse it with my "voice." She reads all the material not only once or twice, but as many times as necessary, to be certain that everything is exactly what I want to have it say. She has the patience to check, correct, re-write, and re-check until she knows intuitively that everything is just the way it should be.

Albert, my husband, has never read even one of my six books because he doesn't have to read what I write to believe in me, and because he's listened to me tell so many of my stories over the years. He was the first one to understand me when I was just 14 years old, more than 50 years ago, and he's trusted me ever since.

He wakes me up with a kiss every morning, makes my breakfast, and then takes me for a walk with our dogs so he can be sure I get my exercise for the day. He knows when I get back that I'll go to my "cave" (my office) where I'll remain for the rest of the day, taking care of others. He understands that this is my life's mission, and he doesn't complain about my long hours, phone calls on weekends and holidays, and shortened vacations.

Although Albert and Colleen are totally unrelated, they do have something special in common. They are both the wind beneath my wings. I couldn't have written this book without either of them. So I want to thank both of them from the bottom of my heart because they each allowed me to be me, to soar, and to fly without worries.

I also know that one of them will never read this dedication, but that's OK, because he'll be taking care of me instead!

Love to both of you, and a huge Thank You!

Contents

INTRODUCTION .... **XIII**
    How do they do it? xiii

PROLOGUE .... **XVII**
    Where Do Animals Go When They Die? xvii
    How Soon After Passing Is an Animal in Spirit Ready to Communicate? . . xx
    How Do Dogs and Cats See Pets in Spirit? xxii

YOUR PET CALLED
Troy 3
Nancy and Kay 19
Dr. Jacquie 22

MESSAGES FROM SPIRIT PROVIDE HEARTWARMING VALIDATIONS
Molly Lisa 31
Ashley 44
Casper 48

SIGNS FROM SPIRIT
Signs from Spirit 55
Harry 56
Chobisuke-san 60

Candela 65
Sukie 72
Daisy 74
More About Signs from Pets in Spirit 76

SOUL MATES AND LIFE MISSIONS
Rocco 81
Charlie. 93
Kirby, Sukie, and Batley 99

REINCARNATION, LIFE MISSIONS, AND LOVE
Rokki 115
Bella 123

PETS AS BRIDGES TO HUMANS IN SPIRIT
Communicating with Humans. 131
Sandy, Bear, and Sweet Pea 132
Heidi 144
A Special Human Spirit Interrupts a Dog's Communication 147

LESSONS LEARNED AND TEN YEARS OF GROWTH IN SPIRIT
Boadicea 151
Ishtar 168
Freya 180
Deuteronomy 184

IMMEDIATE FEEDBACK
The Benefit of Immediate Feedback 193
Mardi Gras, Gumbo, Bayou, and Satchmo 196
Pluto 205

PERSONALITIES
Reiki 213
Opus and Alex 230

Tinker	235
Stevie	240
He Never Does That!	242

UNIQUE CASES

Cinco and Dion	249
Horton	252
Kismet	255

CHANGING A BEHAVIOR . . . OR NOT!

Changing Pet Behaviors	263
Plato	265
Lucy	268
Luna	272
Gaby	277
Lily Mae	286
Leo	289
Ace	293
DJ	307

GIVING SUGGESTIONS AND GETTING RESULTS

Spence and Harold	317
Sneakers and Georgie	320

PETS AS DIAGNOSTICIANS FOR THEMSELVES AND OTHERS

Sully	327
Rocky	329
Bacardi	331
MacKenzy	336
Sweet Pea	342
Cali	345
Bear	351

REMOTE HEALING
Kintaro 363

LOST, STOLEN, OR PRESUMED DEAD
Why Lost Pet Cases Are So Difficult............................ 371
Maggie's Mexican Adventure 376
Vinny.. 384
Soxsie 388
Murphy 395
Moe.. 401
Franny.. 414
Timmy... 418
Franklin.. 420
Chloey.. 424
Thunder Beans.. 430

LETTING GO IS HARD TO DO
Aiko... 437
Paquito... 444
Zac.. 448
Wilfork 452
Thoughts About Letting Go 456

COPING WITH GRIEF
Hana and Snow 461
Coping With Extreme Grief..................................... 465

ALL ABOUT ANIMAL COMMUNICATION
Picture Telepathy 475
Some Frequently Asked Questions and Answers 478
Puzzles, Images, and PTSD Reactions 482
When Pet Parents Help to Complete the Translation 485
Conveying Difficult Information 489

CONTENTS

The Do's and Don'ts of a Consultation 492
Pictures. 498
What About Skeptics? 516
How You Can Communicate More Effectively with Your Own Pets . . . 519
Communicating with Pets in Spirit. 521

Epilogue 524

Acknowledgments 527

Author's Note 529

About the Author 531

Introduction

Contrary to what most people think, animals DO have their own language, and they've been trying to communicate with us since the beginning of time.

Many people laugh at the idea that animals have feelings, needs, and wishes, or that they can express empathy and love, or that they can purposefully decide the where, when, and how of their actions. But animals most definitely do, and they can often tell us very clearly what's on their minds.

How do they do it?

Animals are able to send pictures to each other, and to humans, but in today's busy society, our minds are usually too preoccupied to be able to understand the subtleties of picture communication.

Instead, we go about our lives wishing we *could* communicate with our pets, when in fact, they've been busily trying to communicate with us ever since they came to live with us. We just don't remember how to receive the information they're sending.

When our human ancestors communicated with each other mainly by grunting and pointing, they, too, were able to communicate, even over long distances, by sending and receiving information in the form of pictures. These images were used to convey something important they wanted to say.

Picture language, or "picture telepathy" as I've named it, was mainly used as a survival tool. Humans and animals would send pictures of where the food and water supplies were, and where the best grazing areas were when they needed to move the herd from one place to another. They could also warn each other about approaching storms or other dangers.

All species were able to communicate very effectively with each other using pictures this way.

Nowadays, though, picture language is all but forgotten by humans, except maybe by children. Their minds are so uncluttered that they easily receive the pictures animals are always sending, and they understand the secrets the animals want to share. This is what happened with me. Because I was born remembering, it was easy for me to communicate with animals from an early age.

In the beginning when I was very young, I had many, many doubts because no one believed me. Although a healthy amount of skepticism is normal... and even I was very skeptical for awhile... when I eventually learned to believe in myself, I was able to overcome the negativity and disbeliefs of others.

Once I understood the effectiveness of this gift, I was then able to become the bridge or translator for your pets, and that's been my passion for my entire life, as well as my professional career for the past 30+ years.

But... *everyone* is born with this telepathic gift. We just have to learn how to use it. It was, after all, the first language of humans before humans ever developed speech, and even though picture language has been forgotten for centuries, it does still exist.

Since I wrote my first five books, there've been so many more pets... so many more surprises... so many new lessons learned... and so much love... that many of my clients have asked me to share even more stories in yet another book.

In this, my sixth book, *Your Pet Called*... you're going to find stories that will make you smile, touch your heart, and maybe even heal your spirit.

INTRODUCTION

This book is arranged so you can easily read it from beginning to end, or you can skip around by choosing whatever chapter or story title is of particular interest to you.

If this is the first of my books that you're reading, you'll also probably want to know much more about how I do what I do. You may also discover that you can do it, too. You can learn all about this in detail in Chapter 18.

Although I refer to these accounts as stories, it's important to remember that they're all true. Each of the pets, their names, and their pictures are most definitely real.

I hope you'll enjoy reading each of these delightful stories as much as I've enjoyed preparing them for you!

Prologue
Things That Are Helpful to Know About Pets in Spirit

WHERE DO ANIMALS GO WHEN THEY DIE?

When my clients request consultations, about half the time they want me to communicate with their pets who are dying, or who have already made their transitions into Spirit.

If a beloved pet has passed on, there are certain questions almost everyone wants answers to . . . Where are you? Are you well? Are you happy? Do you have any pain?

Based on thousands of replies, the simple answer is . . . pets who have passed on say they're in the light, or surrounded by light, or they're now beings of light.

Each of them might describe their state of being just a little bit differently, but there's always an all encompassing light that surrounds them. This light is a living light . . . it gives them love as a Mother would . . . it calms them . . . it gives them joy . . . and a deep understanding of knowing they're well taken care of and safe.

If I ask them to tell me who they are or what they look like, even pets who passed when they were very old usually present a younger version of themselves. They never want to be remembered as they were in their last days. Instead, they see themselves as healthy, happy, and enjoying life. And that's how they want us to remember them. They often ask us to choose a picture of them at their very best and display it where it can be seen by everyone.

Some animals remember their mission in life. Some remember their human friends and interactions, or the animals they used to live with.

All of them know who we are, what we did for them, and how much they were loved. Many, whose spirits remain around us for the duration of our lives here on earth, tell us they'll be reunited with us in the light.

Often they can tell us what we did after they left, how we remembered them, the little things we did for them, and how they feel about what we did.

Sometimes their comments are very specific. For example, pets have told me they saw the color of the urn used for their ashes, or their names engraved on an object, or their name tag being carried on their human's key chain.

They're also each focused on helping their humans in different ways. One animal might tell his human that it's time to pick up his food bowl from the floor and put it away, while another might say that her human needs to carry her collar around for awhile longer. Still others will say it's time for their humans to stop grieving and start loving a new pet.

Usually, my clients want specific answers from their pets about a whole list of questions, but sometimes, they'll want an answer to a more general, but very important question, as one of my clients did.

She asked: "What about those animals who died of abuse, neglect, or torture? Those who never knew a loving touch or a friendly human? What happens to them?"

The answer was first given to me a long time ago, and then, over the years, as I continued talking with animals who are in Spirit, it became even more clear.

When animals, who have experienced love, transition into Spirit, their spirit energy often tends to remain around their human family during the family's mourning period. After that, some of them simply continue to learn on the spirit side, while others, who may be a bit more advanced, want to become "greeters."

PROLOGUE

These greeters, I'm told, have a very special responsibility. They're the ones in charge of receiving animal souls who are just making their transitions into Spirit. This time of transition is often called crossing The Rainbow Bridge.

The greeters receive the souls of all new arrivals at the edge of the light and guide them until they're completely embraced within the heart of the loving light.

Being met by a greeter is especially important for those animals who have suffered abuse or neglect at the hands of a human. The greeters will never leave any of these precious beings until they know for sure their souls have recovered from all the suffering they experienced during their last incarnation. These new arrivals will be guided, loved, and cared for with more dedication and diligence than any other souls until their emotional scars have healed.

In a way, these troubled souls are better tended to than regular souls. They've returned to Spirit after volunteering their suffering in order to try to bring attention to the need for better treatment of their species.

This is what I've been told over and over again, although I've never been told why certain individual animals have had to endure what they did. There just seems to be something bigger at work here, about which I've never been given any further information.

But what I do know is, there's great love on the other side, and animals are very involved with helping each other. They're all benefiting from the sacrifices of those who have gone before them.

I never hear a reproach, never a complaint. Those animal souls who have been abused, neglected, or tortured are the best and most centered souls I've ever spoken with. I say this because no matter what they've had to go through, their last thought is to send mankind unconditional LOVE.

So, it is with love that I approach these wonderful spirits, and it is with love that we're able to maintain an open channel of communication.

How Soon After Passing Is an Animal in Spirit Ready to Communicate?

It's easy to understand why humans, who are grieving the loss of their dear pet friends, want to talk with them in Spirit immediately after they die.

But . . . my answer is always the same. It's important to wait at least 30 days before we attempt a communication with a pet who has recently made his or her transition.

There are two reasons for this: we need to give newly departed souls enough time to adjust to their new environment in Spirit, and we need to give the humans enough time to grieve for their deceased pets.

Since I've been communicating with animals my whole life, I definitely know there are only very, very few who will be able to communicate almost immediately after passing.

The souls who are capable of communicating right away are very old souls who have certain memories and understandings imprinted into them after many lifetimes. Younger souls, however, are simply just not skilled enough to be able to maintain a good communication very soon after they find themselves in Spirit.

It's equally important, though, for humans to allow themselves enough time to grieve the loss of their pets, and begin their own healing journey.

If you're in the throes of pain, disbelief, and sadness, or if you're feeling guilty and want to apologize for something you did or something you didn't do, you're going to be blocking yourself from receiving any important messages your pet wants to send you.

If you're not sleeping well, not eating, and continually asking God why He let this happen to your pet, you're not ready to hear your pet's important messages.

You need time to heal so that you can be open to everything your pet in Spirit wants you to know.

To wait at least 30 days before you attempt communication with an animal who's now in Spirit will give you a chance to accept your loss and be

PROLOGUE

more open to communication with your loved one. It will be a much better experience at that point because your sadness won't cloud the information that's coming through.

So many of my clients want to receive clear signs from their animals in Spirit. They want to know if they're still around them, but if the human is going through a time of extreme sadness, once again, they're blocking themselves from receiving the signs, as well as the messages, that their loved ones are trying to send them.

Even if the animal is sending them some visual signs or auditory messages, it's impossible for the human to receive them because all of their attention is still focused on how they feel, and on how they can make their sadness or guilt go away.

After around 30 days, though, both pets in Spirit, and their humans who are missing them, are usually ready to enjoy a good communication.

Is communicating with a pet in Spirit different from communicating with a pet in human experience? The answer is, "No."

As an animal communicator, I'm able to receive images from animal spirits in the same way that I'm able to receive them from the spirit of a being who's in human experience. That's because all communication is actually spirit to spirit, not body to body.

While the way we communicate is the same, the things animals in Spirit want to talk about are usually quite different though.

Pets in Spirit always communicate about love, about accepting, about their mission, about everything they're learning. They don't want to be asked questions about pain. They don't experience pain anymore, so it's difficult for them to have to remember what it was like. Instead, they send wonderful messages of hope, of healing, and of guidance for your life.

All pets in Spirit also tell me that when it's your time to cross over into heaven, you will be reunited with them, and they'll be there waiting for you.

How Do Dogs and Cats See Pets in Spirit?

My clients often ask me, "Why is my pet able to see other pets who have passed into Spirit, but I can't?"

This is one of the best ways I can think of to explain it:

We can all clearly see the spokes of a bicycle wheel when it's at rest.

When the bicycle starts to move slowly we can still see the spokes.

Then, at some point, the wheels begin turning so fast that it looks as if the center of the wheel is hollow and the spokes are no longer there at all.

Similarly, when people are using earthly bodies, they're vibrating at much lower rates of energy. When souls are in Spirit, however, their energy is vibrating at such a high rate that our human eyes can no longer see them.

Our animals, however, are able to see a much wider range of vibrations than we can, and therefore most cats and many dogs are able to see spirit energy.

They may at times appear to be looking off into space at nothing in particular, but when they do, they may be observing energies that most humans just cannot see.

You'll be reading true stories in this book now. They're about pets in earthly experience, as well as about pets in Spirit.

Hopefully the information in each of the articles in this Prologue will have provided you with some insights ahead of time about pets in Spirit so you'll be able to better enjoy the wonderful insights they have to share with us.

Chapter 1

YOUR PET CALLED

Troy

Your pet called . . . he has something to tell you!

I met Troy many years ago, around 2003. He was just a young Sheltie puppy, maybe 4 to 6 months old at that time. Even though he was still so young, he was already deaf and almost blind.

It was a nice spring day, and I was at a clinic in Highland, California where I met with clients every Wednesday.

But I'm getting ahead of myself. Let me first go back a couple of years in time to tell you how I came to be in a place where I would one day have the privilege of meeting this very special dog.

YOUR PET CALLED

TWO YEARS BEFORE...

Sometime in 2001, I received a call asking me to do an in-person reading in the city of San Bernardino, California. This was about an hour and a half drive away from where I lived at the time.

This new client had read my first book *What Your Animals Tell Me* and liked it. Now she wanted me to do a reading for each of her *nine* dogs.

I recall thinking it was a long way for me to drive, and it would be a very costly appointment for her with so many pets. I wasn't even sure I wanted to do it, but she's a very persuasive person, and she wouldn't take no for an answer.

I finally scheduled her for a day in the future, half hoping she'd have time to think about the expense and decide to cancel. But she didn't!

The appointment day finally came and I found myself knocking on her door. From all around, I could hear barking, barking, barking coming at me from several different directions. And those were the barks of big dogs.

She opened the door and invited me in just as four huge Dobermans came excitedly lunging toward me. I was a little taken off guard, but she wasn't correcting them, so I didn't feel there was any cause for concern. Things then quieted down fairly quickly.

Once I was inside the house, we went into the first room to my right, which was perfect because it had a glass door.

There were four Doberman Pinschers and five Manchester terriers, nine dogs in all, waiting to talk with me. I asked her to bring only one dog into the room at a time while the others waited on the other side of the glass door.

Because I'd done readings for many multiple dog households in the past, I knew if the dogs were too close together that my pictures might get confused, leading me to say something about one dog that was actually coming from another. That's because, when there are multiple dogs present, all of them are listening, even though I'm directly speaking to only one of them.

Many times, in group situations, I'll hear multiple and differing answers to my questions. That can become confusing if I can't be sure who said what, especially if they're mostly the same breed of dog. It's a chance I have to take, though, for the sake of my clients, even though it can be quite a challenge at times.

I did end up talking with all nine of her dogs, and I felt my client was satisfied.

INTERTWINING OUR SKILLS...

She was so satisfied in fact that she invited me to come to her clinic in Highland so I could watch *her* in action. She's a chiropractor who treats both people and pets.

The way she worked with her animal clients was impressive. I thought I was just there to observe, but she kept asking me questions. Her questions were specific and they took me by surprise because, at that time in my career, no one had ever asked me questions like these before. Things like: After I made this adjustment does he feel better or worse? Is the pain dull or sharp? Is it static or does it travel?

As I listened to the information coming from the animals and shared it with her, she was then able to make certain adjustments she wouldn't have thought of making before. She could make them now because of what the animals were able to tell us.

We each have a special love and compassion for animals, and as we began to work synergistically together, we quickly became friends.

She then asked me to come to her clinic every Wednesday. She believed in me so much that she made sure I always had clients waiting to see me every week. And on Wednesdays, when her own clients would bring their pets in for an adjustment, she would often recommend that some stay to talk with me.

I truly thank her for her faith in me, and for giving me the opportunity to be able to help so many more pets and their humans.

TWO YEARS LATER...

It was one of those Wednesdays, almost two years later, when I first met Troy in the clinic waiting room. Two ladies came in with three dogs. I spoke only briefly with Troy and his moms before they were all called into a treatment room.

Then a couple of weeks later, Dr. Jacquie knocked on my door to tell me she had some clients I *really* needed to talk with.

The same two ladies came in. I didn't remember them, and I didn't immediately connect Troy with my first encounter in the waiting room, so for me, it was as if this was my very first meeting with all of them.

One moved to a corner, sat down, and didn't even want to look at me. I can spot a skeptic a mile away because, in my line of work, I encounter a lot of them. The other one was holding a young puppy. She sat down in another corner of the room.

The puppy, Troy, was a Sheltie, mostly white with a big black spot on his right eye, but he wasn't doing the normal things puppies do. He was anxious and moving, sitting and lying down, standing then sitting, and he never looked at me. I sensed something was wrong but I had no idea what it might be.

Normally, a dog processes information through his nose, so I put my hand out for him to sniff, watching to see what his reaction would be. Most dogs would sniff then look around, but it seemed as if Troy was trying to take in the scent of my entire body. Because this was such an unusual reaction, I asked one of his moms if he was blind. She told me he was mostly blind and deaf. Those are genetic problems many white Shelties are born with.

At this time, bells went off in my head. Usually I'm very visual. That means animals and I communicate by sending pictures back and forth that I then translate into words so people can understand what the animals want to say. But in this case, Troy couldn't communicate with me in either a visual or a hearing way.

Add to that, such young puppies can't usually send me a lot of information either, because they don't yet understand life the way adult dogs do. Even so, I was still able to communicate with him empathically by connecting in a special way with his feelings.

My first conversation with Troy...

I wasn't expecting to find out anything very important, but was I ever in for a surprise! He knew a lot more than any of us thought he did.

The first thing Troy said was, "They think I'm stupid because I can't hear them giving me commands. I'm not! I'm very smart, and if they do a good job of training me, I'll be the best dog they've ever had. I'm not stupid, I'm just deaf. Plus, I can't see them from far away, so they have to come really close to me if they want me to see their hands."

When I relayed this information to my two clients, now even the skeptic was listening. Nancy, who is now one of my friends, couldn't believe what their little puppy was saying. Kay, the one holding Troy, was laughing.

While this was going on between them, Troy interrupted me to say, "Tell them my tail can move up if I want it to. They're wondering why my tail is always down. I'll move it up for them." And he did!

Laughing even harder now, they both told me they were wondering that very morning if there was something wrong with his tail because he wasn't moving it. Later I was told that as soon as they got home he wagged his tail for the first time.

Troy had come in for a spinal adjustment and Dr. Jacquie, the chiropractor, wanted to know how he felt after she'd manipulated his spine.

He said he was feeling fine now and he thanked her for helping him. He told his humans to be patient with him because he was going to respond to his training in time.

Learning about Troy...

Since he was deaf, he'd never heard a single command, but with what little eyesight he initially had, he did at least learn to respond to sign language.

Kay and Nancy have an agility course at their home where they teach other dogs how to practice agility techniques. They also do other types of training so they know dogs very well, but Troy was their biggest challenge.

Although he couldn't hear, and his eyesight was seriously impaired in the beginning, Troy still managed to become a Grand Champion in agility. He was often instrumental in teaching others how to do it, too, and he loved the excitement as well as the rush of competition.

As he aged, though, he began to have a significant number of *really* difficult health challenges. Among many other things, his eyes developed severe cataracts that even two surgeries couldn't help, so eventually, he completely lost his eyesight.

Once he lost his eyesight altogether, his humans began to use the leash as their communication tool. Kay and Nancy never gave up on him and he went wherever they went, navigating stairs, and confidently going up into either their truck or motorhome and back down again.

When he just couldn't handle agility competitions any longer because of his many health challenges, he'd still be there on the sidelines cheering his sisters and brother onward.

Troy had been doing poorly just before he turned 14, but he would still champion on for a while longer. When he turned 15, though, his health became even more compromised, and he promised he'd let his humans know when it was time.

He was doing so poorly one day that they sent me an e-mail asking me how long they should wait. After I connected with Troy, his answer was, "Until I tell you otherwise." He was always very strong, very hard headed, and he had a huge personality. He wanted to stay until he was ready to leave.

It's a rare instance that someone's pet initiates a communication with me to tell me their time is up, but it has happened before. I had such a special connection with Troy, that one morning, about six months later, he did reach out to me to tell me his time was up. I didn't hesitate to write Nancy an urgent e-mail letting her know what Troy had told me.

She already knew. He'd been doing so very poorly again that she and Kay had talked about what was best for him. They'd wisely made a decision to have the vet come to their home that afternoon. Everything was taken care of very peacefully, and Troy, who was then 15 ½ years old, crossed over The Rainbow Bridge on October 31st, 2017.

I felt a rush of emotions that day. Someone who'd taught us so much was finally leaving, and there'd be no more Troy for us to enjoy, but at the same time, I was so happy that I'd been able to listen to him whenever he needed me throughout his entire life.

The Idea of Reincarnation . . .

During one of the last times we had a conversation with Troy about death and dying, one of the questions Nancy and Kay asked him was whether or not he'd consider coming back to them again in the future. At the moment, he told them he wanted to come back, but he didn't know when or where.

The question about reincarnation often does come up with my clients, but the fact is, animals can only determine the whens, wheres, and hows of any return after they've been in Spirit for awhile.

We need to wait patiently until they're ready to make the decision about coming back. And even when they do, they might not think coming back to the same humans is necessary, either for their own soul's growth and development, or to help their humans grow and learn more lessons. So . . . the topic would not come up again until after he made his transition.

Imagine my surprise, when one day in early July 2018, I was sitting at my computer and I received a message from Troy in Spirit asking excitedly, "Did you find me yet? Did you look for me yet? I want you to look for me. I'm back! Did you look for me yet?"

I told Troy it wasn't my place to look for him, but I'd contact his moms right away and ask them to look.

I immediately e-mailed my friends to let them know that the soul we'd known as Troy was back as another personality, and it was time to start looking on the internet for another Sheltie to see if they could reconnect with this special soul.

At this point, you may be wondering how I'm able to communicate with an animal who's no longer physically present on earth, so let's answer that question before we continue with Troy's story . . .

COMMUNICATING WITH ANIMALS IN SPIRIT

When I first started communicating with animals, I didn't know I could communicate with the soul of an animal who'd moved on into Spirit. Then in time I came to learn that, even though the earthly body ceases to function, the energy or soul of an animal never dies. The animal soul doesn't use a physical earthly body anymore, but it does continue to exist using its spiritual form. The same is true for people.

While both people and animals have to use physical bodies while they're in earthly experience, a body is nothing . . . and can do nothing by itself . . . *unless* it is animated by the soul of a being.

When we're using earthly bodies, we usually think we're communicating body to body, but that's not so. Even when we're using bodies, communication is always taking place soul to soul. This is because it's the *soul* that is responsible for all thoughts, actions, and communications, not the body.

So, I'm able to communicate with animals in Spirit in the same way I do when they're visible to us on earth because we're always communicating soul to soul.

When an animal is in Spirit, the conversation might be a little different because things that happened on the earth plane don't really interest them anymore.

For that reason, they seldom answer questions about what their favorite toys or favorite foods were, or even about how they felt during a vacation when they were left alone. Those things are not what's important to them once they're in Spirit. But I can ask them about reincarnation . . . which brings us back to Troy . . .

WATCHING, WAITING, AND SO MANY COINCIDENCES . . .

In July, when I told Kay and Nancy to start looking online for another Sheltie, they wanted to meet with me in person as soon as possible. Just a day before I was to leave on an extended trip to Argentina, I met with them and we talked with Troy, in Spirit, about the fact that he wanted to come back to his moms again in a different body, and as a different personality.

This time, though, he wanted to change a few things. But what he *didn't* want to change was the fact that he was going to be deaf again. He said . . . and we all laughed about it . . . "They talk too much, but if I'm deaf, they'll have to communicate with me in a more quiet way."

Troy then said he was going to be born at a breeder who was far away from them. He also said his coming was going to be like a surprise or coincidence for them and they needed to be "ready" for anything.

It's not often we're given the opportunity to share life with a special being who's willing to come back to us a second time, so of course, Kay and Nancy were delighted with the idea that Troy wanted to be with them again, albeit as a totally different personality.

They asked him if the new puppy could wait until the end of August when renovations on their home would be complete. He said this would be ok.

On the morning of September 1st, Nancy was surprised to receive word from a friend who wanted her to go on Facebook and look for a particular breeder. That breeder had just posted a picture of a young Sheltie puppy.

While Nancy's friend already knew about this breeder, she didn't yet know that this particular puppy was deaf.

If the picture had been posted any earlier, the puppy could already have been adopted by someone else, but come to find out later on, the breeder hadn't even thought about posting the puppy's picture until it was around three months old. When the time came for posting, it was exactly when Kay and Nancy's renovations were complete.

So here was a friend . . . telling them about a breeder who was far away from them . . . who had a puppy, whom they would come to find out was deaf . . . and the risk of someone else adopting the puppy had been completely eliminated because the breeder had "coincidentally" waited to post the puppy's picture until Kay and Nancy's renovations had just been completed. Could these be some of the many coincidences Troy had talked about?

Nancy e-mailed me right away with a picture of the puppy. She asked me to see if Troy had anything to say about it.

"YES!" he said from Spirit, "that's me. She's the opposite of me."

Of course, at that time I had no idea what he meant. When I asked him, he started by telling me what her name should be.

OK . . . the opposite of Troy . . . Oh, I get it . . . Cassandra or Kassandra, as Helen of Troy was also known, depending on which spelling was used in ancient writings.

He also said she'd have his markings.

I thought that was it, so I told Nancy, "Yes, Troy says she's the one. Go get her!"

Nancy then told me she could think of several reasons why Troy said the new puppy would be the "opposite" of him.

This special little soul would be female instead of male this time.

She'd be smaller than Troy had been. (Troy had been quite large for a Sheltie.)

She'd be named Kassie, a name that was, in a sense, the opposite of Troy, but it was a name Kay and Nancy had always loved.

And . . . she'd have the same markings as he did, but on the *opposite* side.

She'd come from British Columbia, far away from where Nancy and Kay lived, and she'd be deaf, exactly as Troy had described.

PREPARING FOR KASSIE . . .

Things began to happen very quickly after that.

The paperwork for customs was approved for little Kassie in record time, and all the arrangements were made to meet the breeder in Vancouver, BC.

Going from the breeder's home to her new forever home would be quite an experience for little Kassie, so Nancy and Kay wanted me to prepare her ahead of time for their first meeting, and for everything that would happen after that.

I replied back that I'd wait to tell Kassie everything until the following week when they were actually going to meet her because she was far too young to remember everything if I told her a whole week ahead of time.

A week later, while I was re-reading Nancy's e-mail message before I even talked with Kassie, I heard Troy's booming voice in the background saying, "I told you! Humans call things coincidences. They're not! When some things are meant to be, we go to great lengths to make our plans work out the right way."

I then asked him, "How's it possible for your soul to communicate with me as Troy, in Spirit, when your soul is already using a different body and a different personality as Kassie?"

He explained to me that at the beginning of a new life experience, the previous personality is temporarily blended with the new personality so there's a transparency, a continuity of sorts. There's something that binds them together for awhile until the new personality is set, and it becomes the personality the soul is now fully using.

I then went on to talk with little Kassie, using the points in Nancy's e-mail as guidelines . . .

I told her that her new moms would be talking to her using both their voices and their hands because they didn't want her to miss anything.

Kassie liked that idea and said she was looking forward to their hand signals and their gentle touch. She also said she was waiting for them because somewhere inside of her she already knew she was supposed to find her forever home with them.

Troy then piped up saying something I translated as "wear your perfume." It seems as if maybe they used a special soap or cream, and he wanted to be sure their first touch of Kassie had that scent on their hands.

Next, I mentioned to Kassie that her new moms already knew how beautiful and smart she was, and they also knew she had a very beautiful and proud tail. I expected a reply from Kassie, but it was Troy who piped up again saying, "YEP!"

I then told Kassie her new moms would be bringing her some toys and a blanket so she could become familiar with the scents of her new sisters and brother. She said she liked toys and was looking forward to meeting the rest of the family.

After that, I explained to her there'd be a long car ride back to Seattle, an overnight stay in a hotel, a two-and-a-half hour plane ride, and then another hour's car ride to get to her forever home in California.

Kassie was ok with all of the new experiences. She said she'd take naps during the car and plane rides, and she wouldn't be scared because she's a strong girl, and she'd be safe with her two moms.

I learned from my conversation with Kassie that she has definite opinions, she's sure of herself, she's open to everything, and she's very loving. I then shared all of Kassie's and my conversation with Kay and Nancy.

Proving the point that Nancy and Kay were paying attention to "coincidences" as Troy had told them to do, Nancy wrote: *Troy is still teaching us, isn't he? He and you have taught us to believe, and we've never doubted his intentions. We've been seeing his signs and have followed all of the bread crumbs.*

Nancy also wrote: *We're so very honored, humbled, and blessed that he's chosen to come back to us here on earth as a different personality. We'll continue our journey of love and understanding with him/her. We'll also honor his name request. Her kennel name will be "Kassandra of Troy."*

I then told Nancy and Kay I couldn't really express the joy Troy felt when I told him they'd honor him, not only with his request for the opposite name, Kassie, but also for her new kennel name. He conveyed to me that it symbolized to him the inner strength and character of her new personality.

He also said she'll be a good teacher . . . but not be so easy at times. Laughingly, he commented that this "job" of taking care of Kassie will be perfect for Nancy and Kay as they continue their "education," which he so expertly started!

Meeting Kassie for the First Time . . .

The next time Nancy wrote, she described their first meeting with Kassie.

The breeder took the new puppy out of the crate and held her up to her new moms. At first, Kassie turned her head away as if she felt a bit uncertain about the meeting. Then she held her head up high and took a really good sniff.

She'd just caught the scent of the good-smelling hand lotion Nancy and Kay had generously applied just before they met. When she recognized that scent, she became so excited the breeder couldn't hold on to her any longer, so she handed her over to Kay.

The two women signed "hello," "beautiful," and "love" to Kassie. And she continued to wiggle and wiggle in their arms, giving them kisses on their noses.

While they finalized things with the breeder, they put her in a small play pen so she could stretch her legs and move around freely. When they gave her the toys they'd brought for her, she romped around, playing in a relaxed and confident manner.

Nancy and Kay continued signing with her. The more they signed, the more excited she seemed to be. It was as if they were each reuniting with the love of their lives. It was a dream come true for all of them!

When they were settled at the hotel, they played with Kassie until she dropped, and then she slept between them through the entire night, wrapped around a bag of ice. Just as Troy always did, she also needed ice to help her settle.

Home, sweet home . . .

A few days later, I received another update from Nancy, starting with, "What an amazing pup!"

Kassie handled the plane ride very well, again sleeping against a bag of ice in her crate.

They practiced walking her on a leash for a few minutes before they arrived home so she'd be ready to walk in on her own for the initial meet and greet.

Micah, Tess, and MacKenzy all approached her, and after everyone sniffed each other, it was life as usual. They readily welcomed her into the pack. They could have been nervous, apprehensive, or aloof around her at first, but instead, all was calm and peaceful right from the very beginning.

Nancy says Kassie is extremely intelligent and *extremely* food motivated. She's aware of her limitations but she's adjusted to her hearing loss very well. So well, in fact, that sometimes it seemed as if she might actually be hearing more and more each day, when in fact, she was just very quickly adapting to their routine and their movements.

Her sense of smell and sight awareness is at a much higher level than most dogs, which confirms how well she's using sight and smell to compensate for her hearing loss. She becomes very excited and attentive whenever she sees sign language.

She may have at least some minimal hearing, but it's very little, or it's limited just to higher frequencies. She doesn't react to voices or most loud noises.

But . . . they've discovered she does seem to hear high pitched sounds, or loud sounds that are near her. For example, she hears the other dogs when they bark.

She could also hear Nancy whistle, but she couldn't figure out where the sound was coming from, so they taught her to run toward their waving hands whenever she hears the whistle sound.

Given her hearing loss, and the fact that she doesn't usually hear anything spoken, Kassie does do something they just *can't* seem to explain yet.

She actually responds to her name when either Nancy or Kay say it. They can say other names in the same tone of voice, but she doesn't react to those. Yet, when they say "Kassie," she does respond. Very interesting!

She's such a happy-go-lucky pup, and most importantly, she's very respectful of the other dogs. She learned right away not to approach them while they're eating. Instead, she waits patiently until they walk away from their bowls, and then she loves to clean up the crumbs.

She's eager to learn everything, and she's already mastered the baby teeter on the agility course. She's also learned to sleep all night long in her crate, and she loves it.

Her most noticeable Troy trait . . . ICE. She has to have ice! A bag of ice under her blanket saved them on the plane ride, and if they want her to take a nap, they just have to put the covered frozen ice block down, and she'll curl up around it and sleep.

Nancy's e-mail was accompanied by many wonderful pictures and videos. I was laughing so hard at the picture of Kassie sitting inside the refrigerator! She definitely has an interest in anything that's cold or that holds food!

She's so smart! Of course, having known Troy, I wouldn't expect anything less.

I'm so excited and so very pleased to be a part of this next adventure in their lives while the lovable soul we first knew as the personality Troy continues to teach and entertain us as the new personality Kassie!

Nancy and Kay

Are you kidding???

After reading and approving Troy and Kassie's story, Nancy wrote up the following first hand account about how we met . . .

Kay and I first met Dr. Monica more than 15 years ago in the waiting room of our chiropractor's office. We had three dogs at the time. We brought the two agility dogs in for routine maintenance. Our new deaf puppy Troy, was just there to tag along.

I remember when we got Troy out of the car we noticed that he'd just chewed through his 11th halter! Frustrated with him and our failed efforts to solve this problem, I carried him into the office, chewed halter in hand.

We really didn't notice Dr Monica sitting there. After all, our focus was on managing two dogs and holding the third. When we got settled in our seats we made eye-contact with her and in doing so, exchanged pleasant hellos.

Soon after, she asked us if the puppy was going to be seen by the chiropractor. "No," we replied, "he's just along for the ride." Then curious, we asked, "Why?"

She said she'd started a conversation with Troy and he'd told her he was experiencing headaches. She strongly suggested that Troy be seen as well.

I can only hope that our expressions were polite, but our minds were screaming, "What the hell! Is she for real!"

Sarcastically, I remember asking her, "Maybe you could ask Troy why he chews through his halters!" She paused, closed her eyes, and started laughing. "It's because he prefers to be carried," she said confidently.

I so wanted to tell her, *"You know, every time we try to put a halter on him he keeps trying to jump up in our arms."* But I stopped myself thinking in my head, *"What are you thinking? Don't encourage this crazy lady. She saw the chewed halter, she put two-and-two together, and just said he wanted to be carried. I mean, what puppy wouldn't prefer to be carried, right?"*

The chiropractor saved us from this extremely awkward encounter by calling us back for treatment. While adjusting our two agility dogs, she made random comments and asked some questions about the puppy's history.

Then she asked, "How long have Troy's runny eyes stained his face?" We told her a for couple of weeks. Then she asked if she could take a look at him. We agreed.

She felt him all over and she gasped when she reached his neck. She asked if Troy had run into anything lately.

We pondered the thought. Then we remembered that a couple of weeks prior, Troy *had* run into a tree while dodging one of the dogs in play. She informed us that Troy's vertebrae were way out of alignment and that would explain his runny eyes.

I remembered throwing a glance at Kay and then sheepishly asking the doctor, "Could that give him headaches?"

"Why, yes!" she exclaimed. "Very bad headaches! Why do you ask?"

Kay answered, "Well this lady out in your waiting room said that's what Troy told her." Then we both followed up with a chuckle saying, "Can you believe it?"

The chiropractor replied, "Oh! is Dr. Monica here?" Then she explained who she is and what kind of work she does.

She followed up by strongly recommending that we have a consultation with her about Troy. She felt she could give us some helpful insights about what he needed from us as a "deaf" dog. We told her we'd consider it.

A few weeks later, and out of pure curiosity, mind you, we decided to set up a meeting with Dr. Monica. Of course we didn't tell another soul, and we both took the pinky swear to keep the whole thing to ourselves.

When we came for our appointment, we know that, as hard as we tried to hide it, she knew we were testing her, but it didn't seem to phase her. She knew she could win us over.

What we quickly learned is that we had a very chatty little dog. It was as if Troy had kept a diary of his few months on earth and he'd given it to her to read to us.

She told us things about Troy that only he could have told her. She told us about things he'd done, as well as his thoughts about us, his new siblings, and his take on life.

Well, Dr. Monica passed our test and the rest is history. A very long and beautiful relationship has developed among all of us.

Through her communications with our dogs, she's become our teacher and mentor in this much uncharted plane of the universe. She changed the course of our lives.

Because of what we learned, Kay and I have now become dog trainers, specializing in agility training, not only for our own dogs, but for others as well. We attribute our success to using the insights she's given us over the years. It's all about "how to learn from our dogs."

We may originally have been among the greatest skeptics in Dr. Monica's clientele, but we're now truly believers!

Dr. Jacquie

Is she for real?

In Troy and Kassie's story I wrote briefly about the first time I ever met Dr. Jacquie DeGrasse. She's the people and animal chiropractor who treated Troy, as well as Nancy and Kay's other dogs. She was another one of my greatest skeptics at first.

Since she was the one who originally introduced me to Nancy, Kay, and Troy, I thought she might enjoy reading Troy's story. She did!

In fact, she enjoyed reading it so much that she, too, decided to write up her own remembrance about how she and I first met, and how we began our work together.

HERE'S DR. JACQUIE'S FIRST HAND ACCOUNT FOR YOU TO ENJOY...

When I read Dr Monica's book, I was determined to find out if she was legitimate!

I called her because I wanted a home visit ... expensive with nine dogs, but it didn't matter. Even though I had many animals, I wanted a consultation with each one ... and I wasn't taking no for an answer. She had a distance to travel to get to our home ... but I didn't care!

I prayed after the appointment had been set. Then, pretending they could understand, I talked to each of my animals about what I wanted to know. I asked them to give me information beyond the shadow of a doubt, so I could really be sure she was speaking to them. I'd decided that if she was a flake, I'd kick her out after just one animal and pay for only some travel expenses.

I was on a mission to find out the truth!

I deliberately did not tell her ahead of time what kind of animals I had. I never mentioned sex, age, or species.

When she arrived, I simply opened the door to let her in. She had no idea that, essentially, I'd set her up.

When I opened the door, a petite woman with a great smile greeted me. I liked her instantly, but wasn't going to let her know that right away.

We entered the very first room so she couldn't see anything else except for a few dogs. I deliberately let my Dobies run around freely, 'cuz if she was a real communicator then she shouldn't be afraid of them as most people are. Nasty little thing to do, I know! Well, they ran and they barked, and she was okay.

Then I brought Janie in. She's my little Manchester Terrier. The first thing Janie told her was that the white cat was deaf.

After that, there was a silent moment when Monica hesitated after listening to Janie's second comment. She looked at me. I told her to just tell me what she heard and not to judge it. She paused, and then she said, "Janie's telling me she plays the piano!"

Bingo!!!!!!! I had a deaf white cat in the other room whom Monica hadn't seen. And yes, Janie sits on my lap, I take her paws, and she plays the piano. OMG! Monica couldn't see my piano, and what Janie had just told her was a very unusual thing for a little dog to say.

I was so excited after all of the consultations because I learned so many personal details about each of my babies. A whole new world had just opened up for me! And it forever changed my life!

When it was time for Monica to leave, I didn't want her to go. Thanks to her gift, I now had a deep connection with my animals, each individual one, like never before.

Then I thought about my work. What if she could help me with the animals I'm treating?

I was an experienced chiropractor for people, but I was fairly new when it came to learning animal chiropractic. It would help so much if I had specific information about some of those animals. Did they have the same symptoms of back pain or numbness in their legs as people do? Were they actually getting relief when I used traction on their necks, or was I hurting them with my hands? How could I make them less afraid? The list of questions was endless.

And she could be the translator I needed!

Working with her, I could really learn how to help my animal patients. She's the bridge between two worlds. And for the moment, she was mine!

I quickly invited her to my clinic to begin working with me, and my work blossomed thanks to Monica's feedback. Oh, life was good!

A short while after the first animal communication session with Dr. Monica in my clinic, my skills as a chiropractor deepened. I specialize in paralysis and was successfully helping more and more animals walk again.

It feels so good to help a family when they have a pet with a serious issue. I know how much the animal is loved because I know how deeply I love mine. I'm very well aware of how special their place is in the home. And to see the smiles all around when the animal is going home feeling so much more comfortable makes that day a perfect day!

I also work with our veterinarian, Dr Sigdestad. I began giving him much more detailed information about how we could better treat each pet based on what Dr. Monica had discovered when talking with them. This one had greater pain, another one felt sick on a certain medication, or a secondary condition was developing such as a urinary tract infection.

He always listened politely, but in the beginning . . . well . . . there was this "look!" You know when someone's trying to be professional, but inside his head he's rolling his eyes and mentally shouting, *"Give me a break!"*

And it didn't stop there. There was also a little "speech bubble" above his head that said, *"You're missing a marble and now you want to take mine! Where do you come up with this information?"*

But, he was always cooperative, and he started to see the incredible results. Then one day it happened.

Dr. Sig's son had a young dog who couldn't walk very far on their hikes in the mountains. He'd examined him, but couldn't find anything wrong. There was nothing to explain why the dog would always sit down shortly after the walk started. Then he asked me, "Do you have that woman's number. The communicator?"

His eyes weren't rolling around inside his head and there were no "speech bubbles" this time because he was genuinely concerned. He was a highly qualified veterinarian but he couldn't help his son. So I gave him Dr. Monica's phone number.

Not long afterward, Dr. Sig approached me one day while I was working at the animal hospital. He said Monica had told his son that the dog seemed to have a problem with his heart. Not only that, but he also said a specialist had just confirmed that the dog did, in fact, have a heart condition. Another big Bingo!!!

After that, Dr. Sig routinely began to work with Dr. Monica to help many of his pet patients who presented with unusual or difficult-to-diagnose conditions.

Later, I introduced her to several other veterinarians and she was able to help them in their work, also. Minds and hearts continued to be opened, and together, we've raised the bar of animal well-being in our little corner of the world.

On a personal note once again, my relationships with all of my animals deepened with the information I received during my initial consultation with Dr. Monica. I now knew many personality traits about each of my babies, but I was about to discover a new one in Janie!

I enjoy taking a cruise at least once a year. Monica taught me how animals count the days by following the sun, so whenever I traveled, she always told my animals how long I'd be gone. She also told them who would watch them, and why I was going on every trip.

The chewing up of shoes, pottying everywhere, and other destructive behaviors stopped because my animals now "knew" when I would leave and return. This was a wonderful change since I do like to travel . . . but then . . . Janie got mad at me! Uh oh.

She decided to try anything she could to get me to come home sooner! That's my girl! Our hearts beat as one. But when you're in Russia, and you receive a message about one of your pets who's in trouble, your heart stops!

I'd left the balcony of the ship I was cruising on to check my e-mail. There was a message from Monica telling me that Janie was hurt!

Everything stopped. I still had a week to go before I headed home, and all I could think about was my little baby. What had happened?

My pet sitter had called Monica to let her know that Janie was walking very slowly, and carrying her right front leg up. She wouldn't put any weight on the leg. Her head was down and she wouldn't look up. She was 15 pounds of a pitiful sight!

Did she break a leg, or worse still, her neck? Did one of my Dobies hurt her? We were always a good family together and the dogs were respectful of each other. I just wanted to be home so I could hold her, but I was helpless.

I immediately e-mailed Monica and asked her to tell the pet sitter to take her to see Dr. Sig. He was her vet and Janie knew him well, which is another whole story! But, with the time difference, it would be another whole day before she'd even be able to be examined. Ugh.

Two days later I received another e-mail from Monica. She'd talked to Janie to tell her that the sitter would be taking her to see the vet the next day, and if necessary, they'd keep her at the hospital until I returned. Monica also explained to Janie why I couldn't come home for another week.

Well . . . needless to say . . . Janie experienced a miraculous recovery. The following morning the sitter called Monica to tell her Janie was acting just fine! She was eating, playing, walking, and using her supposedly injured leg.

Talk about manipulation! My little girl had had enough of Mommy being gone and she was going to try to bring her back home sooner!!!

But thanks to Monica's unique gift, and just the very thought of a possible hospital stay, the problem seemed to resolve itself overnight!

The most significant thing I've experienced since Dr. Monica began talking with my animals is the change in their behaviors. They "listen" to me now. I'm learning to be more careful with my words, and I can "see" the extra effort my pets put forth when it comes to behaviors that I ask for.

I can feel our relationships continuing to deepen because I know their personalities better, and I'm more aware of their needs. The changes in their behaviors have continued to improve over the years, and everything I've learned has made me become a better animal mommy. I thank you deeply my friend!

Is Dr. Monica for real? Does animal communication really work? You'd better believe it! I've not only seen it! I've experienced it!

Chapter 2

Messages from Spirit Provide Heartwarming Validations

Molly Lisa

She saw "you" in Spirit

    Talking with pets who have passed on is always an enlightening experience. The messages they give us can be both encouraging and uplifting.

In my work as an animal communicator, though, it's sometimes quite a stretch for some of my clients to accept the thought of talking with pets who've made their transitions into Spirit. Some may be supportive, but they tell me right away that they're also very skeptical. Others will tell me, in no uncertain terms, they simply don't believe in what I do.

I usually say, "That's fine! I love skeptics!" Sometimes I'm a skeptic, too. In fact, on occasion, I'm my own worst skeptic. Because of that, I have to be very careful not to get in the way of any of the messages I'm receiving.

Take for example the case of one of my skeptical clients who called me in October, 2012 to set up an appointment on behalf of his wife. Their golden retriever had passed on and neither of them could find the solace they were seeking. The skeptical husband said he was doing this for his wife in order to help her find closure.

Initially, he thought he wanted to have only an e-mail conversation, but because the death of a pet is such a sensitive situation, I encouraged the two of them to have a phone consultation instead.

There are so many subtle things that I just can't put into my written notes, but I can convey those things much more easily in person or by phone . . . the inflection of the pet's "voice," the intensity of a word or a sentence, or the feelings behind what they say.

Before we got together by phone, they sent me a list of questions, and I connected with their precious golden retriever, Molly Lisa, writing down notes to share with them.

Molly Lisa was a great conversationalist and she didn't take any time at all to start communicating with me.

The very first question on her mom and dad's list was:

Did anyone meet you when you passed over?

Immediately, Molly replied:

Yes, of course, no one comes to this side alone! I had several friends who came to take me through the light. It was so beautiful! Everything about dying was beautiful. It was such an easy transition for me.

My body simply went to sleep and although I exited immediately and was able to look down on you touching me, I was no longer weighed down by my body and I could feel everything you were feeling.

I stayed around you for a while because I needed to share in your feelings, but soon enough it was time for me to continue on my way. The light was patient and was there for me.

This healing light I'm talking about is all around us, both loving and healing at the same time. As soon as I was in it, I started to remember who I was, and how I belonged in Spirit.

As we continued our conversation, one of the first images I received was of Molly entering the bright light. At the far end of the light she saw a human. Molly told me that she could see "her mom" from far away. She rushed to meet her, but as she got closer, she realized it wasn't her mom at all, but someone who looked very much like her.

Well, the skeptic in me wanted to stop right there and not write down what I'd just seen, exactly as I saw it. The skeptical part of me kept thinking this just couldn't be right! I didn't want to say it to Molly's mom and dad this way. The human part of me thought . . . what if I'm wrong . . . and if I'm wrong, the skeptical husband will never, ever be able to trust me, or believe in what I and other animal communicators do.

My rational thinking self wanted me to edit what I'd just seen and simply write that Molly saw a human standing at the far end of the light ready to welcome her when she crossed over. That would make more sense, and be safer, wouldn't it?

Yet, the experienced intuitive side of me prompted me to write the message down exactly the way it came through. Over the years, I've learned how important it is not to go back and change anything. It may not make any sense to me at the moment, but it could definitely make sense to the people who'll be receiving the information.

Molly Lisa then continued:

It wasn't my mom but it was a spirit very similar to her and I knew it belonged in my group of humans.

She came to tell me that whenever I wanted, she'd be next to me. She also mentioned that if I did get a chance to talk with you, Mom, I should say she's now doing well and that everything has been "settled."

(The idea of "settled" seemed to mean that there was something she'd been working on and finally understood or fixed.)

I don't usually connect directly with the spirits of humans, but on rare occasions, I will receive information from them coming in through a pet. I couldn't ignore the fact that this message contained what could be a very sensitive piece of information, so it was important to translate it just the way it was given to me.

When the date of our phone consultation arrived, I recounted my conversation with Molly exactly as I received it. I was fully prepared for a skeptical, judgmental, or negative reaction, but instead, I was very pleasantly surprised.

I shouldn't have worried in this case, even for a moment. My intuitive sense was right on target. What Molly told me was exactly what convinced them that, truly, it was their Molly who was doing the talking.

Molly's mom knew immediately that the person who was there to greet Molly was, in fact, her sister who'd passed tragically a year and a half ago. Coincidentally, out of the blue, two people had just recently told her how very much she and her sister looked alike.

Later, after our phone consultation, Molly's mom sent me a beautifully confirming e-mail. This was the first part of that e-mail:

> *I wanted to say a very heartfelt thank you for your help in contacting our dear Molly. My heart has been broken but you gave me so much comfort and peace.*
>
> *When Molly passed, I came across many websites but I felt so pulled to yours. Your compassion and love for what you do is so evident. Your understated, genuine approach is refreshing in this day and age where everyone wants to be a celebrity. I kept coming back to your page*

and watched you on You Tube. I soon told my doubting husband and he jumped right on board with a leap of faith!!!

I was glad you suggested we speak on the phone and not just by e-mail. You were right - there was information that I would have missed or perhaps not understood - thank you for that!!!

I have to tell you that when you told me Molly saw someone who met her as she crossed - someone who appeared similar to me - well - what a wonderful gift!

My sister passed tragically a year and a half ago and our family was fractured prior to her death. We were divided as a family and before we knew it, she was gone.

My sister was a wonderful giving person who always wanted to help - it would be so like her to run to greet Molly - to step in to help me - to be there for me - and for Molly.

Prior to our phone call - two different people had mentioned how much I looked like my sister. At the time - I thought it was strange that on two separate occasions - two people would each make such a fuss about how much I look like my sister - but now I know why - those words would come back to reinforce what you told me.

Also, the word "settled" - it has always been with much sadness that we could never "settle" what happened in our family. We all live with great regret for how we lost focus of what's important. To have the affirmation that my sister wanted me to know she'd finally understood/ fixed something - that things were "settled" - well - when I read that paragraph - it offered so much peace.

The moral of this part of the story is: Always follow your first instincts. Never let your rational thinking self overrule what your intuitive self is telling you, lest you end up rationalizing away the truth!

(The rest of her mom's e-mail will be continued after the next part of my conversation with Molly.)

You can see immediately how well Molly answered the first question that was on her mom and dad's list, but she had even more wisdom to impart as she answered the rest of their questions.

Are you with any family members or friends?

When we go back to Spirit we belong in groups that are like families. We usually travel together with each other, as well as with those close to us you call friends.

On your side, there are times we might not have called them friends at all, but enemies. However, here we understand that sometimes it's necessary to be with those who oppose our views because it helps us understand what "good" and "bad" are on your side. Sometimes even evil. We've chosen to be with these others, even before we go back to your side, so that we'll have the experiences we need in order to learn the lessons we've chosen to work on.

Regardless, I'm never alone. All my family and friends are always here with me, and also with you when you call.

Were you in pain?

Pain is a word that I didn't often care to use when I was living with you. I was not myself. I knew my body wasn't working well anymore and I felt tired. It was getting hard to do my normal routine. No, I don't think it was painful as far as my body could tell, but my mind realized I was coming to the end of my life.

Did you know you were going to pass, and if so for how long?

It's very interesting that we always know we're going to pass when our lives are nearing their end. I can't tell you if it's a knowing, or if we're simply ok with that "feeling." I do know that all animals know and understand death, unlike humans. We're OK with the passing of our bodies, because at some level we understand that those are simply vehicles for our minds and souls.

Besides, when we're close to dying we receive "visits" from the spirit side that prepare us for our journey. It makes everything a lot more real and less frightening.

We long to feel you. Have you, or will you, give us any signs, and if so what should we look for?

I already did. At least I tried very hard to give you the impression I was still sitting next to you. I walked on the floor really hard so you could hear my toenails. And I brushed against the back of Dad's legs too.

Of course, I'm new when it comes to doing these things, and I might not have done them hard enough, but I want you to know that I've tried to do things for you at different times.

For example, I was with you in the car on your way back home from the vet's, but your grief was so intense you couldn't feel me.

Just know that I'm always around you because the love we feel for each other will never end just because I'm in Spirit. On the contrary, I'll be here for you when your turn comes, and we'll be together again.

Are you still around us?

I am, and I'll continue to be. Every time you say my name, every time you think about me, I'm right there next to you. Know this . . . I will never leave you.

Do you come to the house and yard to visit?

I do go now and then to visit if you're around, but otherwise, I'm busy in Spirit reviewing my life with you, studying and understanding more and more each day. My soul is evolving, learning, and growing in unison with our group, and eventually with the Universe.

What was your happiest time/memory with us?

I can't answer that question because each day, each moment, was part of our grand plan. There was never a moment that was more important and happier than another.

My purpose in this lifetime was simply to find you, both of you, so that we could spend as much time together as the body I was wearing would allow.

Remember when I talked about our group . . . when you were in Spirit you were also part of our group. We decided a long time ago that we'd go back to your side to experience life together and be able to love together.

That's why it's so hard for you to heal. There's a hole in your soul that can only be filled by me. I understand that because it works the same for me.

We're soul mates. We are, and will always be, part of the same soul, and as such we've always understood each other more and better than the rest. We are, and have been, a reflection of each other.

If you can, please help me to understand the feeling I had of your life force leaving your body.

It's because we're part of the same soul group that you were able to feel me. When my life force elevated, you felt it in your own body because it was as if a part of you was leaving.

This is what it feels like to lose part of your self. The feeling of emptiness will go away in time, but it will never be filled by someone else.

This, of course, is not to tell you that you shouldn't invest your love in another being. No, on the contrary, you should. You have a lot of love to give. I'm simply stating a fact. I was special. I completed your soul, Mom!

Do you know how much we love you and how much joy you gave us?

The feeling was mutual because I came back to your side with the sole purpose of being with you again, and to give you joy. It was a wonderful life, and one we'll all remember for a long time.

Thank you for giving me this gift of communication on my anniversary date of being reborn into Spirit. This is my natural state, and I'll be waiting for you patiently until it's your time.

The second part of Molly's mom's e-mail then continued:

I also thank you for the detailed notes. At first - there seemed to be so much information - very deep. I read each answer over and over and I don't think I've ever understood anything as much or as well as I did those responses.

Every word has a purpose and place in my life. In 12 years of Catholic school, I never saw a glimpse or understanding of insights like I did reading those answers - and I continue to see more when I read the notes again and again.

So many of the answers provided were from questions I struggle with - the words "my soul mate" - which I totally have always called her - helped me to move to a different level of love and understanding. It was as if she knew my questions and tried to provide clarity for me - and she did - with your generous help!

In closing - I want to say how special you are and how wonderful it is that you give "a voice" to our beloved animals. My husband is working on trying to open himself so he can experience touch and feelings that perhaps are out of the norm for him. You helped him greatly with that! He is so willing to try!!!

I love my Molly so much - my daughter with the blond hair, curls, and TAIL!!! I always told her - after having sons - you are the best and most beautiful daughter I could've ever dreamed of!!! I always wanted a girl with blond hair, big brown eyes and curls - I just never expected a tail - but how perfect you are!!!

I try to temper my tears with gratitude. Gratitude that a beautiful creature like my Molly touched my life and taught me so much about love and kindness.

I'll continue to read the notes and hope one day my heart can catch up with the reasoning of my mind - that 11 years and 8 months is a good run, although I don't think 100 years would have been enough!

Life can be so strange - the table Molly died on was the very one she sat on at her first puppy visit.

Molly was 6 weeks old at the time. The vet told me to take her paw and to always place it in the palm of my hand - that I would be "imprinting" her to me.

Well, just before Molly died - she reached out her paw and placed it into the palm of my hand - I know she was "imprinting" me into her soul. A gift I will always remember - a gift I will cherish.

Thank you Dr. Monica and may God continue to bless you with your kind and loving work.

During a phone or in-person consultation, my clients are able to ask other questions they didn't think to write down ahead of time . . . anything they can think of to make it more real to them.

MOLLY LISA

Molly's mom and dad also wanted to know about Molly and their son, and their son's cat. Molly's mom then wrote:

> *We asked you on the phone about our son and if Molly had any messages for him. The photo you described is one that sits in the drawer - and yes - it is of a young boy - our son with a golden retriever - Molly's father - whom you also mentioned.*
>
> *When I asked you about Chip the cat - you said the word "savior" came to you. When I told our son about that - he said - it totally described his relationship with that feral cat when he was away at college - he said the cat saved him and he saved the cat.*
>
> *Our son was so comforted to know his first love Molly is happy and safe! He had a wonderful dream about her visiting his apartment.*
>
> *Also, during our phone call, when Molly was talking about the fact that she's always around them, her skeptical dad said jokingly to Molly that he wished she'd bite him so he'd know for a fact she was there next to him.*

I responded that any biting would have to be done by proxy since Spirit wouldn't do something like that. And I added, with a warning, "You just may not know what you're asking for." We all enjoyed a hearty laugh, and that was the end of our session.

Some time later, I received another e-mail from Molly's mom:

> *I'm not sure if you remember me - Molly Lisa our golden girl passed and you helped us find so much comfort and peace in dealing with her passing.*
>
> *I don't know if you remember when you spoke with us on the phone that my husband asked you to tell Molly to bite him so he would know Molly is in fact still with him. We all laughed and you said any biting would have to be done by proxy!*

YOUR PET CALLED

We were in Philadelphia recently. I got out of the car to go up to a client's house when I saw the most beautiful Golden looking at me from a few doors down. I went up to that door and the dog had her nose pressed against the glass and was so sweet.

The homeowner came to the glass storm door and I explained that we'd just lost our golden retriever and it was wonderful to see the big blond fur ball looking back at me! The lady was lovely and invited me into her home to meet her dog.

You can imagine how thrilled my husband was when, after he parked the car, he came to find me visiting with such a beautiful Golden. The dog immediately took to my husband and he sat on the floor while she kissed him and rolled onto her back for a belly rub - all the things he shared with Molly - interactions he misses so much.

We stayed for a while then went on our way. Later as we drove home to the Shore, my husband said how sweet Rosalita the Golden was, but wow - he said - she's a biter!!!

I asked him to explain, and he said she kept biting him - he was surprised that a 2-year-old dog would bite like that.

I couldn't help but laugh - I asked him to remember his request!

He had to think about it, but when he got it - it was like a light went off in his head and certainly in his heart!!! It was a wonderful experience. I wanted to share it with you!!! I think Molly heard his request!!! Hope you are well and continuing your wonderful work!

Molly definitely had heard her dad's request, and she found a way to fulfill it, by proxy!

My communication with Molly took place in September, and the phone consult with her mom and dad took place in early October, so imagine my surprise when in December I received this e-mail:

MOLLY LISA

Wishing you and your family (furry members as well!) a very Merry Christmas and a healthy, happy, prosperous New Year!

As my husband and I reflect on the past year with the New Year approaching - we are so thankful we connected with you and that you connected with our dear Molly Lisa.

It was a different Christmas without Molly, and we had a good cry when the grandchildren, my 94-year-old Mom, and our sons and their wives all went home after a great dinner as a family.

I find great comfort in re-reading the notes you sent us. It seems we have many friends who are now going through the same loss with their dogs. I tell them about you - you truly are an answer to prayer!

Thank you again!

It was very heartwarming to have a client remember me at the end of the year, and confirm for me once again how much my work helped to relieve their sadness. I can only say a very special Thank You.

I love my work, and I do it from my heart. And I especially love Molly Lisa's story because it brings together the answers to so many of the questions people ask me all the time, namely: where do our pets go; do they meet someone else in heaven; do they know their purpose; do they see us, feel us, and stay around us.

Molly Lisa had so many important thoughts to share with her mom and dad . . . thoughts that were so loving and healing.

Communications with pets in Spirit . . . when they contain such important messages . . . remind me that Spirit is always in control.

Ashley

Play my song!

In the summer of 2012, Al and Iris came to see me in person. They wanted to be present when I talked with their dog, Ashley, who'd already crossed over The Rainbow Bridge into Spirit. Ashley was a 14-year-old brindle and white female Shih Tzu.

The communication itself was what you might consider a typical conversation with a pet who was now in Spirit, but there was one very important thing Ashley mentioned that came as a complete surprise to me.

Ashley told me that, when she was living with her mom and dad, one of her favorite things was when Daddy would play a special song for her. She loved it, and she'd often use that time to relax in a special way.

At first, I thought she meant Dad sang to her. But no, she very specifically said he "played her song."

The picture she sent me was of herself, when she was on earth, sitting next to the piano, watching her dad with loving eyes. The feeling that accompanied this picture was one of Ashley knowing this music was meant just for her.

When I told Al and Iris, they became emotional because this information was so powerful for them. After they had a moment to reflect, Al told me he's a composer. He said Ashley was always there when he played the piano, and he also told me he often played a special piece that he'd composed just for her.

ASHLEY

I was absolutely amazed because this was the first time a dog ever told me that a person was playing a piece of music that was dedicated specifically to her. No dog had ever sent me a picture, even similar to Ashley's, with those particular feelings associated with it, as if someone was romancing her. It was truly a very special and very loving image.

I was very surprised to hear from Al a few days later when he sent me this e-mail, along with two audio recordings:

Hi Dr. Monica:

Iris and I really enjoyed meeting you and having Ashley back in our lives again for a few precious moments. We both miss her terribly and try in our own ways to move on.

I wanted to share a special song with you that Ashley inspired more than she could ever know. The song is called "Here with You." It's my way of dealing with the profound sadness her loss has caused. She'd sit at my feet whenever I started to play the piano and would remain there until I finished.

I pray she's able to hear me when I play for her now, but I can't tell. It's my hope, however, that possibly she'll hear it better if you play it. If that's possible, please just thank her for sharing her life with us and let her know how much we miss her. She brought more happiness into our lives than we ever thought possible.

Thank you, Dr. Monica, for sharing your special gift with us. I'm also enclosing a song that I believe was Ashley's favorite, called "Gentle Pain." It's a very simple melody that I would play over and over again as I'd pray and meditate with her.

I think it lulled her into a very peaceful, tranquil, and happy state... at least I hope it did.

With warmest regards,

Al and Iris

This was my response to Al's e-mail:

> Dear Al:
>
> Thank you for sending me your music. I really enjoyed having you here. When you left, it had been a fast two hours of conversation that went by so quickly I hardly noticed the time until we were all finished. I'm glad you enjoyed our meeting as well.
>
> Well, Al, I have to tell you something first. I'm not a musically inclined person. I do enjoy songs, but most instrumental music doesn't usually have an appeal for me. Since I lost 85% of my hearing, instrumental music has to really mean something to me in order for me to be able to enjoy it. That's why what I'm about to tell you is so important.
>
> I received your e-mail yesterday but was too busy to open it right away. I received your second e-mail as well.
>
> Today, I had a little time between clients, so I opened the second e-mail, hit download, and started to listen to the music of "Gentle Pain," with Ashley in my mind (as well as the two of you, of course!).
>
> I actually FELT the music! I loved the piano because it made me feel relaxed, almost as if I were in a dream. When the five high notes played every now and then, I'd get goose bumps on both my arms.
>
> At the same time I would "feel" Ashley telling me that's why she loved the song so much. Those five notes were so important to her that she sent me a picture from Spirit of her running in happy circles. It was as if those five notes had a very special significance for her.
>
> I'm doing the best I can to describe my feelings here, which I understand were actually not just my feelings, but also those of Ashley. She absolutely LOVED that piece of music, and because of how I felt, so did I! Apparently, Ashley wanted to be present today to tell you how much she still enjoys that piece.

ASHLEY

I was interrupted, so later on, I came back and opened the music for "Here With You." Although it didn't give me the same feelings that the other piece evoked, it too, is so beautiful in its own way, and I did like it also.

Thank you for sharing this beautiful music with me, Al. It's been a great experience, and I'm sure Ashley also loved to hear it one more time.

Love and light to both of you, and let's keep in touch.

Dr. Monica

Yes, it's true! Ashley clearly showed us that animals do enjoy instrumental music and singing, as well as different melodies and sounds . . . whether they're on earth or in Spirit.

You can listen to Ashley's special music (*Gentle Pain*), and to the other melody she inspired (*Here With You*), by going to:

www.petcommunicator.com/music/

Casper

A single flower meant so much

In January 2015, Christian wanted to talk with his beloved dog who'd gone back into Spirit at the age of 15.

Casper was an all-white, male miniature maltese who'd been a special member of the family while Christian was growing up. As a young adult, Christian had moved out of the family home, but he'd come back often to visit. He felt a very strong connection with this little dog.

As I called Casper to come talk with me, I just couldn't connect with him as easily and quickly as I usually do. The date Christian had written for

Casper's death (January 2014) indicated that it had been a whole year ago, but it was as if Casper hadn't yet made the connection that he'd been in Spirit for a whole year.

Because my client and I were talking by phone, I asked him if he was sure Casper had been gone for a whole year. He then realized he'd accidentally typed 2014 instead of 2015 in his e-mail to me, so that meant the little dog I was trying to talk with had been gone for only a few days.

Because we were talking with him before he'd really had time to adjust to being in Spirit, it's no wonder I was having difficulty connecting with him. But I'd already made the initial connection with Casper, and although he wasn't giving us as many images as pets in Spirit often do, I was still able to translate important things for Christian, and he was able to provide several interesting validations.

I explained to Casper that Christian wanted to find out how he was doing now that he was in Spirit.

He replied:

I'm so happy to hear that you want to talk with me! I never imagined we could have a conversation, and you'd be able to understand what I was thinking, but this is a great gift and I want to make good use of it.

I always wanted to tell you how close I felt to you. Granted, everyone in the family was great to me, and I have no complaints, but you were my buddy, you were my special friend, and I can only hope I let you know time and time again how very special you were to me, and how much love I had for you in my heart.

Then I began asking him his dad's questions:

Did you feel loved?

Of course I did! Actions sometimes speak louder than anything you could say. I felt loved, and at times very special, particularly during my last weeks with the family. I knew I was loved and cared for then, perhaps more, or maybe a little differently, than at any other time.

Did you like your sisters?

I never considered them my sisters. They were simply housemates.

At this point Christian was laughing as he validated that Casper never considered his sisters family. They just ignored each other.

Why did you cry whenever you saw me?

Maybe I couldn't talk, but somehow I was trying to communicate to you how much I missed you, and how happy I was that you were home again visiting with me.

I'd wished for a long time that you'd take me with you, but then I was going to miss the others, so I was fine staying where I was.

However, when you were home, I felt you were there just to visit me, to be with me, to love me, and to play like we did before. I longed for your hands, your touch, your words. And even when you didn't talk to me, I just liked being close to you.

Who do you love the most?

When I was on your side I had a very special attachment to you. Even though I didn't know why then, now I understand because I'm able to see things a lot more clearly on this side. We continue to find one another to work on our issues, and we've crossed paths many times before. That's what makes our relationship so special.

As a matter of fact, humans and animals often travel through lifetimes together in groups. That means we'll all see each other again and again as we continue to evolve and learn.

What memories do you have growing up?

> I remember my hair having to be brushed. I wasn't sure I liked the feeling of my face hair being pulled, but I knew that letting her brush me would make Mom happy.
>
> I remember playing with you and enjoying your company. I remember there being times in your life when I mattered a lot, and times when I didn't matter that much, but I forgave you quickly because I loved you.
>
> I also remember having fun with kids, enjoying our silly games of hide and seek.

Christian said that he'd had many dogs and none of them played hide and seek the way Casper did, so this was also a good validation.

Is there anything you wish we could do for you now?

> It's important to me that you keep my memory, that my picture stays in the house so everyone can see me when they come in. It was my home, and I want to continue to be there. My name, which I loved, has to be prominent, too. I LOVE the flower!

In the image Casper sent me, I saw a single flower close to his picture.

Christian could hardly believe what he was hearing. He said his girlfriend had given his mom an orchid with a single, beautiful bloom, and they'd placed the plant next to Casper's picture.

What a wonderful validation! This one even made my jaw drop in awe when my client shared that information with me.

I told Christian his little Casper was amazing. He'd confirmed the special love they had for each other, told us about playing hide and seek, and how he considered his sisters to be only roommates, not family. That he was then able to show me a single flower . . . and to make sure I would translate exactly that . . . was quite incredible. So many clear validations in just one consultation. This was a great day for Christian, and for me!

Chapter 3

SIGNS FROM SPIRIT

Signs from Spirit

When I talk with clients about their pets who are now in Spirit, many times they tell me how very much they want to receive some specific signs from those pets. They want to know if their essence is still around and still watching over them.

When I talk with pets in Spirit, they say they're *always* around us and sending us clues. They may name the various ways in which they try to catch our attention, and still, we often don't pay attention to those clues, or we may just think that what we're experiencing is a coincidence. At other times, we're just too sad, too worried, or too focused on our own pain and grief to understand, or comprehend.

The stories in this chapter clearly show the many signs that pets try to send us.

Harry

Gone in 45 seconds

Recently, I was talking with Janis during a consultation about Harry, her 8-year-old male Shetland sheepdog mix.

Harry had been attacked and killed in front of her when Janis was taking care of a German Shepherd while his owners were away. Because the big dog had a history of being aggressive, she'd wisely secured him to a tie out in her back yard.

HARRY

All her dogs were outside in the yard, but she needed to go back inside the house, so she called them to follow her.

As Harry turned to come to her, he walked right past the German Shepherd, oblivious to any danger. The larger dog promptly grabbed him and pinned him down on the ground. All efforts to break the bite were in vain, and in a mere forty-five seconds, Harry was gone.

You can imagine how inconsolable Janis was, and why she sought my help to see if she could find some way to understand how such a senseless act had occurred.

Harry was able to help his mom overcome some of her grief with his answers to her questions.

Why did you choose to die this way?

> I didn't know it was going to happen exactly the way it did. We understand from here that we have a finite time to be on your side with you, and we know, more or less, when that time will be up, but what we don't know is exactly how it's going to happen. In fact, I would call what happened an accident. Neither of us thought it was going to be my end.

> But Mom, don't worry. Because it was an accident, I'm permitted to come back to finish my time with you, and to continue my teachings with you.

> Isn't this exciting! Yes, I can come back to you, but in a different body of course.

> Now, I need to caution you about something. My soul will be the same, but my personality might be a little different.

> The reason for this is that the only way I can come back to the same human is not only to wear a different body, but to make this journey important for the growth of my soul, also.

Therefore I'll be there to learn new things and to look at life a little differently by having a different personality. That's the only way I can continue to grow.

That means I will not be the same Harry, but I will still have some things about me that would be exactly the same as when I was Harry.

If you'd be ready to receive me back, I can start planning, and I might be available by the end of this year.

Usually humans want to know how you'd recognize any of us coming back to you.

It's easy if you put your heart into it. You see, you might not recognize me right away because I'm in a different body, but your soul will recognize my soul.

When you look into my new eyes, and you spend a little time with the new me, we'll understand and recognize each other's souls, so much so, that neither of us will want to be separated from the other.

Your heart will tell you.

So when you're ready, just talk with me and let me know, and I'll take care of the rest.

Will you send me a sign that you're here with me now?

Even though it's difficult to make energy move in ways that I want it to, I do try to leave some "bread crumbs" around to let you know I'm there with you.

Did you find my fur? I made sure I put a few strands of hair in a place where I knew you would clean, and yet my hair was still there.

Janis was laughing! She told me she has a good cleaning crew that comes in and does a deep cleaning, so regrettably, she never had the opportunity to find the hair herself.

HARRY

While I was talking with her, Harry chimed in, and said that if she saw a flying being where it seemed to be out of place, it was him telling her that he's always next to her, and that he's now free and happy.

In response to this, Janis mentioned to me that where she lives in Seattle it's now very cold, with freezing rain and snow. But just the other day when she walked out to her chicken coup, she'd seen a dragonfly. It was totally out of place for that time of year, and it shone brighter than usual with a green and blue shimmering hue to its body. It so caught her attention that she talked to the dragonfly saying, "Well, hi, beautiful! I haven't seen you around here before."

She confessed that for an instant she thought it might be Harry sending her a sign, but at that moment, she dismissed the thought from her mind just as quickly.

At least she dismissed it until after Harry made his comment during our consultation about sending her a "flying being."

Now, the appearance of the dragonfly the other day became much more real and meaningful to her. She knew it truly was a sign from her Harry.

Chobisuke-san

Follow the crumbs

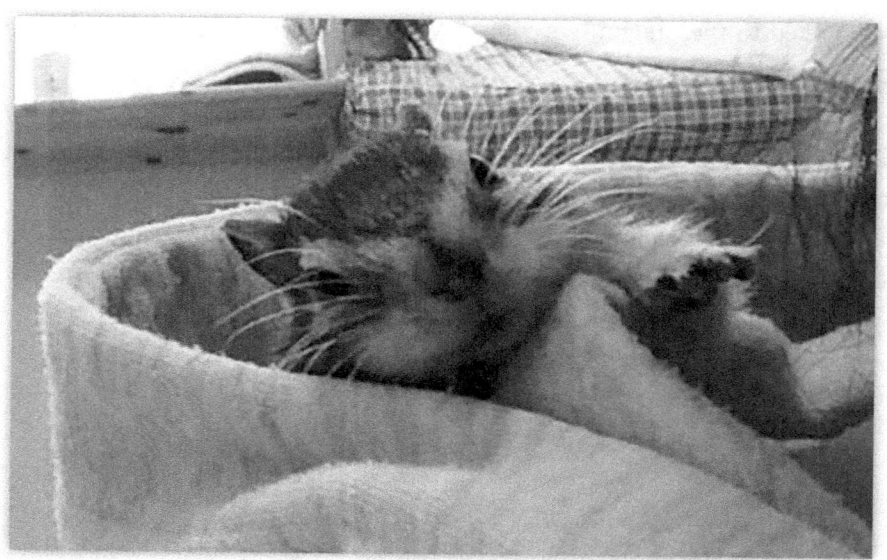

Chobisuke-san was a chipmunk who lived with his family in Japan until his death at nine years of age. Chipmunks, who are cousins to squirrels, may live up to eight years of age in captivity, but to live to nine years old is amazing.

He was very much loved by his people, so when the time was right to talk with him in Spirit, they requested a consultation.

We had a long communication over several emails. One of the main things they wanted me to tell him was that they wanted to "feel" him around them.

Chobisuke-san replied:

When I sent you a picture of a heart in your window, I wasn't sure you'd notice it. I'm so glad you did.

You know, it's difficult to change the energy around me so that I can send you signs you can see. Sometimes I'm not able to do it, although I really want to.

I'll leave you little clues around the house, and if you look closely you'll find them.

When you notice something that I'm trying to do for you, it makes me extremely happy, and I want to do more.

After a few weeks, I received an email back with this information to convey to Chobisuke-san:

We found your long hairs and short hairs near our favorite window. We also found what looked like a spill near the empty food tray that was in your cage. A new spot appeared even after we'd taken everything out, cleaned it, sanitized it, and put the empty tray back in place. We checked before, but the spot wasn't there until this morning.

Then you reminded Dad to move the futon. When we did, we could smell your scent coming up very strong, and we could see a spot on the floor that wasn't there before. We both noticed this. It was great to know you're still here with us.

I also felt you on my knees a few times, and Dad felt you on his shoulders. Even if we can't see you, we know you're by our side. I've also saved all the other clues you've sent us.

Thank you Chobisuke-san!!

YOUR PET CALLED

Here are some pictures his mom sent with the evidence that this little chipmunk was sending them signs to let them know how much he cared . . .

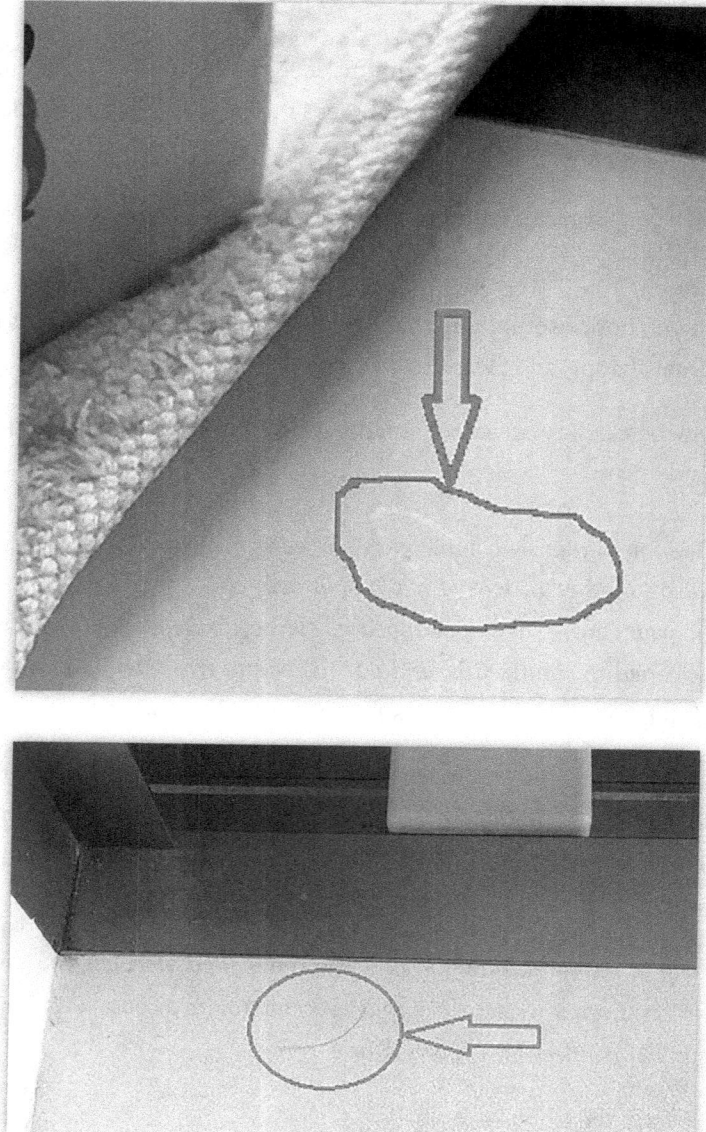

CHOBISUKE-SAN

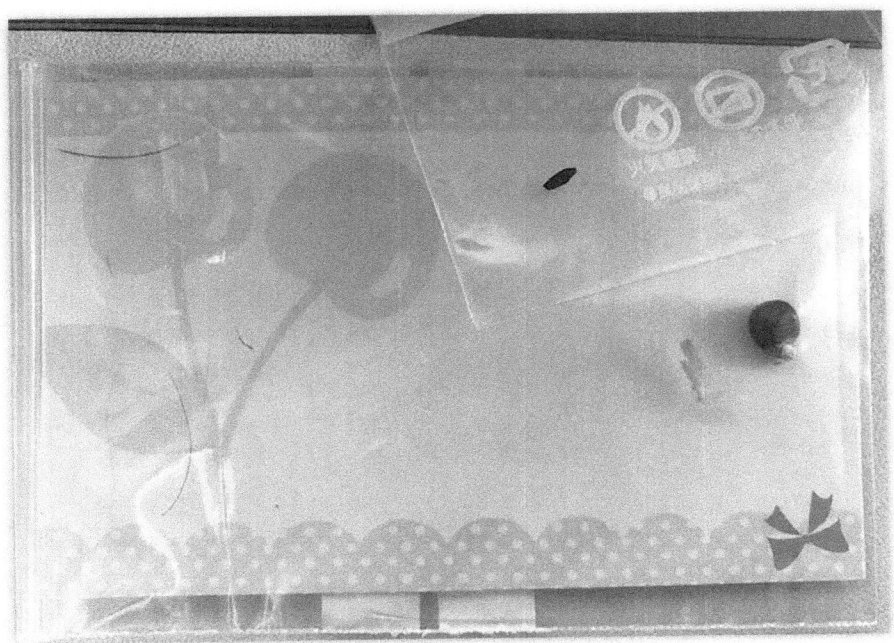

Above: pictures of saved items

Above: Pieces of food from one bowl are now on the floor of the cage some distance away

What impressed me most was that these Japanese clients continued to receive these signs from their pet well into the first year that he was in Spirit. It was such a nice confirmation that our animals are always around us.

As Chobisuke-san said, look closely for the clues, and you, also, may find some wonderful signs that your pets in Spirit are always around you, too!

Candela

Feathers of my soul

Candela had originally been found with her mother when she was just a tiny puppy and had been rescued by a kind person in Argentina. Federico and his wife, Julieta, then adopted her when she was about 2 months old.

Sadly, at the age of just 4½, Candela developed kidney failure. After fighting to save her life for more than a month, and going into debt with all the veterinarian bills, the family decided it was time to let her go because she was suffering and crying constantly.

They asked me to talk with Candela in Spirit because they were traumatized by having had to do this, and they were devastated by their loss.

During the consultation Candela responded to this question:

Is Candela with us? I've read so many things about reincarnation and about the spirit of animals staying around us. I need to know if she could give me a clear sign that we're definitely talking with her. How can we know if she's next to us?

Daddy, Mommy, Feli, I'm always there, and I'll be with you wherever you are. That's my promise. The only thing I need to complete this promise is that you never forget me.

Every time you remember me with love, it's like it's raining petals on top of me. They're so soft when they touch me, and they give me so much happiness because I know each one is a little bit of love you're sending me.

In Spirit, there's not just a single place to be. We can be in several places at the same time. That's why, no matter when you think of me, I'm by your side. It doesn't matter if Mami is at home with Felipe (their 1 ½ year old son) and Papi is working, I'll always be there next to each of you.

I've also spoken with my sisters (the other dogs in the house) and I've apologized. They understood me well. They know I'm learning more every day.

Reincarnation is possible, but there's a lot of time to wait between one lifetime and another because there's so much to learn. I'm not going to return to this family, but maybe I'll go back to Felipe when he's big.

If I do that, don't worry because the part of me that was Candela will remain here with you in your hearts forever. That part is never going to go away.

I also have to tell you that I'm always showing you signs that I'm with you. And by the way, the only thing you have to do is to be attentive and watch and listen.

For example, not many days ago, I left something at the entrance of the garage where the street makes a unique angle. It was a feather of a bird who's a friend. Every time you see a feather, I want you to know that I was there and that I'm sending you a "hello." It also tells you I'm here and I'm fine.

Another thing I did, I hid a toy from Felipe and then you found it. I like to do that so you have a smile on your face, and so you remember me with happiness.

There are other things I try to do, although moving my energy so that I can be felt around the house is a bit difficult because you have so many distractions. But if you pay more attention, you'll see that sometimes I try to be close to you where I've always been, and you can feel me walking around there too.

Look at Felipe because he'll always tell you when he sees me.

Also, don't worry about the surgery one of my sisters will need to have because the tumor is "encapsulated." She'll have an infection afterward, but it can easily be treated.

I had to do this consultation in two steps. There was a five hour time difference between us, and because of Federico's work hours, it would be several days before we'd be able to connect by phone.

After talking with Candela, I sent an e-mail to her dad with my notes so he could read them right away. Then when we were finally able to connect via phone, we were able to clarify some things Candela had said.

When Federico called me, he said he lives in an apartment and not a house with a garage, so he definitely hadn't seen any feather on the ground.

Alarm bells started going off in my mind. How could I be so wrong?

I immediately asked Candela the question again, and the same answer came through. I then explained Candela's picture to Federico like this: The garage has a small double door with bars in it. The street comes in at a sloped angle for the car to go up, but there's a misalignment at the edge, right where the garage starts. The feather is right there, but you didn't see it.

On hearing this clarification, Federico told me this garage is at his mother's home where he often parks his car. He explained the misalignment as being a small step that goes into the garage. Now, he knew the correct location, and my alarm bells stopped ringing.

The next item that needed clarification was about what Candela described as a toy she'd hidden from Felipe, which the family later found.

Federico said Felipe didn't lose a toy, but there was "something" that had been lost and then found. He pressed me for more information, but the only thing I could tell him was that Candela kept telling me it was something for personal use, not necessarily a toy, but something that belonged to one of them.

Only then did Federico tell me they'd lost Felipe's pacifier, and they finally found it stuck in a toy truck. So there was a toy involved after all!

As I try to translate from Spirit, I do the best I can, but once in a while, what I'm being told by a pet might not seem to be accurate at first. However, with a little detective work, it's often easy to validate the message the pet was sending me.

When we were almost finished, Federico shared a validation about something that happened before we ever had our phone conversation.

He said that as soon as he read my written notes, he realized he was supposed to be looking for a feather. He was disappointed that he hadn't found one yet. So, while walking to catch the bus on his way home from work, he decided to talk to Candela in Spirit. He asked her over and over again to please send him some feathers so that he'd know with certainty, before talking with me on the phone, that she was around him.

Just as he was approaching the bus stop, a couple turned around and said, "Look! There's a pigeon stuck on that fence. She's upside down! She must be impaled there because she's not moving. Let's try to help."

So Federico, still with the thought of Candela in his mind, turned around and welcomed the opportunity to help an injured pigeon. As soon as he reached out to touch her, she simply let go of the fence and shed a single feather at his feet.

When he recounted this incident to me during our phone call, he told me he cried with joy all the way home!

Imagine my surprise when, just two days later, I received an email from Federico with two awesome pictures that you'll see below.

Above: feathers at the entrance to the garage

Above: feathers inside the house

Four months later, I received an e-mail from Federico with yet another validation.

He said one of their other dogs did have to have surgery to remove a mammary tumor. The family was worried sick while they were waiting for the surgeon to give them a report after finishing the operation. When the surgeon came out, she calmly said, "Don't worry. Her tumor was encapsulated."

Federico told me their mouths dropped open and they were absolutely stunned to hear the surgeon use the very same word to describe the tumor that Candela had used when she told them about the surgery several months earlier.

Everything was exactly as Candela had said it would be, including the fact that her sister developed an infection after surgery that was successfully treated with antibiotics.

But that wasn't all. Federico also told me that while they were waiting for Candela's sister to come out of surgery, he looked down and found another feather. He knew immediately that Candela was right there waiting with her family. He exclaimed with such joy, "I know she's always with us wherever we are!"

Sukie

Look Pops, she looks like me!

When I was talking with Laura about how our furry friends in Spirit try to send us signs to tell us they're around us, I mentioned that many times we think those signs are just coincidences, when in fact our pets actually have a hand (or a paw) in it.

I told her we often see an article, a movie, a show, hear a piece of music, or see a picture that will remind us of the one who's gone.

She knew exactly what I was talking about. She told me that a few weeks after Sukie passed, her husband picked up a magazine, only to see a picture, right on the cover, that looked exactly as if it was Sukie looking right at him.

The best thing about it was that Laura had a picture of Sukie on her phone. When they compared the magazine picture with the phone picture, they noted that, even though their fur colors were different, both dogs were posed in exactly the same position with their faces at the same angle in both pictures.

For Laura and her husband, this picture was truly a sign from Sukie that they would treasure for a long time to come!

You'll be reading much more about Sukie in the next chapter about soulmates.

Look at the remarkable resemblance between the dog in the magazine picture, and the picture of Suki on the cell phone!

SUKIE

Daisy

A heaven-sent message

A client from Spain requested a consultation when she was mourning the passing of her dog Daisy. Once again, I talked about watching for things that seemed to be coincidences.

She then wrote to me later saying she was walking out to her car when she saw a sticky paper on the ground that was shaped like a teddy bear. She thought it was cute so she picked it up.

As she turned it over, she saw that it said: A space in my soul bears your name. She looked at it in awe as she realized she'd just been sent exactly the message she needed to receive to soothe her soul.

She knew it was heaven-sent to her because it was exactly how she felt at that moment. She then placed it for safekeeping with some of Daisy's fur so she'd have two precious keepsakes.

Always remember, whether it's a sign, a gift from another animal, a reminder of who the pet was because of something that belonged to him, or a simple photograph, our animals are continually finding ways of letting us know they are, and will always be with us.

DAISY

Above: Daisy's fur and the teddy bear paper saying: A space in my soul bears your name.

More About Signs from Pets in Spirit

Many of my clients are upset that they can't at least *feel* the energy of their pets when they can no longer see them. They think not feeling their energy means their pets aren't around them any longer. This just isn't true.

The energy of pets who've been with you for any length of time, and felt your love, will often be by your side, even when you haven't reached out to them.

Just know that everything they do is meant to give you a sign that their spirit is still around you all the time, so don't dismiss these instances by thinking they're merely coincidences.

In this chapter, you've read about a number of signs pets used to let their humans know they were with them. Here's a more comprehensive list of the kinds of signs your pets might use to let you know they're with you:

1) Hearing - they'll try to send you a familiar sound; you might hear a bark or meow, the sound of breathing or panting, their footsteps or the familiar click of their toenails on a wood or tile floor, or some other sound that was specific to them

2) Feeling - you may feel as if your pet just brushed against your leg; you may feel as if your pet is lying next to you on the bed or on the sofa

MORE ABOUT SIGNS FROM PETS IN SPIRIT

3) Seeing - you may see what appears to be a form or shadow moving out of the corner of your eye; you do a double take because what you thought you saw happened faster than the blink of an eye, but it was your pet's energy making it happen

4) Smelling - your pets may send you their scent, and you detect it even though none of the things they used to use are still around

5) Music - they may make a certain song come up that reminds you of them when you turn on a radio, play a CD, or use your MP3 player

6) Pictures - they'll use a picture in a book or a magazine, or on a sign or on flyers to catch your attention; the picture is of a different pet, but the resemblance to your own pet is almost identical; or they'll use something you read to trigger a precious memory

7) Orbs in photos - many times we don't see these images with our eyes in real time, but with better cameras we are able to capture the orbs of our loved ones more often now; they're there to remind you that your pet is still part of the family, and to let you know their energy is still around you

8) Butterflies and Dragonflies - these amazing creatures don't live very long, so when you see them it may mean a transformation has taken place; it may be a sign from a loved one that they've completed their transition to the other side; in Chinese legend seeing a butterfly can mean a soul has come to see you from the other side, so if a face or a voice comes into your mind, it's the soul of that person or animal acknowledging you, letting you know they're around you, and that they love you

9) Feathers - a feather will often appear out of nowhere and this, too, is a sign from your pets

Loving signs and messages are all around you. You just need to become aware that your beloved pets in Spirit are always trying to remind you that they just want to say hello, I'm fine, I'm well, and I love you!

Chapter 4

Soul Mates and Life Missions

Rocco

An old soul, a mission, and a lifetime of love

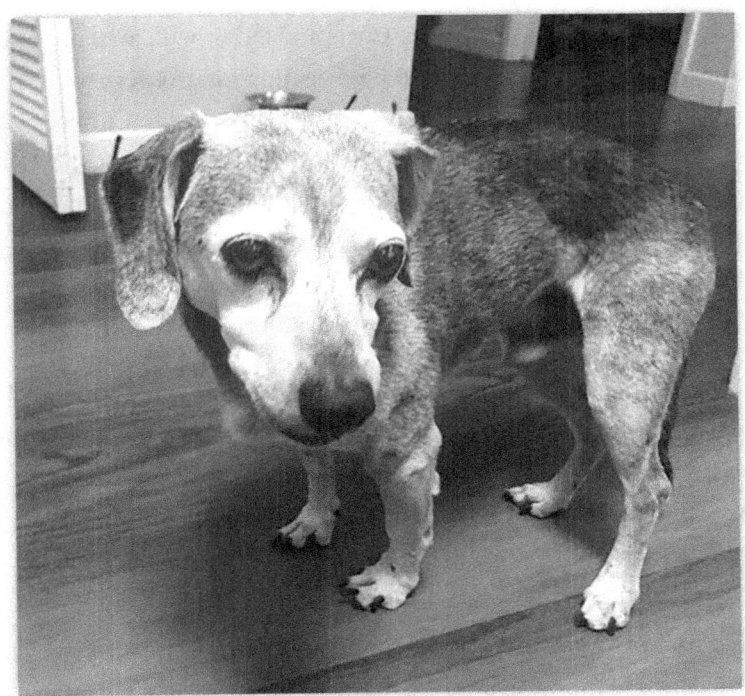

I n a recent e-mail message, Chris and Sarah reminded me that I'd helped them with their younger dog, Cali, when she was so very sick. (You can read Cali's story in the chapter about "Pets as Diagnosticians.") They felt my communication with her had led to a significant change in the outcome of her situation, so now it was Rocco's turn. He's a male Beagle mix, about 17 years old.

As soon as I connected with Rocco, I could feel that he was an old soul. He was very sure of himself . . . who he is, what he wants, and what his mission is. I explained that his dad and mom wanted to ask him some questions.

Then, as if he was speaking to only one specific person, he said, "It would be my pleasure to talk with you. You already know me better than anybody else. We have the type of understanding with each other as if we'd been together before. You hardly need any explanations. Still, I'd be happy to answer your questions."

I remember at one point asking Chris and Sarah who actually wrote the questions because Rocco seemed to be directing his answers to only one of them and not the other. Chris then told me he'd adopted Rocco when he was in college, so at first, it was just the two of them. Sarah and Cali both came later. He also told me he'd written the questions. Then I understood perfectly.

Here's how my communication with this very old soul went, starting with his dad's initial question . . .

Rocco, first let me tell you how much I love you and what an incredible 17 years it's been with you. You've taught me so much about life by sharing your incredible energy and unconditional love. I want to communicate with you to see how you're feeling right now, so can you describe to me what you feel?

It takes courage to be old, and I happen to have an abundance of that.

Some days are more difficult than others, but I know how to enjoy life and live in the moment. I don't care how I feel as long as I'm able to move around and still do what I want. I can honestly say that I don't mind being old. In fact, I think it's a badge of honor.

When others look at me, they don't see a tired being. They see a courageous one who's still enjoying everything and is very much HERE.

I think that being old doesn't necessarily mean being wise, but I happen to be both.

I don't want to talk about my aches and pains because I try not to think about those things unless my body really isn't working the way I want it to, so I'm not going to complain. I'm still me, still able to do all the things I need to do to survive, and I still feel all of your love.

Are you still enjoying your life even though we know you're 17 and have slowed down?

Absolutely! Slowing down doesn't mean anything. On the contrary, I'd say slowing down has allowed me to really cherish everything around me. I enjoy smelling everything a lot more than I did when I was younger and always in a hurry.

I see less now, but what I do see fills me with wonder. Lights, and the energy that moves around them, fill me with awe so that all I can do is stop and look at them. I appreciate everything a lot more.

Do I wish I was younger and more energetic? Of course! But I had my chance to do that already. Now with age, I enjoy other things. Naps, for instance, are wonderful when I'm in a warm place!

Laughingly Chris said this sounded exactly like him. He confirmed that when Rocco was very young, he was so energetic it was hard for him to stop at any one place for any length of time during their walks.

Do you like going for walks with us in the stroller when you're too tired to walk?

Yes, and that won't change. When I can't walk, or I'm just too tired, it's still wonderful to be outdoors and enjoy all the smells. Just make sure I can see all around me.

The picture he showed me made it look as if, at times, his dad wanted to close the top of the stroller using a zipper, but Rocco was trying to explain to me that he'd much rather see outside while he was lying in the stroller. Chris then said it was true he zippers the stroller top to create more warmth because sometimes it's too cold. When I told him Rocco needs to see outside,

Chris then settled on the idea of using an extra blanket for warmth instead of closing the stroller cover.

Can you tell us how you figured out how to open up gifts on Christmas and your birthday? No person we've ever met has heard of a dog doing that.

> It started when I could smell something I knew was inside the package for me, and I couldn't wait until my nose touched it. I could see and feel how happy you were that I could smell something inside the wrapping, and as I grew, I realized it made you very happy to see me open my gifts. Later on, it didn't matter if it was something smelly or not. I'd just have fun opening whatever you gave me.

Chris said this was absolutely true.

If there's anything we can do for you that we're not currently doing, can you please tell us?

> I think you know me so well that there's little I can ask for that you don't already do for me. However, I notice that sometimes when I'm walking on the wood floors, my back legs are giving out on me. I don't want to slide and end up having my legs spread out because I won't be able to get up. It would be nice if you could put a carpet there for me.

Sarah kept saying "Wow!" as Rocco was giving his answers. Now she explained to me that she noticed exactly what he was talking about, and she was worried about this for him, too. She quickly agreed to put another throw rug on the wood floor for him.

Rocco, you've always had a very curious yet alert face, and have always paid close attention to everything I do. What was your reason for always wanting to know these things?

> I don't think I had a particular reason, except for the fact that, since you're my life's mission, it was important for me to stay constantly aware of what you were thinking, doing, and experiencing at all times.

But my job as a teacher also included being your nurse, your confidant, and your soulmate. Without you, I'd be nothing. Without me, you wouldn't have been happy, or have learned as much as you did. It all worked out, and we've made a great team.

What's your favorite part of our relationship?

The favorite part of our relationship is how well we know each other. It's almost as if I'm your kid. You know everything about me and nothing escapes you.

We talk by looking at each other. I know that I communicate with you telepathically, and that many times you understand me immediately. Sometimes it might take you a little longer, but in the end, I know I can always count on you to understand what I need.

That's why I trust you implicitly, and I don't worry about the future. I'm certain you'll know what to do for me when the time comes to say goodbye. I'll give you a clue, or send you a message, and I know you'll get it. There should be no regrets then. I had a wonderful life with the people I love the most. I came here to find YOU and I DID!

Can you tell me how you've enjoyed the last 17 years? Do you feel as if you fulfilled your purpose in this lifetime?

I have. My mission is nearly complete. I came here with a set of instructions about what I needed to do. I knew what was expected of me, and I followed it to a "T."

Also, very early on, I remembered you from a past lifetime, so I knew my life this time would be complete and I wouldn't want to find anybody else. I knew you were my mission, and I was thrilled to understand that fact, even when I was very young.

I'm a teacher, and one of the best. My job was easy because I encountered two great students. So I'm extremely happy with this lifetime. I know that when we meet again in Spirit, we can go over everything and understand many more things together.

After Rocco talked about having two great students, jokingly, I said to Sarah, "Finally, you've come into the picture!"

Do you want to stay with us a little while longer? If yes, will you tell us if and when you may want some assistance so that you don't have to struggle anymore?

> As long as I can eat, drink, pee, poop, and sleep I'll be happy. When I can't do one of those things anymore, then it would be clear that my time has come.
>
> I'll try to let you know in my own way when my time is up, but I'm very dignified, so I don't expect to cry out loud. I might give you a little "unbecoming" sound like a grunt or a whine so you'll know the time is now.

Chris said that he absolutely understood this. I told him Rocco insisted on using the word "unbecoming," and Chris told me that was a sure sign I was definitely talking with Rocco. Then his questions continued . . .

Once again, I love you and we love you. Your nanny and poppy love you too. You've brought so much joy to our lives and have touched so many lives in a magical way. You're such an extremely unique and special friend that I've always wondered what you were in your past life. We feel as if you were always trying to tell us something. Were you?

> You know, I've loved everyone I've come in contact with. I think this is my greatest talent. I simply LOVE, and my job has been to show everyone that you, too, can do the same thing. Life is simple. We're here to learn to love. Once you understand that, the rest is so simple.
>
> To answer your question, in a past life I was also a dog. But I was a big dog, and you and I were partners. You depended on me and I depended

on you. We made a great hunting team and we shared a lot together. We'd sleep together, eat together, hunt together, and fight intruders together. It was also a great life.

In the image Rocco sent me, I saw Chris as a nomad and Rocco as a hunting dog. They did everything together.

Chris told me that Rocco has always had a Big Dog complex, even though he weighs barely 20 pounds. He'd go up to big dogs and try to fight them, and he'd never back down.

Is there anything else you'd like to share with us about your life?

I picked you. Coming in to see you again was one of my greatest accomplishments because, when both of us were in Spirit, we'd made a pact to find each other in your next lifetime.

I wasn't too sure we were going to be able to have this connection again right away, the same way we had it before. I wasn't sure if this would be a wonderful life again. But, much to my surprise and delight, both of our souls happened to remember each other so clearly that we easily picked up where we left off before.

Once I found my soulmate, it was easy to love this life. I've had a great life and wouldn't change a thing.

As you can see, Rocco had many wonderful thoughts to share with Chris and Sarah.

Not all animal communications go as smoothly or as beautifully as this one did. It truly depends on the individual pet, how old or how young their soul is, and how willing they are to share information.

Some of them will only speak in mono-syllables, while others like Rocco tell me enough to fill up pages. And what's always so fascinating to me is the fact that I have no idea ahead of time what incredibly interesting information they may reveal.

Sadly for Chris and Sarah, the time did come when they finally had to help Rocco make his transition into Spirit.

After they'd had time to cope with their own grief, and Rocco had time to adjust to his new surroundings, of course they wanted to have a conversation with him in Spirit.

His dad started out this way:

Rocco, first let me start by saying we miss you more than words can express. I have never been so heart broken in my life to have to say goodbye to someone. We decided to have the vet assist you in your crossing since you couldn't eat anymore.

It's been incredibly difficult not having you with us, but we're also very happy that we were able to say goodbye to you at home and that you did not appear to be suffering too much when we helped you to pass.

Rocco replied right away . . .

> Hello again! I'm so happy you're reaching out to me!

> From Spirit, I see a lot more things than I was able to see on your side. It's because of this that I can tell you I know beyond a shadow of a doubt how much you do love me and how sad your heart is now.

> I can't do anything to change that from here. This sadness and immense mourning goes hand in hand with love. You can't have one without the other. And since I know how much you loved me, it stands to reason that I know how much you miss me.

> Since we're soul mates, the best explanation I can give you is that a part of your heart has left the earth plane and now your heart feels empty, or a better explanation is that it feels like it has a hole in it that no other being can fill.

> But I also know that in time you'll be able to look back at our life together and be in wonder of what we had, and to know that we'll meet again sometime in Spirit.

Were you happy with how we said our goodbye (for now) to you? And do you agree that it was the right time to help you? It was an incredibly difficult decision to make.

> I knew I could trust you to make the best decision for me. Therefore I'm very happy with the way we spent our last hours and said goodbye (for now). As far as being the right time, it was.
>
> I promised I would give you a clue, or send you a message, and I did. I knew you would get it and you did.

Cali is really missing you and hasn't been her normal self since you haven't been here. She sleeps in your bed at night next to me and is doing her best to continue on. Is there any way you can show her any signs that you're ok, and try to help her cope with the reality that you're gone?

> My dear Cali is very aware of the fact that I'm no longer there. I come to her often and she knows it's me.
>
> What she's doing, other than missing me, is trying to help you cope with your loss. She's begun sleeping next to you in my spot so that you don't feel so lonely and your soul will think it's me there and not only her. In fact, I'm there with both of you when that happens. She's trying to create a place of healing where our three souls occupy the same space.

We're certainly not trying to replace you because you're one of a kind and our bond is for eternity. However, we would like to get another beagle pup for Cali. We think it will re-energize her since she's always had you as a companion. Do you think this will help her?

> I agree with this. Cali doesn't know how to live by herself and even though it's nice to feel like a queen, she'll do much better with someone who can play with her and make her feel young again.

YOUR PET CALLED

Can you describe to us where you are and what you're doing in Spirit?

The first thing I need to say is that this is a beautiful place. There's a peacefulness, a serene vibration, and the most beautiful colors I've ever seen.

It's a place, yes, but it's also a state of being. Since we no longer have earthly bodies, we don't need to worry about illness, about not feeling right, about eating, drinking, or pursuing other things the body needs to be happy.

We're all beings of light and energy and therefore able to be anywhere we want to be in the blink of an eye.

For instance, I can be with you, and just by thinking about it, I can visit Mom, too, no matter where she is.

I can understand why humans call this place Heaven.

As far as what I'm doing here . . . well, for right now my job is to be next to you and all the people who loved me and think about me.

This is my first duty. I have to be close and send you my love so that your mourning subsides as fast as possible.

Once I know that everyone can think about me without pain in their hearts or tears in their eyes, I'll be able to continue my studies and continue to evolve too.

Granted, I am, and have been, an old soul, and my travels have been many, but I'm still learning.

However, and more to the point about what I'm doing, I like being a greeter. That means I'm at the edge of the light when someone comes over from your plane to this one. If they don't have a loved one to help them navigate into the light, I'm there to greet them. I simply help out until they get to the light at the end of the bridge.

Are you ever with us at home in spirit, and if so is there anything you can do to let us know when you're around?

> I'm always around you, always. My first job is to help you cope without me. Then, when you're ready, I start sending you little messages.
>
> Cali has helped me by doing some of the things I used to do. I want you to look at her and think, wow, this is something Rocco would do! How interesting!
>
> Then I try to send you small messages with the help of beings who have wings. You see, wings for us in Spirit means we're soaring, we're free. So every time you see a butterfly, a dragonfly, or anytime you see a feather floating in the air, it's my message to you: " I'm here now, and I'm free."

I noticed a few days before we said goodbye, I was holding you on the couch and you looked at me intently as if you were trying to tell me you couldn't continue much longer. Sarah and I felt as if this was the hint you said you'd give me when you were ready to be assisted in crossing over. Am I right about that moment we had together?

> You're absolutely right! It was the right moment for me to see if I could send you a definite message. I knew that when we were in the same space and using the same energy we could communicate with each other, and I tried to see if my message would get through to you. I can't thank you enough for understanding and following your heart.

I am so blown away that you told me we were soul mates from a past life. It makes sense now how we always seem to be able to read one another and had such an amazing bond. I can't wait to be with you again someday. I love you so much and thank you for all the love, laughter, and life lessons. You were the best teacher and there will never be a day that passes that we don't mention your name or think of you. So many people reached out to me when you passed and

said how much they loved you. I just want you to know you had an incredible impact on so many lives even if it was just a brief encounter. You're so special in so many ways. You'll always be my best friend. You have a special place in my heart forever my dear, dear boy.

> Our connection will never end, we will be together again, and we will remember all the good times we had together.
>
> I'm so glad I was able to fulfill my life's mission while at the same time being able to reach out to so many other people whom I met during my long life.
>
> Yes, my job as a teacher was important, but my job as your soul mate was my life's mission, and I'm so glad I had such a good and wonderful student. I'll be here at the edge of the light waiting for you when you come back to Spirit. In the meantime I send you all my love today, and always.

Rocco definitely enjoyed a wonderfully long life with Chris, Sarah, and Cali. He truly was an old soul, which was apparent in each of our conversations when he was on earth as well as after he was in Spirit. He always understood his purpose, his mission, and he fulfilled it magnificently as he lived a life full of love.

Charlie

"I Do"

I received an e-mail from a long-time client in Australia asking me to talk with her horse. She'd sold him a few years ago, but she'd recently received a call from the new owner saying she was getting a divorce and was willing to give the 18-year-old horse back to her at no cost.

The problem was, my client had since moved from her ranch to the city, so she no longer had the right kind of space to give him a home. She was torn about what to do and she wanted her horse's input to help guide her.

Charlie had been living with someone else for four years now. I usually only talk with pets and their current owners, but I felt this occasion was an exception.

Also, because this was a long-time client of mine, and because I'd spoken with Charlie before, I felt confident he'd be able to give us some helpful answers.

When I do remote consultations, I want to be looking at a picture of the pet I'm talking with. Usually I don't use a picture that includes people because it's simply too distracting for me, although I can crop the human out of the picture if the picture of the pet is particularly good.

As I was looking at the pictures my client sent me, and trying to decide which one best conveyed to me who Charlie is, he chimed in and told me I needed to use the one where my client was with him. He said he's nothing without her. He told me to look attentively at his face and I would know how much he loves her and how much he enjoys having her ride him. That's why, even though I had three pictures of Charlie to choose from, I had to pick this particular one with my client in it. He was right. It truly shows how he feels about her.

I then told him she had some very important questions for him, and he needed to take this opportunity to say everything he wanted to because his future depended on it.

He agreed, so I began.

Does Charlie wish to come back to me to live out his days? I no longer own land, so I'm trying to find a suitable place for him close to my home if possible . . . this I'm finding a bit hard. May the gods find me something! He can come and stay at my home overnight at times.

> If we can be together again because I can't stay where I am any longer, I'm ready to jump at the opportunity. We had a good time and I know we both learned a great deal together as well. I would very much like to be with you again, so the answer to this question is YES, I would.

His welfare and happiness are paramount, so it has to be right for him. What does he think?

> I can't think of anything I'd like better.

Is his health ok? He's had Ross River Fever, a mosquito born complaint, but apparently he's ok now. Is there anything else?

> I think I'm doing OK for now. Every once in awhile I have a flare up that lasts for a few days, but in general I'm OK.

> I still spook easily if I feel something is wrong around my mid-section, and I think there are times when my hip is a little sore, particularly when it's very cold, but there's nothing major.

He would be social here, lots of walks around town seeing people.

> You know how much I enjoyed our walks, so this is something I would really look forward to.

Does he wish Chelsea to live with him? She's 25 years old now. (She's a miniature pony who's lived with him for most of his life.)

> I have two thoughts about Chelsea:

- I'm very social, I know, but she's been my constant companion and I happen to like her very much. I've lived with her for many years now and it would be hard not having her around.

- It would be sad to know that just because she's old she wouldn't be able to make the move with me. Even more important, because she is old, we need to do everything we can so that her routine is not changed all that much. I know she'd suffer greatly if she were to be moved and be alone. I wouldn't want that to happen to my best friend.

So, if you ask me whether or not I want her, I need to give you a firm YES.

Is he happy to be ridden lightly?

You said the magic word. Lightly, yes. Remember to take care of which saddle you put on me and not pinch my tummy. Everything else would be OK.

I've had an offer for him to live about 5 miles from here, but I feel this is too far away. He needs to be closer to me.

It would be ideal if I could live close by so that I can see you every day. I don't need to be with you all day, but it would be nice to be able to see each other at least once every day. I'll leave it to you to figure out where I should live. All I want is to be able to continue our journey together.

This is a big decision for me to make considering his welfare, the cost, and the time, but it's a decision I'm happy to have to make. I've owned many horses, but with him I felt such a strong bond. He's my soul horse.

Indeed, and I feel the same thing. Something inside of me is telling me that our companionship, our learning, was not finished in the time we had together before, and we need to continue to be together for further learning. I'll be happy to do that for the rest of my life.

CHARLIE

It's up to Charlie to decide!!!

> I love having the final say when it comes to this decision because it's a simple one. Yes, I want to be with you.

When I sent the e-mail to my client in which I recounted my conversation with Charlie, I told her there was something very special about the last image he sent me. It was a picture of him and her standing in front of each other, face to face. I was in the background, like an officiant of a ceremony, or a witness. Charlie made me feel as if he was saying "I Do," as a groom would promise his soon-to-be bride that he'd be with her and love her until the end of time. It was such a beautiful picture that I needed to share with her exactly what I saw, instead of only using words to express the thought he conveyed. His picture was so special!

My client was both excited and worried. She still needed to find a place close to where she lives that would be able to take Charlie so she could visit with him daily.

It was a couple of weeks before I received another e-mail from her, but it didn't have the news I was hoping to hear.

She wrote: *It's with a heavy heart that I have to ask you to tell Charlie that, at this stage in time, I cannot take him back. It breaks my heart as I so wanted this opportunity to have him spend his last years with me. I've told his owner that I haven't been able to find a place, but I also said if the offer stays open and my circumstances change, as in finding suitable land for Charlie and Chelsea to live on, I will advise her.*

Tell Charlie I love him and that I want the best for him, including a good living environment, but I couldn't find it near me. He's my soul horse, and yes he always felt like my special man as in a marriage bond and love, as you said in the reading.

But just a day later, she wrote again with exciting news:

> *Would you believe, a friend who lives an hour away has offered to take both Charlie and Chelsea. It's a wonderful horse set up where I can*

> *visit fortnightly. There are children there and people all the time, and Charlie and Chelsea will be loved. So tell him he's coming back to me and that he knows my friend, and she loves him. Thanks!*

Although my client wouldn't be able to visit the two horses as often as she'd like, she'd still be able to be an important part of their lives. And Charlie and Chelsea would still be able to enjoy living together in a wonderful home with lots of love and companionship.

After some time had passed, she sent me another e-mail with even better news:

> *I've found a paddock close to my home and Charlie and Chelsea are now back with me. They returned and went into their new paddock calm and relaxed. Its like they never left me. They're two old friends together, and we've picked up where we left off. We go for walks around the town daily with the dog, and they love it. Financially it's a cost, but their love and companionship, and having them near me again is such a gift!*

The Universe definitely works in mysterious ways! When we're on the right path, everything always works out for the best, even when things seem impossible at times, as they did for awhile for Charlie and Chelsea. Many people would call what happened a coincidence, but people who have spiritual understanding know otherwise. We might call it God's love at work.

Kirby, Sukie, and Batley

Unlikely soulmates

In 1999, I became one of the first animal communicators to write about pets and reincarnation. At the same time, I felt I had to address another unique subject . . . the concept of "soul mates" or "twin souls."

Over the years, I'd already learned a lot about those topics from all the messages I'd translated for pets who'd crossed over The Rainbow Bridge. Twenty years later, I can still say that I'm continuing to learn from the pets I now communicate with. Sukie and Kirby are excellent examples.

Shortly after moving into their new home with their cat Kirby, a stray dog wandered onto the property where Laura and her husband now lived. The stray then had to spend a few days at the shelter hoping her owner would be found, but when no one came to claim her, Laura and Kevin adopted her themselves. They named her Sukie.

Laura, a dedicated cat person, told her husband that Sukie could stay, but only with the understanding that Kirby, the cat, came first. He was, at that time, a very special and spoiled "only child," and if Sukie didn't get along with Kirby, Sukie couldn't stay. But there was absolutely never any cause for concern because, from the very first day, Sukie and Kirby became the very best of friends.

You can see how very much they enjoy each other's company in the picture below. They're simply content to just rest together.

Above: Kirby and Sukie

Batley, who was named because of the mask-like markings on her face, joined the family a few months later. When everyone was sitting outside one day, she simply walked into the yard and immediately acted as if she owned the place. That was an attitude that never changed. She was a difficult cat, always wanting to be first, and never truly feeling happy about having to share her life with other pets in what she considered to be "her" house.

Shortly after she arrived, she delivered a litter of five kittens. She was eventually diagnosed with kidney problems, and when I talked with her in 2015, we knew she wasn't going to live much longer. She crossed over The Rainbow Bridge soon after that, and I later talked with her again at an appropriate time after she'd made her transition into Spirit.

Several years later, I spoke with Sukie when she was nearing the end of her time with the family. She was already suffering, but she told me Laura wasn't ready to let her go, so she was going to stay around for a little while longer.

Then, in early 2019, just a couple of months later, I received an e-mail from Laura telling me Sukie had also crossed over The Rainbow Bridge at the age of 15.

Laura wanted to make an appointment to talk with her in Spirit. She wanted to be able to tell her precious dog how very much she was missed, and she needed to hear how Sukie felt about her passing.

Only a couple of days after that, she contacted me again telling me her cat Kirby had pooped on Sukie's bed and was showing other signs of mourning. He wasn't eating well, he was restless, and he'd spend much of his time lying on Sukie's bed, all of which made it very obvious how depressed he was.

Laura told me they'd thoroughly cleaned upstairs so it wouldn't smell so much like Sukie, and they'd also plugged in a Feliway for Kirby, but she wanted to know what more she could do to help him find some comfort.

Above: Kirby and his sweet disposition

I then did the consultations with Kirby and Sukie back to back.

It was a cold January morning when I finally connected with Kirby. He was in such bad shape emotionally that it took me a while to connect with him. When I did, our conversation revealed the depth of his sadness and his very deep love for Sukie.

I began asking him all the questions his mom had sent me in her e-mail...

Kirby has not been sleeping with us as he used to when Sukie was here. Instead, he's been camping out on the sofa all night long. Sukie used to sleep on the sofa when it became too difficult for her to come upstairs. I don't know if he's hoping Sukie will come back??? We miss Kirby sleeping with us.

> I'm so sad. Sleeping on the sofa where Sukie used to sleep helps me cope with my grief a bit. I do understand my parents would like me to be with them and I need to be strong in order to do that, because when I'm with them I have a job of protecting them from anyone who comes in. Actually the job was Sukie's, but she told me what to do and how to behave, and I simply have to follow her lead. Since she's not here, the job belongs to me now.

(Monica to Laura: I told Kirby he didn't have to be in protection mode, that you just want him close to you on the bed where you can feel his soft fur and he'll be keeping you company. He told me you can remind him by taking him upstairs with you if you wish. If he feels he can't stay, he'll jump off the bed and go downstairs again.)

He has this howling meow that started about eight months ago and it continues. I don't know if he knew Sukie would be transitioning soon . . . maybe the two are unrelated . . . but he was never this vocal before.

> Of course I knew that Sukie was sick, Mom. But that's not the reason I'm complaining. Well, complaining is kind of a broad term. I complain a little bit, yes, but many times I howl, not because I need you to do anything, but simply because I'm so sad or so worried that I don't know what to do with myself. I howl like dogs howl at the moon, or call each other. I howl because I'm sad, and I'm calling out to my friend.

Please ask what we can we do for Kirby to ease his sadness . . . toys? treats? cuddles? We've been doing all those things, but we'll do whatever he asks to make him feel better. He was just two years old when we moved into this house and Sukie moved in, too. He and Sukie became instant best friends. They were together 24/7, wrestling/playing/napping together.

Oh Mom, I wish I could tell you what to do for me. Believe me, if I knew, you'd be the first to know, but I just don't know what I want or what I need. I can tell you that Sukie was part cat, and that I have always been part dog. So when we met, we just knew each other and we understood each other better than anybody else.

He must be so lonely without his companion. Please ask him if he'd like another friend. Sukie was a wonderful buddy but we know not all dogs would be, and Kirby's experience with other cats in the house has not been pleasant. Batley did not play well with others. We'll respect his wishes, whatever they are.

Even if you want to bring in another cat or another dog, it's never going to be the same. Sukie and I, we were special. You could call us twin souls. That's how we felt. There's no one else on this side who can fulfill my heart the way she could. I'm completely lost without her. You are so nice, though, for trying to please me and I really, really appreciate your efforts.

Unfortunately, no one else can take her place. My other half, the part of my heart that was beating happily, is gone. In time, I must realize this and start coping with it as soon as my soul is able.

We'll never find another Sukie, Mom. She was this unique being who was at home in either kind of body. She allowed me to be me, while never being angry or upset. She was always happy to play or to rest together. We simply understood each other and no one else could take her place.

Please tell him we're hurting for him and his loss, and thank him for accepting Sukie into his house and being such a good friend to her.

Thank you for understanding my feelings and for knowing how empty I feel now. I only had to be with Sukie for a few hours before I realized I'd found my soulmate, and we never looked back again. She loved me as much as I loved her and I'll always remember that. They were the happiest years of my life.

We comforted Kirby as much as possible and knew he'd eventually be all right again because he'd already acknowledged that, when his soul was ready, he needed to resolve his feelings of grief.

Next, we were ready to talk with Sukie in Spirit.

I loved receiving so many pictures of her to choose from. I'd already chosen one to use when I was ready to connect with her. But, as soon as I spoke to Sukie, she told me I should use the picture where she was looking out the window instead.

She preferred it, not just because she was young and looking her best, but because this picture showed her spirit better than any of the others. Sukie then said it represents who she was, always happy and always with a smile on her face. She loved life and she was happy every single day.

Once we'd selected the best picture to use, we spent a few more moments connecting with each other, and I then began asking her mom's e-mail questions and sharing her mom's comments with her . . .

We'd like to know about her transition and hope that she's feeling like a young pup . . . that her back legs are strong again and that it isn't hard for her to breathe like it was here sometimes.

> Before I even start to tell you anything else, I have to thank you for doing everything exactly the way I wanted you to. It was wonderful having you there with me, and I didn't mind making my transition. In fact, it was very smooth. I enjoyed seeing the light above me while at the same time watching you stay behind with my old and broken body.
>
> You won't guess who was the first one to come and say hello to me here. Yes! Believe it or not, it was Batley! She apologized to me several times and told me she'd been so wrong in her attitude toward me when we were all living together. She's trying to make amends now, and that's why she came as my guide to walk with me to the main fields.

Above: Sukie in the picture she wanted me to use

She was sincere and happy to see me, and I want to report that she's learning about her mistakes so she can improve and do better in the future.

As for me, I haven't been able to do much since I arrived here because all of you are mourning, so my job right now is simply to be by your side. Every time you think about me, I need to be next to you.

And of course, there's Kirby, my best little friend. He, too, is very sad, so my job is also to be next to him as much as possible.

Believe me, I'm with him all the time. I talk with him, I visit with him, and I tell him I'm doing fine and I'm very happy. But his feelings of loss are so deep that he has to take his time to adjust. We need to let him do that.

Please convey to Sukie that she was the light of both of our lives and brought us more joy than I ever could have dreamed. I was a "cat person" before Sukie. Now I understand the love of a dog.

> You just don't know how close you are to the truth. In fact, I do have a lot of cat in me, having been one for many, many incarnations. I decided to come back in a dog's body this last time to give me an opportunity to experience something different. I'm glad I did. What I learned was very gratifying. And I found you, in particular, so we could learn together. I also learned a lot from Dad about how to play like a dog, but my heart belonged to Kirby because he reminded me how I could be in either form and still enjoy my life.

I hope I was a good mother to Sukie and that there's nothing she could have wished for that we didn't do for her.

> You were great parents and I had a lot of fun with you. Whether we were home watching a movie or outside watching the birds, my life did not feel complete unless I was always next to you. I couldn't have asked for better humans.

It bothers me that Kevin and I weren't getting along very well that night and I worry that anxiety about our bickering stressed her out.

> No, Mom, I wasn't really listening. I'd given you more than two months of extra time and that was finally as much as I could give. I knew it was my time and I was ready and willing to go. You shouldn't blame yourselves.

Please tell her that our hearts (and house) feel empty without her, but we know she'd want us to embrace life the way she did and be happy as she was, so we'll try very hard.

> I know you'll try to do that, and I thank you for listening to what Kirby needs to have you do around the house. It's good that you've tried to

eliminate my scent, especially upstairs, because it's important for him not to smell me so much so that he, too, can embrace life and be happy again.

We have her ashes here. If she has any wishes for where she'd like them to be distributed, we would honor that, or we can keep them with us always, even if we leave this property. If there's anything else she'd like us to do to honor her memory, we certainly will do our best to do whatever she asks.

> The old body that is now ashes doesn't hold any further interest for me. It's like an old pair of shoes that have been worn out beyond repair. Although you may have loved them, there's nothing else you can do except to throw them away. My ashes are not me, my spirit is. So, keep them, throw them away. It doesn't matter to me. The only important thing for me is that you keep me in your memory. To do that, keep my pictures with you. Show them, talk about me, and most of all, think about me often. That's the only wish I have.

I think that's about it other than to say thank you to her for being such a good friend to Kirby, (and Batley, even though Batley was not a friendly kitty to her). I would ask her to please send some comfort to Kirby because he seems to be missing her so very much. They were best friends and together 24/7.

> Oh, Mom, Dad, thank you! You took me in without knowing anything about who I was and what I needed in order to live a happy life. And while doing so, we all learned together. There's nothing I would have wanted in that lifetime that you didn't provide for me. I'll be next to you for as long as you and Kirby need me, and just know that Spirit, my spirit in particular, is always there helping you to cope, to laugh, to learn, and to continue your learning experience in this lifetime and beyond.

Because she loved her so very, very much, Laura not only sent me her questions, she also sent me a letter she wrote with all the thoughts she wanted to convey to her beloved dog. Sukie commented on each part of the letter as I shared it with her.

>My Dearest Sukie,
>
>My heart is broken to bits but bigger because you chose me.
>
>It was 14+ years ago, when Papa, Kirb, and I had just moved into this new (old) house. You showed up that first week, running, just running in the field behind us. A couple more days passed and finally you came around and ate what I had to offer, and you slept and slept in front of our garage.

Yes! I picked them after they showed me I could trust them.

>It was clear you'd had puppies recently but where were they? We were also worried for your safety. Papa had the dog warden come when you got so close to our busy road that people beeped their horns. He told the dog warden, "This is a good dog. If no one claims her, please call us."

I didn't know Papa had said this, but it was definitely love at first sight for all of us.

>Sukie, your mama was a devoted cat person and didn't think she wanted a dog, but three days later, when no one claimed you, you came home with me. Your sweet panting face was all I could see in my rear view mirror. And my heart opened up little by little, and then a LOT . . . and I fell crazy in love with you!

We were meant to be!

>The rest is our history . . . so many stories . . . the way you escaped from two crates meant to make you feel secure, so that we finally said "no more crates for you, Sukes," and that was that . . . the way you and Kirby became instant BFFs . . . and what a gentle mama you were to the foster kittens who passed through here . . .

KIRBY, SUKIE, AND BATLEY

I loved being a mother, but they'd taken my babies from me.

. . . your honey ears, your popcorn paws . . your "chopping" when you wanted something . . . your backward dancing that had me calling you Ginger Rogers . . . the 98% dead possum you brought me one day . . . the time you took me "skiing" on the wet grass through our backyard, holding onto your leash, first on my feet and then on my face . . . the time you stole the tail off the Flying Monkey at our Halloween Party! . . .

I knew how to have fun, too!

. . . the way you stole treats from the kitchen and took them upstairs to enjoy on the bed . . . the laughs Papa and I had over how you were stealing corn stalks from my fall display to eat the corn, and I didn't catch on for ages! . . .

I was sneaky, and I was surprised it took you so long.

. . . the time Mama and Papa left you for ONE WHOLE DAY with Uncle Kim, and Grammie & Grampie Bache coming to visit you a couple of times . . . and the next day when we got in the car for a quick errand you jumped in and refused to get out so you could be sure we weren't going to leave you again!

Oh, yes, I recall that. I wasn't taking any chances. Although they were all very nice, my heart belonged to the two of you, and I couldn't imagine not going home with you.

Ahhh... the Grammies and Grampies . . . how they loved you! Grampie Bache adored you, Grampie Barrett asked about you until the very end, and you even wooed Grammie Barrett, who didn't believe pets should be on the sofa. Ha!

I was partly cat, after all, so being on the sofa was my default position.

There will never be another you, Sukie. I wish I could turn back the clock and give you more love than I did. I wish I wouldn't have been dis-

tracted sometimes when you wanted my attention. I'll never regret one single time Papa and I opted out of all-day excursions, or came home early from an outing so we could be here with you. I'll never regret that Papa took road trips without me so I could stay with you. Kennels were NEVER an option.

Absolutely, kennels were never an option. But Mom, you don't have to turn the clock back. We'll meet again, and you and I will continue our studies. I know this will not be the only time we were able to be together. We'll make plans again when you also come to Spirit.

    I love you forever Sukie! Thank you for coming into my life and opening my heart. I want you back, I want 15 more of you, or at least enough Sukies to last until the end of my life. I don't want a life without a Sukie. My heart feels like it's been crushed into pieces but I'll be forever grateful for the time you chose to spend with us, my beautiful dancing, chopping clown.

No, you won't have another Sukie, but you should certainly find someone else to love.

    Godspeed to the Rainbow Bridge, my sweet Sukie Lou . . until we meet again.

Indeed. And so we will. I love all of you today and for all eternity.

After our conversation Laura sent me this e-mail:

    Dr. Monica, as I read your notes . . . for about the 10th time! . . . I feel such tremendous gratitude that these two unique and wonderful beings chose US to share their lives with. Thank you again for confirming what we already knew . . . that they are beyond special!

    Love & Light....

    Laura and Kevin

KIRBY, SUKIE, AND BATLEY

There are several things I like about both consultations, but the thing that struck me most was when Sukie said she'd been a cat many times before.

I remember Laura laughing hysterically when I translated that information. She told me that both she and her husband used to have nicknames for Sukie and Kirby . . . Puppy-cat and Kitty-pup! It wasn't a conscious decision to call them by those nicknames . . . they just seemed to come naturally. After talking with Sukie and Kirby, it's easy to understand why!

In many, many years of doing consultations and talking with pets who're in Spirit, I had no idea that two animals of different species and ages could be such soul mates. At least not until Kirby explained it to me, and Sukie agreed.

I'm always in awe of the information I receive from animals, whether they're living, or in Spirit, and I can only thank them for their great explanations so that we too can continue to learn and evolve.

Chapter 5

REINCARNATION, LIFE MISSIONS, AND LOVE

Rokki

I'll be back . . .

When I do consultations for clients in Japan, they're usually done by e-mail because my Japanese clients often feel they don't have enough command of the English language to engage in a conversation. This was true for Yukiko, who sent me an e-mail request saying she wanted to connect with her little Chihuahua.

He'd recently passed in a most unusual way. He'd been running with his brother when he hit his head so hard on a piece of furniture that he died instantly.

The accident happened when Rokki was only two years old, so the information he shared with us from Spirit was particularly heartwarming, surprising, and delightful.

In the notes I wrote to his mom, I said:

> *Sweet Rokki was very happy to hear his name when I called him. He felt I'd made him wait a long time to have our talk.*
>
> *I'd had his picture on my computer since the first day you wrote to me, so every morning when I'd open up my Word documents, there he was looking at me with his loving eyes, but I didn't start my conversation with him until a few days later.*
>
> *As soon as we did connect, I told him you had some questions for him and he said he was eager to answer them. He wanted to talk with you and he welcomed the opportunity to do so right now. Then I began asking your questions.*

It's been five months since your departure. Do you miss us? We miss you. Do you visit us sometimes? How will I know if you're here?

> I'm so glad you decided to talk with me. I do visit with you every day! I know when you think about me, and I try to be right there by your side.
>
> I know your heart is broken, and I don't know how to fix it. I know how much you miss me because I can feel what you feel. But I wish you could see things from my point of view and understand how well I'm doing now.
>
> I do miss your happy face. I do miss the touch of your hands, and the feeling of being cared for that you always gave me. But I can't miss you in the same way you miss me because I can still see you and feel your energy.
>
> Please know that I'm still next to you on the bed. I also walk around and try to make noises that you can recognize.

(I told Yukiko that he sent me the sounds of his little paws as his energy body walked across the floor.)

> I want you to know that I'm always with you and I'll continue to be by your side.

Are you sad that you left us behind? Why did you have to leave us so suddenly when we were not prepared?

> I was very sad I had to leave, but that was only for a little while. Once you're here, you're able to understand things so much better than before! It's almost as if a book of your life opens up in front of you and shows you the reasons there were for everything.
>
> It's also true that I wish I didn't have to leave so soon, but I have plans to return to you as soon as I'm able to do it.
>
> I don't believe I was able to teach you and Dad all the things I needed to teach, because I left earlier than I wanted to, but I want to try to do it over again because I didn't get it right the first time.
>
> I'm hoping Dad will get over his feeling of not wanting another small dog and instead wanting only a bigger dog next time, and I do hope the way in which I left doesn't cause either one of you to hold onto any lasting impressions.
>
> I mean to say that I wouldn't want you to stop me, or any other dog you get in the future, from expressing our feelings of happiness and gratitude just because you're afraid the same thing will happen to them. IT WON'T!

Are you happy at the place you are right now? What do you enjoy most now in your life there?

> I'm so happy to be here that at times it's difficult to describe the happiness I feel.

We're surrounded by a beautiful white light that gives us warmth and embraces us all the time, as if we were in the arms of our mother. It's a feeling that's new to us but everyone here cherishes it. You can't be outside this light, and you really would not want to be. We no longer have bodies. We are all light, or spirit. But our "minds" are much more open and we can think so much better than before.

We also have a good memory and remember all things, not only of this recent past life, but of many other lives before this one.

I think what I enjoy the most is the knowledge that I have. It makes everything crystal clear to me, even those things that are difficult to understand.

So, not only do I enjoy being here, it's the most wonderful feeling I've ever experienced. The reason I'm telling you this, is because I want you to know that I'm willing to give all of this up for you, and come back again, just so I can spend some more time with both of you.

Rokki, do you know we loved you so much and we still love you and talk about you? Were you happy living with us? What did you enjoy most with us?

I know of your love now, and I knew it then too. But now I understand it even better. I was always happy to be with you because I always felt that you understood me. I had a good friend in you and I was happy to be me.

I know now that we can pick our humans. We always try to pick those who have energies similar to ours, and who are willing to learn things and teach us things. The choice has to be important for both of us. We can't be in each other's lives without learning something from one another, so I feel my short stay with you was very important for my future, and that you also learned from me.

Are we able to meet again someday? Will you come back to us? How soon will you come back to us so that we can be together again?

I can tell you now that I'll start to make preparations to come back to both of you. I didn't know how soon I'd be able to come back before this because I needed confirmation that you'd be able to take me if I were to return. But now that I know you're open to having me again, I'll start to prepare things.

One day, I'll send you a message. It could be in your dreams, or it could simply be an overwhelming feeling that you need to go out and get a new dog. Don't fight that feeling because somehow, it will be me telling you to go out and look for me.

Please don't be too concerned about all the different circumstances. Just know that you will look at me and "know" this is the dog you need. I will take care of everything! You won't miss finding me.

Do you want us to do something for you at home? We pray for you with incense and your food and water placed at Buddhist altar. Do you want us to place something you like there? Please let us know if you have anything you'd like to have done at home for you.

I enjoy seeing what you did for me and I like my picture too. I'd very much like it if you would also put a picture of the breed you wish I would be if it's something different from the kind I was before when I was with you. Please put it facing down, under my picture. It will give me an idea of exactly what I need to search for.

Also at my one year anniversary, I need you to take the offerings down. That will be my cue that I need to come back. I'm planning on coming back next year.

I want to tell you I love you both very much and I'm hoping we can be together again soon.

Yukiko was overjoyed, and she responded:

YOUR PET CALLED

Dear Dr. Monica,

Thank you very, very much for your communication with my Rokki, so much quicker than I expected.

I can't help crying with happiness to know that Rokki is willing to come back to us next year! How wonderful!

I cried because he will sacrifice all the joy and happiness he feels where he is now in order to be with us again.

I will think about what kind of breed I want when Rokki returns and place a photo as soon as I find out. My hubby doesn't want to get a teacup size dog anymore as its body is too fragile and easy to get hurt. I will think about it :)

I am so happy to know that he is always by my side sleeping with me. I will try to imagine his energy and his love so that I won't feel lonely anymore.

I believe he will definitely return to us someday soon in another puppy's body. When the time comes, I will find Rokki.

Thank you 1000 times, Dr. Monica for doing this in the midst of your busy schedule!! I can't thank you enough.

Kind regards,

Yukiko

About two years later I received another e-mail from Yukiko:

Dear Dr. Monica.

I would like to thank you so much for the reading you did for my beloved Rokki two years ago.

ROKKI

I should have sent you a thank you note much earlier to report to you that my Rokki did return to us last year!

After 1st anniversary of Rokki's passing, I stopped giving offerings at Rokki's altar.

After some time, I did some internet search to look for my Rokki in the form of a puppy.

Then, I found a photo of a chihuahua puppy who looks quite similar to the first Rokki.

I contacted the breeder right away and drove two hours to see the puppy. In an instant, I knew this is my boy! The rest is history! I will attach his photo.

Above: The new Rokki

His name is again Rokki. I couldn't find anything else. He has the same personality as Rokki 1, to my surprise.

YOUR PET CALLED

I really appreciate that my Rokki came back to our life! We are so happy and feel complete with Rokki around.

Thank you so much for saving me when I was at an emotional loss.

Yukiko

What surprised me most about this story is the fact that Rokki knew exactly when he was going to come back. He made his return just as he'd said he would.

Usually when we're talking about reincarnation it takes pets anywhere from three to five years to come back, but in Rokki's case, his sudden death enabled him to return a lot sooner to the same parents so he could complete his life's work with them.

Bella

Second Chances

Six years ago, Juan had to make the incredibly difficult decision to give away their puppy Bella. No one could be home all day, and they'd been unable to resolve her very severe separation anxiety issues. They hoped that letting her go to a different home would be the kindest thing they could do for her.

However, a month ago, he received a call from the local animal shelter telling him they'd found Bella tied to a tree at her current home. A neighbor had contacted the local animal shelter complaining about her treatment. They'd confiscated the dog, checked her microchip, and called Juan because he was the previous owner of record.

When he heard about the sad situation Bella was in, Juan decided to bring her home again and give her another chance. But Bella, a now six-year-old female pit bull, still proved to be very difficult.

She continued to suffer from the same anxiety issues and, since her return, she'd already destroyed two steel kennels, several partitions, several doors and window sills, and other items in the house. She'd also jumped a six-foot fence.

Juan didn't know much about me, but thinking I was an animal trainer, he called because his mother had told him he should contact me.

Before even having a consultation with Bella, I told Juan that, in my experience, pets with such severe separation anxiety were difficult to manage when they had to be left home alone all day. I suggested that maybe Bella should be adopted by someone who would always be home with her 24/7.

He then asked what kind of work I did. I explained to him that my role is to be a translator between the pet and the owner, and that I'd be able to explain Bella's side of the story to him. He thanked me for my time and we ended that phone call.

About a week later, he called me again asking if I'd communicate with Bella to ask her how she'd feel about being placed in a home with someone else. We agreed on a date and time for an appointment.

After first checking in with Bella, I told Juan that she's actually an extremely nice dog and quite subdued. All she wanted was company, love, and attention. She said when she was given up as a puppy, it was the saddest time of her life. She couldn't understand what she'd done so wrong that would cause her family to give up on her so easily.

She'd never been as happy as she was with her original family, and now that she's with them again, she feels she's back on track to being happy the way she used to be.

I told Bella that her family loves her very much and that her dad wanted to ask her some questions so he could better understand her feelings. She said she'd be happy to answer everything.

I then began with the questions Juan wanted to ask Bella:

Why do you follow me, and why do you only want to be next to me when other family members who love you are there too? Why are you so attached to me?

> Because I need you. I also need to see if there's something I can do this time to be sure you won't give me away again. I have to make sure you're ok with me and that you love me.
>
> Besides, I do have a special attachment to you because we've been together before. Not only this time when I was younger, but even before that.

Were you someone close to me in previous lives?

> Yes, we were very close and you loved me more than anybody else. In this lifetime, even though I was very young, I felt the same love from you, and for you, from the very beginning. I still do, even though I was hurt when you gave me away, but I forgive and forget easily.

Why did you come back into our lives?

> You need me and I need you. It's as simple as that. It's something neither of us can fully understand, but our hearts and souls do. We belong with each other.

After a few hours of being alone, if someone other than me gets home first and greets you, why do you still keep looking and looking for me?

> Because when you leave me, I have to make sure you'll come back to me. I know that I'm acting strange now, but it's because I don't understand why you sent me away before. It will take time, but I'm hopeful that at some point it will sink in that you're always coming back.

Why does my mother feel afraid of you?

> Please forgive her. She doesn't understand me. She thinks I'm dangerous, but I wouldn't hurt a fly. Yes, I'll defend you and yours if anything were to happen, but I'm incapable of hate. I'm just your protector. She shouldn't be afraid of me. The only thing I ask is for a little bit of attention.

Can you help us by being ok when you have to stay alone for a few hours during the day?

> I get so fearful when I'm alone that I overreact sometimes. The worst of it is, I don't know if I can remember that you're coming back. My first instinct is to go out looking for you. I have to work on this. It isn't easy for me. I've been tied up and forgotten about for so long that I'm afraid humans will always forget about me.

We've tried everything to help you. What would help you cope with your anxiety? Please tell us if you need someone to be there with you all the time.

> If someone is inside the house, I need to be inside the house, too. If I see someone inside and I'm outside, I get nervous. I want to find a way to get inside to be with them, or leave the yard and go looking for you.

> Ideally I need to be with someone all the time. Then I can be a lot more relaxed and not destructive. When I get upset, I really get upset and I don't care if I'm hurting myself or anything else in the process.

(I told Juan we needed to talk about giving Bella some Xanax or something stronger when she has to be alone for very long. I explained to her why Juan had to give her away when she was just a puppy. I also gave her lots of reassurance, and I suggested ways she could learn to cope with being alone. Of course some special training was also needed.)

Would it be ok if we give you to someone who won't leave you for long periods of time and will always be with you?

I can assure you that I'll be ok, but if I go live somewhere else then I won't be able to complete my life's mission with you, and we'd have to do this all over again at some other time. We're meant to be together and there's nothing that can change that.

What is your life's mission?

You are! I can't explain it, but I know it with every fiber of my being. My mission is to be your teacher and at the same time to give you unconditional love, no matter what your decision is. Your lesson is one of loving and living, of accepting me for who I am, and of commitment.

You're my son Liam's dog. What's your mission with Liam?

Liam already understands me and my mission. He loves me no matter what. His heart tells him to love and not to give up because it's hard. I'm just reassuring him that what he feels is right.

Liam has asked about you every year since we had to let you go, and now you came back during his birthday month as if he called you to come back. Are you somehow connected with Liam, and if so why is that?

Our three souls are connected . . . Liam, you, and me. We've been together before in other lifetimes, and although circumstances might have been different, the love was the same, and it's the love that binds us together now.

You found me again this time because my mission has not been completed. I'm not ready to leave this existence before I try one more time to complete it. It's what I'm supposed to do. I have no control over it.

You're such a sweet dog with everyone. What do you want or need from us?

Understanding, love, and affection. That's all I need from you.

We love you so much and thank you for being in our lives again this past month.

My love for you is not only unconditional, it's eternal. I'll understand whatever decision you make.

Why do you think we're together again?

Because you had a second chance at life, and now it's your turn to give me a second chance, too.

I didn't understand the meaning behind what Bella said until Juan explained that he'd had a brain tumor when he was young and wasn't expected to live into his teenage years. His family moved to the United States when he was 11 so he could have the operations and medical care he needed.

Juan was very emotional. He was given a second chance at life, and now it was his turn to give Bella a second chance at her life.

He asked me to tell Bella he was very sorry for having given up on her so many years ago, and he promised he wouldn't do that again. She would stay with him, and they would finish this lifetime together so he could learn the lessons he needed to learn, and she could complete her mission.

You might also enjoy reading about Juan's childhood experience, and about his own special life mission at:

www.mygivingspacenow.com/the-story-1

Chapter 6

PETS AS BRIDGES TO
HUMANS IN SPIRIT

Communicating with Humans

My life's work is to communicate with animals and to translate for them, but on rare occasions, a human who's already in Spirit will also take the opportunity to get a word in edge-wise. When that happens, it's as if the animal I'm communicating with has become a "bridge" between me and the human. The stories in this chapter nicely illustrate how that sometimes happens.

Sandy, Bear, and Sweet Pea . . .

plus Laddie and Crash in Spirit
Someone has a special message for you

Above: Sandy, Bear and Sweet Pea

This is a very special story about five Silky Terriers and their loving Mom and Dad. They were all adopted into the same family at different times. Some are purebreds and others are mixes. Each one has a very distinctive personality, and each one has a special mission in life, as well as in Spirit.

SANDY, BEAR, AND SWEET PEA...

On his veterinarian's recommendation, Jeff requested a first consultation in 2011 for three of his Silky Terriers, Sandy, Bear, and Sweet Pea.

Essentially, I asked each dog the same basic questions: Do you like your home? Do you like your family? Do you like your name? Is there anything you'd like to tell me?

Bear answered first:

- I love my home and my family; everything is great here; my only complaint is that it often smells like pee.

- I love my family; when I first arrived, Sandy and I had to take some time to get to know each other, but we're fine now.

- After she joined the family, Sweet Pea and I used to play all the time, but since *she's* gone, Sweet Pea has become nasty and aggressive, so I don't like playing with her anymore.

- Our dad gives us all equal attention; if one of us gets a treat, we all do; if one gets held, we all do.

- I love my name, except lately I don't like it when my dad calls me by my formal name, Oliver; I think it means he's about to scold me; I prefer it when he calls me by my nickname Bear.

- My role is to be a healer; that's my job.

- What I don't understand is where *she's* gone; her scent is still so strong but I can't find her, so I have to look for her; I don't know why *she's* not coming home.

As I recounted for Jeff all that Bear had said, he took copious notes, as he'd do for each of the other two dogs as well.

His jaw dropped to the floor when he heard Bear say he wanted to be called by his nickname because he thought he might be in trouble when he heard his dad calling him by his formal name, Oliver!

Sweet Pea answered next:

- I love my home and my family; everything here is great, especially when I get my way.

- Sandy's ok; he's older and in his own world, so he doesn't get in my way.

- Bear has become a whiny baby since *she's* gone so I don't like to play with him anymore.

- It's ok that *she's* gone; I'm in charge now, so if I don't get my way I let my dad know it.

- My dad gives us all the same treatment and that's fine; if he does what I want, I'll be good, but if he's not listening, I'll let him know I'm unhappy, and I'll keep doing it until he gives me the attention I deserve.

(What she was doing was peeing, and more, in the house, right by their doggy door, instead of taking just a few more steps and going outside. That's why Bear was complaining about the smell.)

As I set Sweet Pea back on the floor, I told Jeff, "You have a real diva on your hands here. This one is very stubborn."

Then it was Sandy's turn:

- I absolutely love my home, my name, and my family; ever since I came here I've felt safe and loved.

- Bear and I had our issues when he first arrived, but we're ok now.

- Sweet Pea thinks she's in charge, but every now and then I have to remind her who's the boss; she's young; she'll learn.

- Bear says he's a healer, but he can only diagnose; I'm the real healer.

- I love how our dad does everything he can to give us all an equal amount of attention and care; it's very considerate of him even though sometimes it's hard to do.

Please tell my dad a few things for me:

- Don't worry because I'm not eating so much at breakfast; I prefer to eat my big meal at dinner; I'm not sick; I just don't want to eat so much first thing in the morning.

- Please thank him for standing with me while I eat; I hate when the other two try to take my food, but with him here, I can take my time to eat at my own pace without worry.

- Please also tell him not to worry about anything; let him know that now that *she's* gone, I'll take care of him, just as I used to take care of her.

- I know *she's* gone, but that's only her body; I can still see her spirit; I can't talk with her, but Laddie can.

(I had no idea who Laddie was, and Jeff didn't make any comment when I mentioned Laddie's name. It would only be later in the conversation that I'd find out who Laddie was.)

While I was talking with Sandy, Bear, and Sweet Pea, and translating for Jeff what each dog was saying, I didn't stop to ask for any clarifications. But after talking with all three dogs, I then asked Jeff, who's this *"she"* they're *all* talking about? Is this another older dog who's already made her transition?

Imagine my surprise when Jeff told me they were all talking about his wife, Janine, who'd passed away only a few months ago.

I immediately told Jeff that Bear wasn't allowing himself to believe his mom had passed on because her scent was still so strong in the house. He was absolutely certain she must be some place where he could find her.

Above: Janine

Dogs almost always know immediately when a person or another animal has died, so it was very unusual for Bear not to acknowledge his mom's passing. It was almost as if he was in denial in the same way many humans are in denial after the death of a loved one.

I talked with Bear again right away, explaining to him that Janine had gone back into Spirit, so he needed to stop looking for her here on earth. His body language immediately changed. He had a look of understanding in his eyes, and he finally visibly relaxed.

Sandy told me he was the real healer in the family and that he was now taking care of Jeff just as he'd been taking care of Janine. He said he loved sleeping in his crate, but he'd been sleeping on the bed next to his dad recently to be sure he was ok.

Jeff told me that Sandy had begun his mission of healing long ago, shortly after Janine brought him home. Their first two dogs, Laddie and Crash, had both crossed over The Rainbow Bridge within months of each other, and both he and Janine had been feeling an intense sense of loss ever since.

But when they brought Sandy home, he soon became Janine's shadow and constant companion, and he gave both of them all the love in the world, healing their souls and mending their hearts.

At this point, I asked Jeff what he knew about the history of each dog. He had some information from each of the rescue groups, but was interested in learning more, so I talked with Sandy, Bear, and Sweet Pea again. After that, Jeff and I were then able to piece together a little better background about each one.

Sandy had originally lived with a couple. The man used a cane and a wheelchair and was abusive to Sandy, often hitting him with the cane. One day, when the front door was open, Sandy told me he ran away and lived on the streets for several years before he was picked up. He was then rescued from death-row by a Silky Terrier rescue organization.

In 2007, when he was around seven years old, Jeff's wife Janine brought him home from a foster family in Pasadena. Because of the abuse he'd endured from his original owner, Sandy was terrified and didn't trust men at first. He was also very shy and wary around other dogs, but with Jeff's and Janine's love, he soon learned to trust, and he became much more confident. It was then that he began his healing work.

Bear apparently walked away from a farm-like environment in northern California when there was a new baby in the family and he was simply left outside much of the time. He told me his first dad would usually find him and bring him back home, but not the last time.

Jeff and Janine adopted him from a Silky Terrier Rescue in southern California in 2008 when he was around the age of two. He'd been microchipped in both Marin County and Sacramento, so how he made it all the way to southern California is a mystery, but he may have had a very eventful first two years of life.

Sweet Pea had been released to a Silky Terrier Rescue in southern California by an older couple who couldn't handle her energy level as a puppy. She'd been adopted by Jeff and his wife in 2009 when she was around a year old, and was definitely a little diva in the making.

In an e-mail Jeff sent me after our consultation, he said:

> Going into our meeting I was skeptical, even though our vet told me he consults with you whenever he has difficulty diagnosing what's wrong with a patient, including his own dogs.
>
> All you wanted to know at the start of the visit were the dogs names, how long I've had them, and which dog I wanted you to talk with first. You didn't want to know anything else. Quite honestly, that impressed me even more than getting a recommendation to see you from my vet.
>
> I'm open-minded about the universe but made sure I treated our encounter like a deposition. I gave only simple yes or no answers, and I kept as bland an expression on my face as possible.
>
> However, by the time you told me what Bear had to say, I was convinced that you're the "real deal." There was ABSOLUTELY NO WAY for you to have known all the details you described about their behavior, relationships with each other, and with me, without having heard it from the dogs themselves. I knew from observing their behavior that everything you were describing was exactly what was going on.
>
> The only thing I didn't know was that Bear was unaware that Janine had died. When she did pass, I put all three dogs on her bed so they could understand that she was gone. After a minute on the bed, Bear lept off, ran into another room and started crying like a baby, so I thought he was the first to realize that Janine had died. But apparently, he still didn't believe it . . . until you explained it to him during our visit.
>
> And do you recall what Sandy said regarding being able to see Janine's spirit? How in the world would you have known about Laddie, by name, if not for having heard it from Sandy? I never mentioned it until later after you talked with him.

I may have been somewhat skeptical at first, but I'm definitely a believer now.

Nine months later, on the one year anniversary of Janine's passing, Jeff again brought all three dogs to see me to find out how they were doing now that a whole year had elapsed.

They'd all had some behavioral issues for awhile after Janine passed, which was essentially why Jeff brought them to see me in the first place, but not one of the dogs was troubled by her loss during this second visit. They'd apparently successfully grieved and moved forward, but for Jeff, Janine's loss was still quite an open wound.

Above: Laddie

After I talked with Sandy, Bear, and Sweet Pea during this second visit, Jeff asked me if I could reach out to Laddie, whom Sandy had mentioned briefly the first time nine months ago.

Laddie barely had a chance to say hello from Spirit before I needed to tell Jeff there was someone with him. This someone was a woman who interrupted Laddie because she wanted to talk with me. It was, of course, Janine.

As Jeff summed it up in an e-mail to me later on:

We had a great, great chat with Janine. She repeated things, through you, that she'd repeatedly told me she wanted me to do after she died - almost verbatim! She shared with you that at that moment she was dancing, and it was rather cute because you had to physically demonstrate the kind of dance she was doing, which once again reaffirmed for me that your gift is REAL.

She also explained something personal through you which enabled me to "tune in" to hear her messages, which I still receive on occasion - usually when I need her the most.

When we were done and my eyes were dry, you told me that you don't usually translate for human spirit because too many people get upset with you if they don't like what they hear. Quite honestly, I agree with you - people are not as pure as dogs, nor are they as intelligent in many cases.

Truth be told, I've been tempted to ask you if you'd be able to talk with her again during subsequent visits, but I've been both shy about asking and respectful to you. I guess if she has something important to tell me that I'm not picking up through other means, she'll jump in, just as she did during our second visit.

Even though my communication with Janine took place almost a whole year after my first visit with Jeff and the three dogs, it was Sandy who initially served as the "bridge" for Janine to talk to Jeff through me. During our first visit, Sandy not only talked about Janine being gone, but he also mentioned that Laddie could talk to her.

After Sandy told me about Laddie during our first visit, Jeff had only told me that Laddie was their first dog, but when he asked me to connect with him during the second visit, Laddie then became the bridge through which

Janine was able to reach out to communicate many important things to Jeff that he found very comforting.

This family story wouldn't be complete without including one other precious Silky Terrier who'd also been a very important member of the family. Crash was Laddie's half brother, same mother, different father. The two pups were born six months and a litter apart. Laddie and Crash were Jeff and Janine's first two Silky Terriers, whom they adopted from a breeder when they were each just tiny puppies.

Above: Crash

Crash was a gentle, passive soul who often "played second fiddle" to Laddie's outsized personality, so it seemed as if he rarely had the opportunity to express himself fully.

He also had some vision issues from birth, and some unknown hearing issues that sometimes made him seem "slow" in comparison with Laddie's advanced intelligence. But when he taught his family about the games he liked to play, his family learned he wasn't slow at all.

He wasn't "slow" either when it came to being a fierce protector. One day when Janine, Laddie, and Crash were out for a short walk to get the mail, they were approached by a snarling Rottweiler whom they weren't familiar with.

Neither Silky Terrier pup required a leash on these walks, so Laddie was free to run back to the house for safety, but Crash positioned himself protectively in front of Janine, stood his ground, and barked ferociously as the Rottie continued his menacing approach. When Crash had had enough, he jumped up, bit the much larger dog on his nose, then proceeded to chase him down the hill until the Rottie ran far away!

Later, when Laddie became gravely ill, another aspect of Crash's beautiful personality emerged, showing what an exceptional little boy he was. He'd remain by Laddie's side to comfort him during the home treatments Laddie required until he recovered. Laddie later reciprocated by offering comfort to Crash when he became so ill near the end of his life.

Crash passed on at the age of 13. Laddie then passed on at the age of 14, just six months later.

Sandy, who'd joined the family just three weeks after Laddie passed in 2007, crossed over The Rainbow Bridge in 2015, so now, these three friends were together in Spirit.

It wasn't unusual for Sandy to "pop in" from Spirit during some of the more recent conversations I had with Bear and Sweet Pea.

On one particular occasion, Sandy said he appreciated what Jeff had done with his music. I had no idea Jeff had recently paid tribute to three of his dogs in a very unique way. On one of the songs for Giving Shelter, his cancer fund raising project in honor of Janine, he'd given credit as a backup vocalist to Reverend Sandy "Sweet Pea" Oliver (Bear's original name). Sandy wanted to thank Jeff for doing that.

After being diagnosed with cancer in 2018, Bear had finished his first chemo cycle in early 2019 and seemed to be doing well. He'd gained 5 pounds, had a joyful spirit, and was strong enough to jump up on the bed on his own again. He also had an ever-present enthusiastic sparkle in his eyes.

But in June 2019, Jeff and Bear came to see me again for an emergency consultation. Bear had fought the good fight for a long time, but he made it absolutely clear during this June visit that he was now ready to go. That very same night, Jeff could see the unquestionable signs it was time, so he drove Bear to "his" hospital where a kind veterinarian helped this valiant little dog pass peacefully.

With Janine, Laddie, Crash, Sandy, and Bear all now in Spirit, that leaves only Sweet Pea at home with Jeff.

She's recovered from her own two bouts with cancer, but she's faced some new health challenges recently, including the need for both gallbladder surgery and eye surgery. However, with her courage, inner strength, and adaptability, this spunky pup has recovered well and has maintained her inner joy for life. She's still busy perfecting her skills as a little diva, and she's definitely still "queen of the castle."

As you can see, everyone in this beautiful family of Silky Terriers has had a special mission in life. There have been diagnosticians, healers, protectors, divas, and maybe most uniquely of all, there were those who, on earth or in Spirit, served as bridges for human communication.

You'll find Bear's and Sweet Pea's individual stories in the chapter about Pets as Diagnosticians for Themselves and Others.

You might also enjoy visiting Jeff's website: **www.givingshelter.net**

Heidi

A message from your mom in Spirit

I was having a consultation day at one of the veterinary clinics when I met Patricia with her dog Heidi, a beautiful German Shepherd who was about 4 years old.

Pattsie is in her late seventies and very petite, weighing 100 pounds on a good day, while Heidi is about 75 pounds of solid muscle, so it was a strange combination to see the two of them together!

HEIDI

Pattsie told me she and Heidi volunteer three days a week at the East Campus Hospital. They visit patients who've had a stroke or suffered trauma from some kind of accident. I understood then that this was a very special dog, a therapy dog.

I immediately tuned in to Heidi who was wearing a collar and leash, and sitting quietly next to her mom. She told me her throat hurt and she had problems eating. It was such a distinctive pain that I told Pattsie it would be very wise to have the vet take an x-ray of Heidi's throat.

As soon as the vet met them in the exam room, Pattsie requested an x-ray right away. It showed that Heidi had a vertebrae out of place in her neck that was causing her to have problems swallowing.

Even before getting the x-ray results, I also suggested to Pattsie that she elevate Heidi's food bowl. Doing so would help her to eat more easily if she didn't have to bend her head all the way down to the floor to reach her bowl.

Because I have thousands of clients, it's not possible for me to remember all the details of every conversation. That's why I was so pleasantly surprised to read in Pattsie's e-mail that this had been another occasion when a pet had been the bridge for a human to come through with a message from Spirit.

She wrote:

> *Your gift of being able to talk with animals is truly a gift from GOD.*
>
> *You were so right when you said that Heidi had problems swallowing, and you said it was probably a birth defect. Well, now she's thriving and enjoying her food again. You told me about raising her food bowl to a higher level and we bought an elevated device for her. Thank you!*
>
> *I was so touched when you shared that my mother was there to visit with me during your communication with Heidi. You were able to quote just what my mother would say to me if she were alive today, and to reveal the very happy and loving Mother she always was.*

> She had multiple sclerosis and was an invalid for most of my childhood. I took care of her from the time I was seven years old until she passed away when she was only 50 years old, and I was 23.
>
> I tell you this because having my mother visit meant so very much to me. As you described it, she's very happy and positive, as she always was.
>
> Thank you so very much! As busy as you are, you took the time to talk with Heidi, as well as with my mother. You are a true angel and I'm blessed to know you.
>
> I'll keep you informed as to what's happening with Heidi. You have, as always, put us on the right path.

It feels so good during my conversations with animals when I'm also able to communicate a long overdue message from someone who's in Spirit. I never know when, or if, this will happen. It's all up to Spirit, but the more insistent someone in Spirit becomes, the more likely I am to tune in.

Because my life is dedicated to working specifically with animals, communicating with humans is not something I normally do, but I'm still happy to translate what they need or want to say whenever they choose to use one of the pets I'm communicating with as a "bridge."

It's a good reminder that those in Spirit, whether animal or human, are always around us and caring about us, no matter how long they've been gone from this earthly experience.

A Special Human Spirit Interrupts a Dog's Communication

Sandy, Laddie, and Heidi aren't the only dogs I've met who've served as bridges to human communication.

One day, a young girl in her teens came to see me with her mother and their two dogs. Only later on during the consultation did I come to find out that one of the dogs was hers and the other one belonged to her mom.

What I do remember vividly is that, as I was talking with the two dogs, a male figure kept interrupting me, insisting that I speak on his behalf. I finally had to stop what I was translating for the dogs because this spirit figure kept insisting he had to say something NOW.

He wanted to reassure the young lady that he was watching over her, and let her know he was the one who sent her this dog.

Of course, there were tears all around. The young girl told me this was her dad. She'd asked him to send her a friend because she'd felt so lonely now that he was gone. Her dad had definitely heard her request, and fulfilled it beautifully.

Even though I normally translate only for animals, sometimes I can't help it when a special human is so insistent. In this case, the mother and daughter came back to see me two more times, and on both occasions, Dad was there to greet them and to just say "Hi!" again, which I was very happy to translate.

Sometimes I laugh to myself on these occasions because, even though humans in Spirit know I'm not there to translate for them, they still insist on finding ways to get my attention.

To me, it feels as if they're hovering around me and moving from my left to my right, tapping me on the shoulder to make sure I'm seeing them, hearing them, and more importantly, paying attention to what they have to say. It might only be a single sentence, but they want to be sure I convey *their* message before I continue my conversation with the pet, which is always my primary focus.

Chapter 7

Lessons Learned and Ten Years of Growth in Spirit

Boadicea

Longest communication from Spirit

I knew Boadicea (Bodie) for about five years before she passed on. She was a very unusual cat who didn't like any other animals. She grudgingly accepted humans, but only on her own terms.

When she passed in 2008, I then started talking with her in Spirit. My last full conversation with her was in 2017. That's a 15 year record for me for continually communicating with one pet, and a 10 year record for me for communicating with any one pet in Spirit!

Each year, her mom Carlotta would send me a list of questions she wanted me to ask Bodie. And each year, her answers showed how Bodie advanced more and more in her spiritual growth.

Even though it will be quite a lot to read, I'm going to share with you at least parts of every communication I've had with her since 2008 so you, too, can see how beautifully she's evolved, and how very helpful she's been to her mom when it comes to providing information about some of the many other cats in the family including Semiramis, Odysseus, Deuteronomy, and Ishtar.

These are the notes I recorded in answer to her mom's questions. Sometimes I have to explain what Bodie was saying in my own words, while at other times, I write what she actually said.

September, 2008

In the first part of my notes to her mom, I wrote:

The first thing Bodie said to me was, "Greetings!" It felt as if she was embracing the wonder of communication now that she was in Spirit. She seemed to be so happy to hear from you that she wanted to embody, in one word, her feelings of welcome, wonder, and gratitude.

The image she sent me was more a picture of feelings than of thoughts to be translated. It was as if she was so very happy to hear from you, through me, that her energy body, and mine, felt it.

First of all, she wanted to let you know that she's no longer in pain. In fact, she said there is no pain, and there are no unhappy times where she is. Everything is good and loving, and there's an everlasting sense of happiness around her.

It took her awhile to understand that feeling. She said she'd never experienced it in her lifetime with humans, so she could hardly believe this feeling could be sustained for such a long time.

Bodie acknowledged that she has a lot to learn where she is now, but she's looking forward to it. She said it doesn't feel like learning at all. It just feels right.

Next I began asking her mom's questions and adding Bodie's answers to my notes . . .

BOADICEA

Who greeted you as you arrived on the other side? Was Semiramis there?

Bodie said that although she could feel the presence of many animals around her as she made her transition, she was wary of all of them and couldn't trust herself to follow anybody.

That's when a human hand appeared in front of her. Because she sensed she could trust it, she became a little more at ease and allowed the hand to pick her up.

It was a transition almost as if she was going from dark to light, and although it didn't take that long, it felt as if she was doing it in slow motion.

She was able to see all around her and knew she was surrounded by others. Some souls she immediately recognized from before, and some were new to her, but all of them had one thing in common. They were all loving her and accepting her.

Even so, it took Bodie awhile to feel comfortable around others of her kind. It didn't take long, though, for her to realize that she was already feeling quite different within herself.

All the animosity, resentment, and distrust she felt during her stay on earth was quickly disappearing as the others came closer and closer to her. Pretty soon she was no longer experiencing any of those negative feelings that she used to experience on earth, and everyone was surrounding her to welcome her in.

She said for the first time since she can remember, she felt accepted for who she was, and even loved by everyone else. It was such a nice feeling, but she hardly knew how to respond to so much love.

I asked her directly about Semiramis and if she knows who she is in Spirit. While that name wasn't familiar to her, Bodie did know that somehow, Semiramis's energy definitely belonged in the family group.

(It's no wonder Bodie didn't recognize Semiramis right away. Bodie had been adopted a few weeks after Semiramis made her transition into Spirit, so she'd never had the opportunity to know Semiramis as part of the family on earth.)

My reply to her mom's first question then continued:

She understands there are quite a number of animal souls in Spirit now who were very close to you at other times in your life. She does know that Semiramis is one of them. They all work together to guide you as you're taking care of all the cats in your home. They help make you aware of what your current animals feel, think, and need. They also work hard to send you, directly or indirectly, the animals you'll be able to help.

I asked her if she was jealous that there were so many others who'd been so close to you.

She responded:

> "There's no such thing as jealousy on this side. We all work together because that's how we evolve. There is not you or me here, there is us."

Then her mom's questions continued . . .

What's your life like now?

> Learning is what I need to do first. When I learn, we all learn. Everyone learns from everyone else.

In what ways is your spirit still with us? Have you come to visit us, or Ishtar, or the other cats in the house?

(Ishtar is Bodie's sister, and was the other cat Bodie lived with upstairs.)

> My first job is learning, but my other job is simply to be around you and to say hello to Ishtar sometimes. I come to say hello often just to remind both of you that life continues, even though we can no longer touch. When we come to visit our former home, we feel the connection with everyone. It's something we never lose.
>
> We also feel it's necessary at times to connect with those who are still in earthly experience to prepare them for their next journey, which will be into Spirit.

For instance, Ishtar will never be alone when she's ready to make her transition. I need to make sure she understands that I'll be watching her and will be helping her every step of the way. That's just part of my job.

About the young ones, I often come to let them know how they should best approach Ishtar and what to expect, what to do, and sometimes even what not to do. But . . . not everyone understands and pays attention. That's why we need to keep trying to help them understand.

I know when I was there, I felt others coming in and trying to communicate things to me, but I was always so stubborn. I didn't want to listen to anything they said. Consequently, I never learned some of the lessons that were so important. I need to make amends now, and in order to do that, I need to try to get messages across to the ones I can help. They're my family.

Are you content on the other side so that you prefer to stay there, or at some time, do you want to come back to this side, to us, or to another family?

When I asked Bodie what her feeling was about coming back again, she said she's nowhere near ready to do that. She feels there are a lot of areas in her personality she needs to work on since she never gave herself the opportunity to be open-minded when she was living with you.

She told me, almost with a smile, that not being open-minded has cost her. It was almost as if she was telling me she had to learn a whole lot more before she'd be ready to return for another earthly experience.

Bodie did say that eventually she might need to come back and do it over again. That's because it can take a lot longer to learn all the things she needs to learn on the Spirit side.

This is especially true when it comes to relationships. She says if she comes to your side again, she can learn some of the lessons a lot faster, but she's not even close to being ready to make a commitment right now because there are so many things she needs to work on first.

For instance, she acknowledges she was very stubborn. This was not a good thing because, although it helped her in some ways, her stubbornness prevented her from learning many new things.

She also needs to learn to be social, and there's no better place than where she is now to learn how to do that, since someone is always available to be a teacher, a helper, a guide.

She does, however, have to learn to adapt to being around others so much of the time because this is a new experience for her.

Do you want to communicate with us again in the future?

She would love to keep you informed about how she's growing and what lessons she's learning.

She's telling me that, after a little more time in Spirit, Semiramis is almost ready to come back as a boy, but she knows you don't like boys so she's not asking you to look for her. She just wants you to know it took her this long to be ready.

They're both sending love to you in the form of pink roses and a yellow ribbon.

MARCH 2009

In response to her mom's question about what she's learning, Bodie replied:

> Greetings! I've learned that cats have been around for thousands of your years, and yet we still have so much to learn. Many of us never really learn to trust humans, and yet humans are able to give us so much comfort and security. Still, not many of us appreciate them. I'm saddened by that and can only hope if I go back to your side I can learn to practice unconditional love.

Her mom's questions then continued:

What are you doing?

No one here tells us what to do and when to do it. It's all up to us, to each individual soul.

The interesting thing is that once you're here, you want to learn, you want to do things, and what's even more incredible, you want to be of service to others. I don't even know how to explain it. It's a feeling that comes from deep within you. It's as if it's your soul's mission.

My biggest task is to work on relationships. It hasn't been easy for me. It's easier to work on myself. It's more difficult to work with others, and for others. This is a big challenge, so I spend a lot of time practicing being social.

Another thing I'm learning is patience. Yes, that's a big thorn in my side, but I know I'm lacking in it, so I'm making an effort to change.

Have you been trying to help me?

This might come as a surprise to you, but actually I've been trying to help you decide NOT to help another cat who has a sad story. I don't believe this is the right time for you to bring another animal into the house because there's so much work you need to do with the ones you already have at home.

June 2009

While Carlotta was preparing for the family's move to a new home, she asked Bodie's advice about what she should do with her two outdoor kitties who are wild.

Bodie replied:

I'm concerned about Odysseus and Deuteronomy. Although we'll look into their needs, it's important for you to know that we each have to follow our own individual life paths. As much as we can, we'll direct them towards someone who'll be nice to them, but it's up to each of them to decide what to do when you move.

Our souls, our spirits, always know what we must do and why. That's very clear to me. I don't know what others, with or without a physical body, will do or won't do. All I know is that somehow our paths are pre-determined by ourselves. But while our general path is pre-determined, we do still have free will, so how we act while we're on that path depends on the choices we make. Things are pre-determined, not pre-destined.

June 2010

Bodie told us:

I'm learning how to be more in tune with others and how to understand older beings. You know I was never too patient, so for me this is a bit difficult.

My main job is to be next to Ishtar right now (her sister was still alive at that time) and I can promise you that I'll do the best I can for her.

Odysseus and Deuteronomy are both busy and doing very well now. They're happy to be here and happy to be evolving. Yes, evolving. They're both doing beautifully. I'm so proud of them.

(In the few months it took the family to sell their house and plan the move, both Odie and Deuteronomy made their transitions into Spirit. It was almost as if the two of them knew it would be better to go back to Spirit than to stay around their familiar yard with new owners, or move over to a neighbor's yard.)

Then Bodie talked some more about her sister Ishtar . . .

Ishtar is slowly realizing she needs to make her transition, but she's not happy about it. She still doesn't know how beautiful and peaceful everything is here. She's not herself anymore, and I don't think we can explain things to her now. I'm sorry she's being so difficult, but it's her stubbornness that's getting in the way. She just can't accept changes.

Her mom then said, **"Dad wants to get a dog soon after we move. I thought he understood that we shouldn't do so while Ishtar is alive, but he doesn't want to wait that long. In fact, he'd like to get a dog a month or so after we move. I'm concerned about how Ishtar will deal with a new pet. Also I feel all the cats need time to adjust to their new surroundings before bringing in a dog. I'm upset and worried about this. I know how important a dog is to Dad in his later years, and I'm happy to have one. I just hoped we could wait awhile longer. I don't think I can convince Dad to wait a long time. What do you think?"**

> The dog is coming! I can assure you of that. We've known about it from this end. You can worry if you want to, but it's a given, so why worry!

September 2010

In answer to her mom's question about what she's learning, Bodie said:

> I'm not sure if my lessons will ever be finished, but I'm continuing to work on patience and being able to accept things the way they are without wanting to change them to my advantage. I try very hard to see things from the point of view of others so that I may better understand those who don't think or feel exactly the same way I do. I hope in the future I'll be able to graduate from this.

> This is very, very hard learning. They tell me this lesson is one that's easier to learn on this side than on your side. That's because we can directly experience the energy of others and feel what they feel so we can better understand them, even though they can't, or won't, provide an explanation. This helps a whole lot because some souls are not good at explanations. In fact, I was made aware that I was one of those. Bummer!

Her mom then asked:

What do you think of Thor (the new dog)?

Thor is exactly what you needed! More to the point, he's exactly what Dad needed! You see, if I would have sent you someone who was already perfect, then you wouldn't have been able to learn along with Dad. This way you're both learning at the same time, and the experience will bring you that much closer. Everybody likes perfection, and we know how Dad is . . . don't we? So, this was the perfect scenario. He wanted a dog so much, but I felt he needed to do the work that comes with having a dog, too.

The cats, with the exception of Ishtar, will learn to live with Thor in time, and even become his friends. I know there's a learning curve, but believe me, everything will turn out just fine.

Is Ishtar ready to make her transition into Spirit?

I think I'm making more progress with her now. She's paying attention, although not for very long. She might still be upset at the thought of having to prepare herself for her transition, and I don't blame her. I was very upset too. That's why I'm a good example for her. Rest assured, I won't leave her alone now, or during her transition to this side.

You need to understand that we start to transition very slowly. First, our body starts to give us signs that we're not the same young things we still like to think we are. Once we come to terms with that, then our minds become cluttered with the many, many thoughts we have to put into perspective.

No one decides when they want to die (unless they feel very badly), but we do think about dying off and on just so that we're prepared when the time comes. To do that, we need the help of those who're already in Spirit. They help us understand each step along the way.

(Ishtar did make her transition into Spirit just six months after this conversation)

July 2011

Is Ishtar with you now?

She is. She's even happier than I was when I first made my transition. Now that she's here on this side, she's beginning to see things in a very different way. As soon as she found herself here, everything became very clear to her.

She's already regained her strength, and her mental abilities are developing very quickly too. She's very happy to be here among all of us.

September 2011

I've been working on respecting myself so that I don't blame myself so much for the things I did or didn't do in my last life. I've also been reflecting on how my attitude affected others, you included. I've been able to discover some of the reasons why I was so uptight then, and I've also been able to release the negative feelings. It's been a good journey for me because I'm now more free to enjoy myself and to help others like Ishtar.

We were part of the same litter, but we were so different back then that I could never understand what made us sisters. We basically felt the same, although we showed it in very different ways.

We spend a great deal of time together now, so we're able to better understand our behaviors towards each other, both then and now. She's smart, and even funny at times, and she continues to grow and evolve.

Dad and I want to thank you for being there for Ishtar when she entered into Spirit.

I wouldn't have had it any other way. I was there with you and Dad while you were on the bed, petting her and making her feel so very special.

You know, when someone's ready to come into Spirit, we all know it almost at the same time. If feels as if an alert sounds, but only those connected to that soul hear it, unless the soul doesn't have anybody here, and then the greeting group is alerted. But no matter where we are, or what we're doing, we hear this "bell" ringing in our beings, and we know that one of us is coming, so we go to greet them right away.

I'm so impressed by your wisdom and by how much you've grown.

Let me tell you that I didn't think I had it in me to grow as fast as I did. I thought I'd become an old grouch, and there was nothing anybody could do for me. Boy, was I wrong!

When I started to learn WHO I WAS, I felt the real me had been hiding behind my heart, but slowly and determinedly, she's decided to shine through. That new being is me. It was always me . . . I just needed to remember that.

SEPTEMBER 2012

I can actually say now that I'm happy. What a strange word that was for me while I was on your side. I don't think I was ever truly happy, but here it's so easy to feel happy that I can hardly understand why I just couldn't feel it before.

I continue to learn about myself and, just as I would in a classroom, I study different subjects at different times. I've accepted responsibility for my actions and how they've affected others around me. I'm still trying to cope with how it affected the "me" I was then.

Before I go on to study anything else, it seems as if I need to work much more on understanding my last personality, and the things I did and didn't do when I was with you. I need to keep learning and improving so I don't make the same mistakes next time.

I know this will create a better "me" next time, and I try to learn and accept everything I did with humility. Wow, another word and feeling I knew little about! This just shows you how far along I've come.

SEPTEMBER 2013

I have great news indeed. I've been able to work on relationships a lot, and I'm now completely at ease when I'm around others. I've participated with some of our family, too, by receiving those on your side who come in by themselves

It was a whole new experience for me because you have to be in the moment. You see, if I think about myself, my surroundings change because I immediately go to the place I'm thinking about. Therefore, at the time I'm ready to receive a new soul, it's very important that I stay in the moment. I need to think only about the new soul and not about me. As you know, this is very difficult because in my lifetime with you, "me" was all I was concerned about.

SEPTEMBER 2014

I need to bring you up to date on how much I'm evolving. I now have FRIENDS! Can you believe that, Mom! Yes, indeed. I'm so happy and proud of myself. I didn't know if I'd ever be able to share with other beings about me, about the things I need to do, and the ways in which I need to grow. Having friends was not normal to the Bodie you knew and loved, but I'm now an improved version of me.

It's not easy to have and to keep friends. We all need to set special times aside to just be together, to talk and to listen. I've managed quite well indeed. It's taken me a little while longer than it has for some of the others, but I'm pleased with the outcome. Even Ishtar is proud of me now.

I continue to try to make those who have no one on this side feel welcome, but I want to let you know that never, not even for a moment, has my energy left your side.

September 2015

I'm working hard on being receptive to others, to listen, to care, and to participate. I'm trying, as you say on your side, to walk in someone else's footsteps so that I can see things from a different point of view. I've learned so much by doing just that.

I know you're proud of me when I tell you how much I've advanced in my learning.

Lately I've been working on what you would call ego. It's not like we actually have egos here, but I'm making sure that what I want doesn't interfere with what others want.

I'm working on being more giving, and . . . this is the difficult part . . . on liking it.

I love hearing from you. Yes, we're always around you watching you, but we know you're often not aware of the thoughts we're sending, so it's always nice to have the opportunity to bring you up to date on everything.

September 2016

I don't remember what I told you I was studying last time we spoke, but right now my focus is on respecting myself, and respecting others. Both of these were difficult for me when I was in the body. Now that I'm a free spirit, things are a lot easier.

But when you're in Spirit, you don't just learn what you're doing wrong here. You have to look at your previous life, and then your past lives, too, to get a broad picture of who you were before, and who you want to be in the future.

It's hard work, but I take it head on with a good attitude toward learning. This has proven to work well for me as I embark on various learning exercises, and also learn to cope with new things I hadn't expected.

This is the true meaning of learning. We need to experience things from both sides in order to understand. If we work on only one thing like respecting the self, without taking into account having respect for others, then we can become selfish. That's why it's important to see both sides.

SEPTEMBER 2017

I talked before about respect for self, and respect for others. It's a difficult lesson to learn and to master, so for right now I'm continuing to delve into all the aspects of respect, knowing that it's one of my most important lessons to date.

I think the most difficult part for me is to find respect for myself. At least, that's what I've been told. It's been easier to learn about respecting others, but I still need to learn to respect myself, too. I have to learn to find the right balance before I can move on. That's the most difficult task for me, but I continue to enjoy every moment of this experience, and I'm delighted that you know just how much I'm enjoying being on this side.

Yes, Mom, I'm happy all the time. That was something that never happened to me on your side. So, no matter how difficult my lessons are, I'm happy to have the opportunity to continue to learn, and in the meantime I enjoy myself. I know you're happy for me, and I won't stop learning until I achieve my goals.

September 2018

My 2018 conversation with Bodie turned out to be quite different from any previous conversation. These were my e-mail notes to Carlotta:

> I wanted to say hello to Bodie and tell her to be ready to communicate with us when we had our annual appointment in a few days, but as soon as I called her, she told me she was busy. She said she was making final plans to come back to this side again, although she still needed to figure out the physical location for this trip.
>
> She said she appreciates that you communicate with her each year, but she must leave those former memories behind for now to concentrate on her next adventure.
>
> She told me it's been a difficult decision for her, but it became clear she needed to come back to work on her people skills because she'd now learned as much as she could in Spirit.
>
> She wants to thank you in particular for being such a good cat person, and for teaching her to believe in humans. As she embarks on this new adventure, she'll remember all that she's now learned when she meets her new parents. She'll know so much more this time around. She says all that learning, both with you and in Spirit, will help her to be more appreciative and less combative.
>
> She's really looking forward to this trip which, as she put it, is imminent.
>
> Last but not least, she wants to tell you that she's always been very fond of you, and her soul will always remember you.

After I shared all of Bodie's information with her, Carlotta then replied asking what kind of cat Bodie would like to be.

When I connected with Bodie again, she said:

I want to be strong: I'll be a boy.

I want to be opinionated: I'll be a Siamese.

I want to be beautiful: I'll have long hair.

Bodie must have successfully figured out the physical location for her journey, because later in 2018 when I was talking to one of her sisters who was now in Spirit, Freya volunteered the information that Bodie was, in fact, at that very moment, as she put it, "in her mom's belly."

Bodie had a very good ending to her ten years in Spirit, and I'm so happy to know that she was ready to embark on a new beginning. She was ready and willing to put all the work she did in Spirit back into practice as a different personality, with free will, and with a new family. I wish her well!

Ishtar

Advancing my social skills and becoming a teacher

Bodie's sister Ishtar and I also have a very long and interesting relationship. I began communicating with her when she first came to live with Carlotta, and we then continued our conversations after she crossed over The Rainbow Bridge in 2011.

As you listen to the important things she has to say, you'll see once again how much a soul can grow during its time in Spirit, and you may even benefit from the many important understandings she's shared with us over the years.

She was one of those special cats who was adopted by my client from a rescue. She then became an upstairs cat in a two-story home.

ISHTAR

For many years, she and I talked about how she reigned over the upstairs, not allowing the other cats to come up. She did, however, have her sister Bodie upstairs with her, but only because Bodie understood she was the boss.

She also had a very special love for her dad. He spent many hours a day in his office upstairs, and she always felt it was her job to take care of him.

In 2011, Ishtar wasn't feeling well, so my client wanted me to have a conversation with her.

Her mom's e-mail began by saying:

> She threw up some dry food during the night on Saturday and again on Sunday morning. She's been meowing more and more loudly at night, but when I give her the liquid medication to relieve her distress, she foams and drools.
>
> I can't give it to her every day, because I don't want to traumatize her by pulling her out from under the bed so often to medicate her. And, because she drools it out, I just don't think it's worth giving it to her any longer.
>
> Tell her I'll stop giving her all oral medication. I'll use just the ear gel so she doesn't need to be afraid of me. Let her know I was only giving her the white medicine because it would calm her and make her less anxious.
>
> Is it almost time for her to go to the other side, or does she want to stay with us awhile longer?

When I tried to speak with Ishtar, she wasn't very forthcoming at first, but eventually she did respond. What follows are the notes from our conversation that I wrote up and sent to her mom . . .

> I started by telling Ishtar that you'll no longer give her the white medicine because it makes her foam and drool. Then I waited for Ishtar to send me a message in return.

She said she really hates that medicine because it makes her feel as if she needs to vomit. Her tummy has been feeling all weird now, and the medicine just makes it feel worse.

I asked her, "Weird in what way?"

She said it's difficult for her to eat anything because she always feels as if she has to throw up. She can hardly eat enough normally, and she can't eat nearly enough to overcome the unusual bodily stresses she's feeling now. She doesn't know why this is happening, but it's something new.

I tried to reassure her that you'd no longer be giving her the white medicine, and she seemed pleased about that.

I also told her you noticed she's crying more at night, and you wonder if there's anything you can do for her. She said she can't think of anything that would help.

Ishtar told me that what she's feeling is not really painful, but it makes her feel so awkward and uncomfortable. She's realizing more and more, as each day goes by, that she's no longer enjoying life as she has in the past. She doesn't know how much longer she can stand to feel that way.

Not even your caring and comforting touch or presence is doing anything to make her feel better, or to make her feel really present in the moment. She says she drifts in and out at times, and doesn't always know where she is when she wakes up. She's often in a state of panic. This reminds me of someone with Alzheimer's disease.

Because she was talking with me so coherently, I asked her, point blank, if she thinks this is the time to leave and go back to be with her sister, Bodie, and all the other good souls who are waiting for her on the other side.

ISHTAR

She said there's just no joy in eating any more and she can't stand the thought of not eating and going hungry, or of eating and then not feeling well.

She's asking me to be very direct with you. She wants me to tell you that when she starts turning up her nose at her food and walking away, it will be her way of telling you the time has come, and it will be soon.

She said that on some days, more than others, she feels strongly that it will be the last day, and then something happens and she's ok again for a little while. She can't stand this yo-yo feeling and she's just not her happy self anymore. She can't even do her job of taking care of her Dad now because she needs to take care of herself.

She has little doubt that she'll be around for a few more days, but she wants you to be aware of her and notice the signs she sends you. She knows you will, but she wanted to make sure I was telling you again and again so she can be sure you really understand her.

I told her that you and her Dad love her immensely, and so do I, as well as many other people. I promised on your behalf that you'll pay attention to her and not let her suffer or linger too long.

I also told her it would be wonderful if she can release her tired body by herself, but she didn't reply at all when I sent her that thought.

Finally, she wants to thank you for promising not to give her any more medicine. She appreciates that gesture more than she can say.

She feels she's lived a long and happy life and we should leave it at that.

I told her we understand.

Ishtar passed into the light 15 days later in 2011. I've had a conversation with her in Spirit every year since.

2011 Consultation

On the one month anniversary of her passing, her mom asked me to have my first conversation with her in Spirit. These are Ishtar's answers to some of her mom's questions. She said:

> I was reborn here. This feels like home to me now. It doesn't feel like this is something new. Rather, it's something I'd forgotten for awhile, but now I remember it well. It's so nice to be here again.
>
> There was a big party here when I made it back. Everyone was lined up to say hello to me and I felt like I was going through a long row of beings who knew me at one time or another and who were there to support me and to welcome me. It was better than I ever would have imagined, and even better than Bodie said it would be. I loved it, and I'll never forget the love that was here waiting for me.
>
> The first thing I noticed was that the pain was gone instantly and I was feeling better than ever. Sometimes I look down and I still see a body, but it doesn't have the same density as before so I don't mind it.
>
> It's later on that we're told we don't really need a body anymore and we can shed the thought of it if we want to. I did right away. I was fine without one and started to glow with beautiful light immediately upon making that decision.
>
> I want to acknowledge one thing I need to have you know. When I asked you to stop the medication you were giving me and you did stop, it was one of the best times in our relationship. I knew then that you were really listening to me and I want to thank you for that now.
>
> What am I learning? I can learn many things if I put my mind and effort into it. Right now, I'm simply allowing all the feelings to surface that I had during my time on earth. By doing this, I can work out the good ones from the not so good ones.

I need to be able to understand the "me" that was with you on earth in order to start working on the "me" I need to become.

I know this must be a little confusing, but it's as if there are two parts to me, the soul part and the personality part. When we're on earth, the soul is there with the personality. When we're in Spirit, the soul sometimes needs to re-visit the personality and those life experiences in order to learn and to grow.

Reflecting on my conversation with Ishtar, I marveled at what incredibly amazing insights we can receive from our pets who are now in Spirit!

2012 Consultation

In our 2012 conversation, Ishtar told us . . .

One of the main things I'm working on in myself is "acceptance." It's a difficult lesson to learn, but it's a very important one.

As we study, there are so many things we learn about ourselves. Some we like, and some we don't like. There are things we want to change right away, but first, we have to accept ourselves just as we are.

After that, we do need to change things for the better so that our souls can grow. At times, the fastest way to do that is in Spirit, but there are certain lessons we can learn faster if we go back to your side.

Sometimes when we go back to your side, we can work on a lot of those faults, or on things we need to grow in, all at the same time, in just one experience on earth. Other times, we may choose to work on only one thing during an earthly experience.

Sometimes we learn the lesson, and sometimes we don't. Sometimes we succeed, other times we fail.

Even when we fail, we must never be too hard on ourselves because the beauty of these lessons is that we have as long as we need to learn them.

But once you're back in Spirit, you need to accept yourself, even if you seemed to have failed during your experience on earth.

This is very difficult to do, especially when your whole life experience the last time was dedicated to just one lesson, to one singular fault you needed to overcome over and over again.

Every time we go back to your side we say to ourselves, "This time I'm going to succeed." But sometimes, we don't. So, in order to feel accomplished and be happy, one of my jobs right now is to learn acceptance. Once I get proficient at it, I would like to become a teacher here, too.

2013 Consultation

I'm happy and always busy. There isn't a need to rest here. If you want to do something, if you want to be helpful, you simply do it. We don't wait for someone to tell us what we need to do. We simply go and make ourselves useful doing whatever it is we're interested in. That gives us true freedom.

For those who don't want to be involved so much, that's all right, too. Those souls may need to just be and reflect for awhile.

For others like me who want to accelerate learning, we must be involved. We must reach out and help others. This is part of our job and part of our learning. I enjoy it so much! I'm doing everything I can to teach acceptance.

I've even started on my sister, if you can believe that! She's been able to find and keep several relationships and I'm very proud of her.

You know, learning goes hand in hand with teaching. The more I teach, and the more beings I work with, the more I learn from their sufferings and their mistakes. It's important work, and I take it very seriously.

2014 Consultation

I've been busy as always here. I told you before that I go out and look for things to do, for souls I can help, and I'm often able to do something good.

Not long ago I was very interested in learning about a past life I had, and I also discovered a little bit about you. I'd like to share what I learned about you so that you might better understand who you were then and the reason for your very devoted care and love of cats now.

When I visited one of my old incarnations, I found I was in charge, or at least one of the ones in charge, of a very old temple. It felt to me as if cats were more precious at that time than in your time right now. Humans would always be around us when we needed them, continually offering us food and milk.

You were there too, but your physical being was that of an older man. I guess you could say you were in charge of the temple, too. You were always there, kneeling most of the time, but sometimes just sitting there.

All the cats knew you very well and approached you easily because they just wanted to be near you. You had the ability to make beautiful pictures in your mind that we could see, so we were good friends.

I think this is when we first met each other and I understood that you'd always take care of us. I remember feeling extremely satisfied that I'd found such a good human to look after me, as well as all of us cats.

We were many, but only those who had the right energy would stay (of their own free will) in and around the temple. You stayed there, too. When my time came, I said my last goodbye to you, and then you took my body and said we would meet again. We've kept that promise throughout many lifetimes.

I hope you enjoyed this piece of information. Now you know why you want and need to care for cats in this lifetime. We're all very thankful that you do.

2015 Consultation

Ishtar's 2014 message awakened something in my client, so in our 2015 conversation, she requested to know about other lifetimes they may have shared.

Ishtar responded . . .

> You're asking me for more past life recollections, so I'll need to pick a couple that I can remember well. . . .
>
> There were two times when I've been a black cat by choice, and those two times I recall being with you for different reasons, but in both of them we forged a very good bond, and our love for each other grew ever stronger.
>
> The first one was a long time ago for you. Your skin was darker then and you were female with long hair that was braided most of the time.
>
> You picked me up from the streets, but at that time you didn't have the opportunity to take me inside your home. Nevertheless, I knew that I belonged with you and therefore I was always around you in case you needed my assistance.
>
> You relied on me for learning certain things. You used the earth and the plants for medicine and you were important in your community.
>
> For some reason I remember your sandals that were made of leather, as well as the sandal strings that were wrapped around your ankles. Maybe I remember these things because they were right at my eye level, but I always knew when you were coming whenever I saw those sandals!

At that time we were able to converse more freely because we understood each other's thoughts. You haven't developed that ability in this life experience, but you still can understand cats much better than most people do.

The second time I remember vividly was a time when people like you were being persecuted for using the same herbs you had used for centuries to help other women.

Some people were crazy then, thinking that herbs and other methods were actually being used by women not of your earth. Those people wanted to get rid of anyone they thought was an evil spirit. It was a dark time for humanity.

I was there with you and saw you being hurt by others who thought your gift of healing stemmed from the dark side. You were a very nice midwife, a very nice human, and yet they banished you forever.

You learned a lot from that incarnation, and so did I.

Unfortunately that's when I got the idea that I shouldn't trust humans, and I extended that feeling to almost every living being, except you.

You see, I'm still learning and still having to erase some of the feelings I picked up from previous incarnations. But I'm on my way, and I know what I have to do. I'm much happier now than I've ever been before.

I hope this helps you to understand yourself a little better now, too. I realize those memories have been erased from your mind for a reason, and I hope this will in no way negatively affect you now. I only told you because you asked!

2016 Consultation

I'm still doing great and advancing in my social skills, but I'm not quite ready yet to come back to your side.

However, I'm learning a great deal, and because there are a lot of family members, we all help each other in our continuing growth.

When we look at your side of the veil, sometimes we're very happy because the human consciousness has been steadily growing. Humans are a little more aware about Mother Earth now and about all the beings in it. We really enjoy seeing this learning process going on.

On the other hand there are other humans who are reverting back to more primitive-like, or selfish behavior. This is a cause of concern for us.

We're working tirelessly with human souls here as well, in order to help humanity, but it's proving to be a difficult task. For this reason, I don't want to go back to your side now because my work is too important to leave here.

My client replied to Ishtar:

You are one very special kitty who brought so much joy to us, and you remain constantly in our thoughts and hearts.

Ishtar replied:

I'm always amazed that you continue to call me a good and special kitty because I never thought I was. I had a lot of baggage then. However, I know you can be proud of me now because, as a being of light, I've grown so much!

2017 Consultation

I continue to work with all the souls who want my help. Sometimes I have to work with animal souls, but most of my time is dedicated to working with human souls.

We'd like to help humanity to better understand how self-sufficient cats are, to help them really connect with our animal nature, and to know that, although we might need them in a home environment, it really is innate in us to be able to independently sustain ourselves.

But . . . we have chosen to be domesticated and to enjoy the comforts of having food and shelter provided for us daily. And that's where I come in. I remind both humans and animals that it was our choice to do that. Humans need to understand that we have free will, and we must also take responsibility for our choices and our actions.

2018 Consultation

My job in the world of Spirit with both animal and human souls will never be done.

As you know, I choose to work with souls while I continue to evolve myself. I'm continuing to teach all of those who need to know about animals, and why we choose to be with certain humans in order to teach them about us, and to help them learn some of the lessons they need to learn.

It's funny that you're asking me about your new cats because in a small way I was instrumental in guiding you toward them.

I felt that you needed to continue to learn other lessons that the first group did not show you. So I asked around, and these were the souls who volunteered to be with you this time. I'm happy with all of them. Especially with the little girl who is such a handful!

I'm looking forward to even more conversations with Ishtar in the future. It's been wonderful for me, as an Animal Communicator, to be able to have such a long relationship with her because every time we speak, I learn something new. Thank you, Ishtar, for continuing to be a wonderful teacher for both animals and people!

Freya

Thank you again

F reya is another one of Carlotta's cats. She crossed over The Rainbow Bridge in 2016.

This year, as the anniversary of Freya's passing was coming up on September 26, 2018, her mom had some questions she wanted me to ask her beloved cat. I had some time available on September 21st, so Freya and I had our annual conversation.

After reminding her that her mom and dad sent their love, I told her they also thanked her for giving her mom some extra energy when her mom was helping Freya's dad recover from a broken hip.

Freya replied . . .

> You're welcome! And boy! You needed it. I don't understand humans sometimes. Instead of being happy to have someone close to them, giving them comfort and company, they get really uptight and complain a lot. I *had* to give you strength because it was such a tough time, but I think both of you are on your way to recovery now.

Carlotta then wanted to know how Freya and all of Carlotta's other felines were doing who were also in Spirit. Additionally, she wanted to know if Freya had anything else she'd like to share.

Carlotta always includes a favorite picture of Freya in her e-mail request, and Freya was very aware that I was looking at it, so her first response to her mom's question was:

> Before I answer your question about how we're doing, I want to be sure to tell you something. Every time you remind me about the picture of me sitting on my special sofa at home, I get warm feelings about it. It was my favorite spot, with my favorite blanket, in my favorite room.
>
> I know you were aware of it, but I still want to thank you for giving me a special place that was all my own. When I first came to live with you, it took me a long time to adjust to being in a home with so many other cats, but because you gave me my own safe space, and because of your patience, I was able to flourish later on, and eventually become part of the family.
>
> So now, on to how we're all doing. I'm doing great here. Growing every day. I like learning new and different things, and I want to stay here a little while longer. It's so beautiful!

Above: Freya on her favorite sofa and blanket

Everyone is doing well and we continue to be together. We're always watching over all of you.

(She was speaking of all of Carlotta's former cats who are now in Spirit.)

I've been helping Bodie prepare for her next journey, and she's now in her new mom's belly."

You may recall from the first story in this chapter that Bodie was Carlotta's cat who'd been in Spirit for 10 years and was just now ready for another earthly experience.

Earlier that month, when I spoke with Bodie, she told us she'd be coming back to the earth plane soon, but wouldn't be coming back to Carlotta. It was nice to have Freya provide confirmation now that Bodie had already begun to embark on her new journey.

FREYA

Freya's mom then wanted to know if Freya had any thoughts about the current animals in their home.

In response, Freya made comments about each of the current cats, but she was very specific about one of the newer members of the family . . .

> Speaking of Cassandra, she's a real hoot! I know she's more difficult, but you have to agree, she's really making you laugh, and keeping you on your toes, too. I think she's just what you needed in your home right now, someone who makes you laugh and who's unpredictable.
>
> I know you love all your kids equally, and there's something good and special about each one of them. We're all watching over your new crew and happy to see all of them working things out. It's so nice they're all getting along, so at least you don't have to worry about that.

Her mom then wanted to remind Freya how much they miss her and love her. She also said she was so glad to know Freya was happy where she is now, and that she still remembers everyone in her family, as well as the special times they spent together.

Freya responded with thanks to her mom for the loving wishes, and reminded her mom that she's always with them in spirit, even though she can't be with them at the moment in physical presence.

When I shared our conversation with her mom, Carlotta told me that was definitely Freya, always strong and in charge, and she asked me to tell Freya she was right about Cassandra!

Freya's reply when I told her . . .

> I *know* I'm right!

Her mom's response: *She's too much! We really miss her. We'd certainly welcome her back anytime she wants to return.*

Deuteronomy

Working on lessons

Carlotta helps several rescues with their cats in her spare time. She often fosters kittens, and has adopted some of the more difficult-to-place adult cats. On occasion, stray cats have sort of "adopted" her. This was the case with Deuteronomy.

Many years ago, when I went to her home to visit with all of her cats, she introduced me to one of her two outdoor felines. Deuteronomy was a female cat, age unknown, who'd been coming around Carlotta's home for feedings for many years.

Communicating with her wasn't easy. She had quite an attitude, which made her a really bad conversationalist. She did *not* want to send me any pictures, but she was ok with me sending her information. The message seemed to be, "You can talk to me, but I'm not going to talk to you."

At first, it looked as if this was going to be a very one-sided conversation, but eventually I was able to get her to send me at least a few pictures.

I explained to my client that this cat didn't necessarily view her and the other cats as her family. To Deuteronomy, this home was more of a place to hang around and be fed. She stayed on and on simply because it had become so familiar, so comfortable, and so dependable.

I wondered if she might be seriously stand-offish because of something that had happened in her life when she was growing up.

One particular impression she gave me was that she didn't ever recall having a family. She remembered being an outdoor kitty and having to fend for herself from the time she was very young. She never had any friends before either, and everything she did was on her own. She was untrusting of both animals and humans, except for her beloved friend Odysseus (Odie for short), who was now the other outside kitty.

Whatever was making her be so aloof continued to make it difficult to maintain a good conversation with her. At one point she even told me I shouldn't bother her with any more questions! But I gently persisted, and I received at least a few more answers during that conversation.

DECEMBER 2009

The two outdoor cats, Odysseus and Deuteronomy, each passed into Spirit one month apart in late 2009, so the next time I spoke with Deuteronomy was in December, one month after she passed.

Of course, I was half expecting her same personality to come through, and I was concerned that she might not even be willing to talk with me, but that was not the case at all!

What impressed me more than anything else was how much growth her soul had accomplished in the short time she'd been back in Spirit.

Her mom asked me to tell her how much she loved her, and to express her sorrow about the traumatic way Deuteronomy had died. She'd fallen from an 80 foot tree during an attempt to rescue her.

Deuteronomy then consoled her mom and explained in detail why she went up the tree when the coyotes chased her, and why she fell when she did.

She said she wasn't in pain when she fell because her spirit was already hovering over her body. She felt more like an observer, and there were also many souls in Spirit who were there to help her.

She was a wild cat, not a domesticated cat, so she didn't mind leaving this human experience to go join her friend Odie in Spirit.

She told her mom how much she appreciated all the care she'd given her during her time on earth, and she thanked her mom for all the love she was sending her now.

She admitted she didn't know how to accept love from humans before, but she was quickly learning how to do so now that she was back in Spirit. More importantly, she was also learning how to give love to others.

I then had several more conversations with Deuteronomy in subsequent years where her continued growth during her time in Spirit was evident. These were her answers to some of her mom's questions in each of those years.

FEBRUARY, 2011

Oh, I'm so happy to be with Odie again! I don't miss or want for anything. I'm beginning to venture out more, and Odie says he's very proud of me. I just follow him wherever he goes and I'm always happy.

Odie has a very special job as a greeter for those animal souls who don't have anyone else to meet them when they come back into Spirit.

I've even been able to go with him recently when he greets some of the newcomers. I won't come close to the new arrivals yet because I don't know what to do or what to say, but I'm very close by and I can see everything.

I believe that I'm making great strides in coming to terms with my recent life with you. My healing is coming along, although it's slow, but

I'm having reassurances from everyone around me that I'm doing fine, and they tell me to take all the time I need, so I'm doing just that. The pace feels right for me.

I'm learning that I can be around others, like Odie can, and that others are eager to help me in any way I need. This is a journey every soul must go through alone, but it's nice to have the support of so many others who are there for you and can help you in so many ways.

You asked if there's anything I want to share with you. I guess this would be a good time to tell you that as I went over my life and saw the good and the bad, I need to make sure you know that giving me a home and being a friend to me was one of the most important things you could ever have done for me. I do, from the very deepest part of my soul, want to thank you for everything you did for me.

I now realize your kindness, not only to me, but I also continue to see your love pouring over all of those who need you. We're all very touched by that, and we're very proud of you.

February 2013

I should emphasize that the longer we're here, the less we remember what it is to feel pain. That's a part of life on your side that we don't carry with us when we cross into Spirit. Here, there is no more pain, and we don't dwell on the past at all.

I do, however, look back at my behavior in the past so that I can make strides to better myself in the future, but at no time do we go over our ills or our pains. We like it that way. We concentrate on the growth of our souls and how to better serve you and humanity. We don't think about our physical bodies any longer.

What am I doing and learning? I've learned to accept myself the way I was when I was with you because I now understand it was all part of an important lesson. From that lifetime, I've learned many other things as well. So that I can master each lesson, I take one thing at a time and make sure I learn it from beginning to end.

Being friendly with everyone who loves me is one of the first steps. I have to learn to mingle with others, to accept and to understand others, and not to be jealous. I need to learn to have harmonious relationships, and in the end, I also have to learn to love everyone who is bonded to me. Those are my challenges.

February 2015

I'm really proud of myself because finally I'm able to understand that I'm also an important being of light, and as such, it's my responsibility to help others as much as they've helped me when I first came here.

I'm working hard on many lessons now, which is also a surprise because I couldn't work on more than one lesson at a time in the beginning. So there's plenty of reason to rejoice in my progress.

Although I've been with Odie many times when he goes out to be a greeter, I know that kind of work is not really my calling. For that reason, I simply get involved with others who, like me, did not have the opportunity to know much about people. We talk about the many ways we can improve ourselves and our relationships now with humans.

We're creating the building blocks for our future, in the hope that when it's our turn to go back to your side, we'll be better equipped to be part of the human experience.

So I'm working on relationships, on understanding the needs of others, on accepting that sometimes I won't be the most important being, and that I won't be able to do whatever I want to do all the time.

As you can see, these things are difficult for someone as wild as me, and it takes a lot of learning on my part. I need to know that I'll be able to cope with humans telling me what to do and what not to do before I can go back and experience what it's like to be a special part of a human family again.

But it's not all learning either. I have fun too!

For fun, I imagine myself high up and trying to fly into other places that I remember when I simply think about them in my mind. I'm looking at the view under me and thinking that maybe, just maybe, I'd really like to be a bird. Time will tell. For now, I'm simply enjoying the view!

Mom, thank you again for giving me this opportunity to talk with you. Just know that your love for us is always felt, received, and appreciated, and all your kids are always sending you lots of love, now and forever.

This little girl has a special place in my heart. She teaches all of us that we shouldn't take anybody for granted because all souls learn and evolve. Some of that learning takes place during their time in Spirit, but to learn other lessons, they may have to come back into human experience.

She's also a good example that to go back to Spirit is to go back to class, to continue to learn lessons, to review your life to see where you went wrong and where you can improve, and that we have more than one opportunity to master a lesson.

Thank you Deuteronomy, for being a great teacher!

Chapter 8

Immediate Feedback

The Benefit of Immediate Feedback

I do many, many successful consultations via e-mail, but what I enjoy even more is having clients present, in person, by Skype, or even by phone.

That's because it's so rewarding to receive immediate feedback from the client, along with validations about specific things their pets have told me.

Being able to talk with both the pet and the client at the same time makes the conversation flow much more smoothly.

The client poses a question from his or her list, and I then ask that question of the pet using picture telepathy.

The pet responds with his or her pictures, and I then translate those pictures into words for the client.

Immediately, the client can respond to that translation to validate what the pet has just told me, or to provide additional feedback.

When it's a simple question and a simple answer, we can go right on to the client's next question.

Many times, though, the pet's answer will lead to another question that wasn't originally on the client's list, and if the client is present, that question can also be asked and answered before we move on.

Before I ask any questions, I usually ask the pets if they want to tell their parents something, or if they want to ask *them* a question. Many times clients are in awe when their pets talk about something that's an answer to one of the questions they haven't even asked yet.

Other times, when the pet responds with an answer the client didn't expect, there's often reason for a big smile, a hilarious laugh, or even a little embarrassment.

This often happens when the pet "tells" on Mom or Dad, revealing something Mom or Dad never planned to tell anybody! On these occasions, any number of my clients have had to say, "I've just been busted!" And we all share a good laugh!

I do understand that some clients simply want to be present and listen to all of the answers a pet gives without giving me any feedback right away. They bring a written list of questions with them and ask them one at a time. Then, when all of the questions have been asked and answered, they can validate the translations, or they can tell me if an answer didn't fit.

If something wasn't clear, by immediately being able to ask the pet a question again in the same way, or in a different way, I may be able to get the pet to give me additional information, on the spot, that clarifies his or her answer for my client.

Because I purposely don't want any information before I talk with a pet, the feedback a client provides helps to tell me if I'm clearly understanding the pictures the pet is sending me, and translating them with the meaning the pet intended.

Usually I know with certainty when my translation is clear and accurate, but there are those times when a pet's pictures may be incomplete, unclear, or even misleading.

In those cases, their pictures can often be interpreted in more than one way. It's especially at those times that I appreciate immediate feedback, so I know whether my translation was accurate or not, and so that I can ask the pet again for clarification if necessary.

The questions that any one pet parent asks, in and of themselves, are no different from those that many other clients ask. The questions may vary from serious to silly, and back to serious again, but the answers to those

THE BENEFIT OF IMMEDIATE FEEDBACK

questions sometimes provide just the insights a client needs to better understand his or her pet.

There've been a number of other stories elsewhere in the book that have included some instances of feedback and validations, but in the following stories, I'll focus specifically on some of the interesting, humorous, and heartwarming feedback pet parents have provided, as well as showing how much we can accomplish during a conversation when the pet, the pet parent, and I are all together at the same time.

Mardi Gras, Gumbo, Bayou, and Satchmo

One validation after another

I love having clients who keep coming back for consultations over the years because I get to know them so well. Many of them live within driving distance, so our consultations can take place in person.

During in-person consultations, it's very rare for me to take notes myself unless something is very much out of the ordinary. However, my visitors often record our conversations, or *they* take copious notes.

One of my clients in particular, who's been doing so for several years, has shared various portions of her notes with me.

She has an affinity for Boston Terriers. They've all been females, and all of them have been named for her New Orleans roots. The oldest was Mardi Gras, followed by Gumbo, Bayou, and Satchmo.

Although I don't have complete notes from all of our consultations, I do have some interesting excerpts to share with you. As you're reading them, you'll discover the many validations my client has provided about both fun and serious information her four pets have revealed to me over the years.

I first met Mardi Gras' mom in 2007, several weeks after Mardi Gras made her transition into Spirit. Losing her very first dog, with whom she'd had such a very special bond, had been a very upsetting experience for her.

Mardi Gras

Later on, my client sent me some of her notes about that consultation. She wrote:

When I asked you to communicate with Mardi Gras, you told me she wanted me to stop feeling so sad and to stop crying all the time because she was now happy and pain free.

I hadn't shared with you how she passed away, but you were able to tell me in detail what happened . . . among other things, that she had trouble breathing and had to be put on oxygen.

When the doctors told me there really was nothing that could be done to heal her, I was faced with the most horrible decision whether or not it was time for her to be put to sleep. I went home, but Mardi Gras spent the night in the hospital.

As I was driving there the next morning, she went to Heaven on her own just minutes before I arrived. During your communication with her, she told you she didn't want to put me through the pain of having to make that final decision, so she just peacefully left by herself.

I'd adopted Gumbo when Mardi Gras was around four years of age, and Gumbo had come with me for this consultation. Gumbo told you she'd "see" Mardi Gras frequently, describing her as a bright light moving about the room, which would cause her hair to prickle with excitement.

This consultation was a very healing experience for Mardi Gras' mom, and it was the first of many we would have with each of her dogs.

Gumbo

Gumbo was quite the talker! And with her personality, she often kept us laughing whenever it was her turn to talk.

She was eight years old during one of our consultations when she came to visit me with her new little sister Bayou.

Among the questions her mom asked at that time was:

How did you feel about the pictures I took?

The images Gumbo sent me came very fast and were very clear. I was a little surprised by their clarity, but I was also a little confused because of how Mom had worded her question.

You see, I thought Mom had been taking the pictures herself . . . *but* . . . Gumbo was telling me she was actually posing as if she were waiting for someone other than Mom to take her picture. Next, she emphatically showed me *how* she was posing, and *how* she needed to wait for the flash.

As I was receiving these images in my mind, I had to stop translating to ask her mom if someone else had been taking the pictures.

Mom laughed and told me that on that occasion she did, in fact, have a professional photographer capturing pictures of both girls. While Bayou was running around the beach, seemingly unaware of what was going on, her sister Gumbo was deliberately posing and stopping to look into the camera during the entire shoot. To prove it, Mom gave me a 2009 calendar with Gumbo's picture on the cover. The following year, Gumbo was chosen as Ms. August 2010, and in 2013 she was once again the cover girl.

Way to go, girl! Don't let anyone ever tell you that animals aren't proud of who they are and what they do. Gumbo certainly proved that to us!

Later on when Gumbo was older, her Mom wanted to talk with her again.

On this occasion, without even being asked, she told me her tummy hurt and she felt nauseated most of the time. She'd try to eat the food she'd always liked so much, but after taking only a few bites, it felt as if her stomach was closing up and she was about to throw up what she'd just eaten. She was craving food, but eating was causing her to feel so uncomfortable. She also asked her mom not to put any food in her mouth because it made her feel like gagging.

YOUR PET CALLED

My client e-mailed me later to tell me that Gumbo had been diagnosed with a stomach tumor shortly after our conversation. I was so sorry to learn that Gumbo had to deal with such a serious problem, but this diagnosis was not surprising after what she'd told me during our communication.

Something else Gumbo told me caused me to say to her mom, "I have a strange question to ask you. Do you have Mardi Gras' ashes?" Her mom replied that she did. I then said, "Oh good, because Gumbo wants her ashes to be with Mardi Gras' ashes, and she knows they're in a special place."

Mom then validated for me that Mardi Gras' ashes were in a pendant around her neck that she wears everyday.

Later my client wrote:

After Gumbo went to Heaven in 2014, I had her body cremated so I could put some of her ashes in my pendant as well as keep the rest of her remains in a special box next to Mardi Gras' ashes.

The day her ashes were ready to be delivered to me, I was volunteering down at a state park at the beach so the driver met me there to make the delivery.

After I received Gumbo's ashes, I stood on the bluff talking to her and crying and staring out at the sea. I told her how much I love her and miss her and that she will always be in my heart. As a spontaneous thought, I said out loud, "I wish I could see a dolphin right now."

I kid you not, at that very moment, two dolphins leaped into the air simultaneously and put on a playful show directly in front of me! It was so incredible.

Although I still miss her to this day, I feel comforted to know she's up in Heaven where she's happy and carefree.

Bayou

Bayou hadn't been into the picture taking the way Gumbo had been, but she was also very smart and had many important things to say. She didn't even wait for her mom to ask any questions. As soon as I asked her if she had anything she wanted to tell us, she took over the conversation!

First, she told her mom, "I don't like the place where you've moved my crate! It gets very hot for me."

Her mom confirmed that she'd recently moved her crate from the hallway into a bedroom under a window. Bayou would stay in her crate when her mom left the house for short periods of time, but it was true, the afternoon sun would shine in and make the room too hot for her. Mom said she'd be moving her crate again right away so she could be in a more comfortable place.

Next, Bayou volunteered that she loves being near the sandy beach and the ocean and wants to go there again. Mom validated that they do live near the beach and go there frequently.

Bayou wasn't finished yet. She wanted her mom to know she likes her new home but she misses the sunshine deck she used to have at her old house. She described the deck as having a big sliding door with lots of sunlight coming through it.

Mom confirmed, "I recently moved to a new home, but my old home did have a sunshine deck, just as she described it."

Bayou then told me her new food is cold and mushy and she really likes it.

Mom was right there with yet another confirmation that she'd recently changed her diet from dry kibble to wet food.

Finally, Bayou wanted me to know she was concerned about going outside because she feels nervous whenever she sees flying things.

Mom said, "She's highly allergic to bees and becomes very sick if she's stung."

Then I began to ask Bayou her mom's questions. Here are just a couple of them . . .

Do you like your babysitter?

Bayou answered, "There's more than one sitter. I like the young girl who loves animals and likes to cuddle."

Mom confirmed that the other sitter was older and more regimented, and not that much of a cuddler.

Do you like camping in the camper?

Bayou responded that she does like camping, but she *hates* the fence. She can see all sorts of adventures just waiting for her, but she feels trapped inside that fence.

Mom acknowledged that she does use a portable enclosure so Bayou can be outside without any danger that she'll wander off by herself.

But Bayou soon proved that she didn't always have to forgo having adventures during camping trips. She clearly remembered going on numerous trail walks. She told me she smelled lots of different animals whom she described as being quite large. She loved being out in nature where it was very quiet and there were lots of birds, and she also recalled riding around in something like a golf cart.

Above: Bayou and Satchmo in a vehicle resembling a golf cart

Her mom explained that they'd stayed on a ranch for a month to relax and unwind. They hiked on trails every day and saw all kinds of animals including horses, goats, deer, longhorn steer, wild turkeys, and squirrels. And . . . they drove around the property in a John Deer utility vehicle that was very similar to a golf cart!

Satchmo

After Gumbo died, Bayou was feeling very sad and needed a new companion, so Mom brought Satchmo into the family.

After only a few moments of talking with her, I told her mom she's one very smart cookie, very focused and active, and always go-go-go. Her mom said this is so true about her.

Right away, Satchmo said, "I have a new name that has two words. I like it!"

Above: Bayou and Satchmo

Mom then told me her original name was Sophie, but she'd changed her name to Satchmo Grace shortly after adopting her.

Next, Satchmo sent me an image of a dog running back and forth and barking on the other side of the fence. She told me that dog doesn't like her, and she doesn't like that dog either.

Her mom then confirmed that they have neighbors who have an American Bulldog. She runs along the fence every day, barking all the way. She's very aggressive toward Satchmo, and Satchmo reacts the same way toward the Bulldog, if not worse.

Her mom then wanted to know, "Were you happy at your previous home and do you miss it?"

Satchmo replied, "Something tragic happened. My owner was sick." The image she sent me was of someone who was lying around all the time.

Mom confirmed that her previous owner had been very ill with cancer before passing away.

Her mom then asked, "What hurts and what does it feel like?"

Satchmo told me her neck hurt. She described the pain as being very uncomfortable, similar to what we might call the pain of a pinched nerve. It was making her front legs feel a little numb. I told her mom the location of the problem seemed to be in the vertebrae between C4 and C5.

Later, her mom sent me an e-mail to tell me that Satchmo had had to go in for neck surgery to repair a herniated disc at C4/C5, but she now seemed to be on the mend and was doing better.

Talk about receiving one validation after another! And also receiving a lot of interesting and immediate feedback. These girls and their mom made my day every time they came to visit me.

Pluto

He's in my favorite place

The following conversation is another very good example of how the client and I can share information as we go if the client is present during the consultation.

Pluto is a Standard Poodle who's approximately 10 years old. His mom and I were present together, thanks to Skype.

Pluto remembered me from a previous conversation we'd had, so he was ready to talk with me right away. He even said he was expecting me because his mom told him I was going to reach out to him.

Since he didn't need to ask or tell his mom anything at the moment, I reminded him of how much his mom loves him. Then I told him she wanted to ask him some questions so she'll know what she can do to help him have a better and longer life.

He told me he was all ready to answer, so I began with his mom's first question:

How are you feeling?

> I'm a little tired. I don't know if something is maybe a little wrong with me, but I feel better when I'm at home and resting. Sometimes I even hide a little, just to get away from it all.

His mom confirmed that she *has* noticed him hiding at times. Sometimes he'll hide only his head under the sofa and leave his body outside where you can see the rest of him, but he still feels as if he's hiding.

Are you in pain?

> I can't say that I have a sharp pain anywhere. It's not like that, but something's not right, and I don't know what it is.

The impression he gave me is that it feels like coming down with the flu when every muscle in your body aches and it's hard to move around, so you feel better just doing nothing.

His mom said this is exactly how *she* feels all the time from rheumatoid arthritis, and she wondered if Pluto felt that way, too.

I agreed that many times our pets will display the same symptoms we have. They may do this to try to take the illness away from us, or simply to show empathy for us. However, this was not the case with Pluto. He was just feeling his own discomforts.

Can you give me a signal when something hurts?

> You're asking me to do something that's completely out of my comfort zone. I can't cry out. That's just not me. It would have to be something *very* painful for me to even tell you that I'm in a lot of pain. I wouldn't

> cry out, but I might whimper. I'm very stoic. I have been ever since I was very young.

His mom said that last weekend he did whimper twice so she took him to see the vet. The vet didn't find anything really wrong, but thought maybe he'd strained some muscles. Mom said Pluto was then given some medicine that might help relieve his discomfort.

What's going on with your diet?

> I'm not eating because all the bones in my head hurt when I have to eat the crunchy food.

I then suggested his mom try giving him half the amount as kibble and half the amount as moist food, or even give him all moist food. She agreed to try those options. She'll also check with the vet to see what else she can do to help minimize Pluto's discomfort.

He's due for a teeth cleaning but I'm afraid to have him anesthetized. Will he be ok with anesthesia?

> I don't know! I have no idea how to answer that question.

It's not uncommon for clients to ask their pets if they know the outcome of surgery, anesthesia, or taking medications, but pets wouldn't know this, just as people wouldn't know.

I explained to my client there are a lot of places now that do teeth cleaning without anesthesia. You just have to google "anesthesia-free dental cleaning close to me."

My client didn't even know this option was available to her, so she was very happy to learn about it.

Do you like the park?

> I do like it, but sometimes I'm not there to socialize. I like to go there for the freedom I feel when I'm off leash.

His mom agreed. She said he loves the park and runs around like crazy whenever he's off leash.

Do you like my boyfriend?

> Sometimes. I'm not always that good around people and sometimes he's in my favorite place. He's nice to me, but I was here first, so he shouldn't take my place.

His mom was laughing because it's so obvious that sometimes Pluto likes her boyfriend and other times he doesn't. Also, her boyfriend always sits on the side of the sofa that Pluto usually sits on, so I suggested she ask her boyfriend to change sides so Pluto could always be in his favorite spot.

How much time do I have with you?

> Every time you have a chance to ask me questions, you always want to know how much time we have together. I don't know, but I can tell you that I think I'm fine, and every day I intend to be here close to you. I love you. I know you're my Mom, and I know how much you love me.

Another way clients often ask the same question is, "How much longer are you going to live?"

I told his mom that sometimes a pet who's very close to dying does have a general idea, but a pet who isn't close to making his or her transition just doesn't know.

Neither people nor animals know the answer to this question, but Pluto's response to his mom was very loving and showed how much he cares.

If I can't take care of you because of my own health issues, Sharon wants to come and get you and take care of you at her house. Will that be ok?

> Yes, that would be OK. It's not something I want to do because I love my own home. I'd much rather she'd come to our house to help with my feedings and other things, but if I have to go, I'll go.

His mom said he doesn't really like to go to Sharon's house because she has a lot of other dogs.

Do you know that mommy is often in a lot of pain from rheumatoid arthritis?

> I know. It doesn't come as any surprise to me to hear you saying you're always in pain. I can see you, and I can feel your energy draining at times. I'm sorry it hurts. I try to be a really good boy on those occasions and chill out so that you don't have to worry about me. Sometimes I even feel what you're feeling.

Via Skype, my client again said she always wondered if her dog might be experiencing health issues similar to what she herself was experiencing. If so, she certainly had an abundant amount of empathy for him.

Once again, we talked about how it's not uncommon, on occasion, for pets to mimic our feelings when it comes to our health.

Sometimes they go so far as to take on our symptoms in the hope that they can relieve our pain or even make us be well again.

In the worst cases, they can even make themselves so sick that they end up dying themselves.

Other times, though, they'll just have sympathetic pains, just because they feel what we feel.

I reassured her that, in this case, though, Pluto was not doing any of these things. He was simply dealing with his own discomforts, albeit somewhat similar to what his mom was experiencing herself.

It was obvious that he didn't want to complain, but from his responses, it was also obvious that something wasn't quite right.

Having this conversation with her dog helped my client to feel even more attuned to Pluto's needs so she could continue to find every way possible to keep him comfortable.

As you can see, when the client, the pet, and I are all in the same conversation together at the same time, that kind of communication can flow as easily as ordinary conversations among people usually do.

YOUR PET CALLED

The pet has an opportunity to express his or her feelings.

The client can receive confirmation about something they already suspected, or they can gain new understandings.

And I have the privilege of bringing the two of them together in a very special way, in addition to receiving immediate validations and feedback!

Chapter 9

PERSONALITIES

Reiki

Mr. Grouchy

One of the reasons I've been able to write so many books is that I have a written record of all my remote communications, and there are thousands of them.

Sometimes I like to select stories of pets who've been my clients for many years to give my readers a clear sense of how they maintain their specific personality traits throughout many consultations. It's also very interesting to see how much they often change after they make their transitions into Spirit.

Reiki is one of those memorable pets. I met him in person in 2004. He was a rescue so my client didn't know exactly how old he was, but she did know that at some point he'd been wild, and lived as an outdoor cat.

He'd been misbehaving and lashing out at her over the smallest things ever since she'd rescued him. She wanted to improve their relationship, so she was making every effort to understand him better.

I remember going to my client's home and meeting Reiki for the first time. He was very standoffish and didn't want to talk. He appeared to have a bad attitude and wanted little or nothing to do with me.

We eventually did manage to have a conversation during that visit, but when we parted ways, I was doubtful our talk would have any beneficial results when it came to Reiki being willing to change his behavior.

Then in 2006, my client requested another consultation. This time I had my first remote communication with Reiki. These were the notes I wrote for the client at that time:

> Reiki says he knows he has a mission with you. He feels he's supposed to be with you to teach you something . . . well . . . maybe to teach you many things. He says he wants to make sure you don't give up on him, and for that reason, he does try at times to be more friendly, just as you'd like him to be.
>
> He definitely wants you to know he loves you very much, and the reason he chose you was because it was clear to him that you need each other.
>
> He agrees with you that he loves Kelly very much. She has a good aura about her and he loves to rub against her aura. (Kelly is one of the client's roommates and pet sitter.)
>
> Reiki also loves her smell. I don't think he's talking about a scent like perfume. I think he's referring to the unique scent that each of our bodies produces because of pheromones. Hers are stronger than yours and maybe that's why he's so in love with her!
>
> Reiki isn't complaining about being sick at all. Instead, he complains about being bored. That's why he likes the outdoors so much. It

> *gives him something interesting to do, and there are so many smells to enjoy.*
>
> *"Open the window!" he shouts at me all of a sudden, wanting to have at least some access to all the outside smells.*
>
> *Reiki also likes having a friend with him, but he says Simpy doesn't play. (Simpy is another cat his mom adopted.)*
>
> *I then told him you were going to have to be away from home for several days each month. He responded that as long as Kelly is there to feed him and keep him company he'll be OK, but he will miss you at night.*
>
> *Reiki expressed a concern about one of your roommates who's getting married. I'll need to talk to him about that when you can send me a little more information.*

As you can see from the last sentence in my notes, if a pet expresses a concern about something, I may need to obtain some additional information from my client first, so I can then go back and explain the situation to the animal in order to resolve that concern. Once I knew enough to be able to explain everything to Reiki, he was then ok.

I had another remote conversation with Reiki again in 2008 and wrote these notes to share with his mom:

> *Reiki has been speaking with me since last night. He said he did remember our last conversation and he told me that since then, his life has been wonderful. You've both made great strides in understanding each other and he cares very much for you.*
>
> *I told him you're very worried about him because he won't eat and he's throwing up what he does eat.*
>
> *That's when he sent me a picture, not of food, but of yellow-greenish stuff that comes out of his mouth and gives him a bitter taste.*

I asked him if he knew what it was that was making him feel so sick.

He then sent me a series of pictures. I understand from them that he doesn't know for sure, but he thinks it was something he ate, some kind of poison, or it reacted like poison in his system. It's affecting his liver.

I don't think there's anything in his system he still needs to expel because he's not talking about having colic or problems in his intestines.

If it is the liver, this is good news because of all the organs we have, the liver is the one that can regenerate itself. With the right medication and diet, it's possible to reverse the bad things that are happening right now.

He doesn't seem to feel that it's anything life-threatening, although not eating for a long time can result in other organs shutting down prematurely. So your first priority is to keep him hydrated and then to make sure he eats something.

I told him you'll be taking him to the vet tomorrow to help you find out what's bothering him and to get the right medicine. He wasn't very happy about the idea, but he understood you're doing this because you love him.

He said he's very sorry to make you worry so much, but please don't restrict his outings in the future because of only one thing he did wrong this time. He said he'll be a lot more careful in the future.

I took this opportunity to tell him you'd be happier if he'd just stay around your house and not wander so much. He didn't give me any response, so I felt he was finished talking for now.

In the series of pictures Reiki sent me, one of them showed that he loved to drink rain water off the cement. His mom later realized that it may have been the rain water that had made him so sick. It was runoff from the roof that had pooled near the garbage containers, and it was very possibly contaminated.

His mom and their vet worked very diligently to help Reiki recover from that episode and he did recuperate successfully.

At the request of his mom, I communicated with him again six months later in January, 2009. He was already about 10 years old. We actually talked on two different days this time, and I wrote these notes for his mom:

> I started talking with Reiki on Friday while I was waiting for my last consultation of the day.
>
> I wanted to give him time to think about everything I needed to convey to him, so I started by telling him we wanted to see him happy again. I asked him if there was anything you could do to make him happy so he wouldn't be so grumpy or frustrated.
>
> He told me he never asked you for this new friend (a third cat his mom had adopted). He feels just too old to have to babysit someone who constantly wants to play. He said he's not happy about this situation at all. I told him you thought a friend would give him some good companionship, and you made this choice for his benefit, too.
>
> He said he was happy being your one and only friend. But then he sent me another picture of him being upset because you seem more interested now in your boyfriend Clark. He said you have plenty of friends to keep you company, and obviously you no longer need him, so he wants to be outside the house as long and as much as possible.
>
> I explained the dangers of being outside and reminded him that every time he comes home he's hurt. But he, in turn, reminded me that he's very strong and very smart, too. He made me laugh out loud because, similar to the joke we're all familiar with, he said, "You should

have seen the other one," implying that he'd been much tougher, and he'd beaten the other cat to a pulp!

I told him it's still very dangerous and you wouldn't want to lose him just because he was allowed to roam. He simply said he always makes it home.

As you can see, he has an answer for everything, which makes this conversation very difficult at times.

For now, I told him he shouldn't be anxious or upset if you didn't open the door for him to go out every morning until around 9:00 a.m.

He shouldn't be aggressive toward you or Clark either, otherwise you won't allow him to go out at all and he'll have to spend the rest of the day in the bathroom. (Using the concept of spending the day in the bathroom was a way I could get tough with him temporarily just to see if he'd react to it and change his behavior toward Clark.)

Huffing, and displeased with me, he simply said, "OK, I'll think about it."

That was the end of our communication for now until Monday when I'd be ready to continue again.

On Monday, while I was waiting for another client to arrive, I once again connected with Reiki and recorded these notes for his mom:

I told Reiki this was a good opportunity for him to tell me about things he doesn't feel are right because I'd be able to share that information with you in another couple of hours.

He told me he hates the other Tom who comes around the house. He needs to patrol his home so the other cat will not come close to the wall. If Reiki sees him, he'll chase him.

I asked him why he can't be a bit more relaxed and maybe stay inside the house longer. He said patrolling outside is his job and he needs to do it well.

He also complained about you not spending enough time playing with him. He then told me he doesn't even want to start playing sometimes because you just don't follow through, but in his heart he would like very much for you to engage him in some cat and mouse play. Of course, he made sure to tell me he needs to eventually catch the prey, otherwise he'll get frustrated!

He said he knows he's with you for a specific reason, and he believes both of you need to learn patience at the same time. He realizes he's not doing very well right now, so I asked him to give it another try. I also told him you'll try your best as well.

I found him to be a little more open-minded today and not quite so grouchy. I'm hoping he'll take today's information to heart.

It was four years later in 2013 when I spoke with Reiki again. By this time he was about 15 years old. His mom's questions came first in this exchange, followed by his responses:

He's talking loudly and wakes us up multiple times during the night and early morning hours. This has been going on for weeks. It's gotten out of control. I'm losing sleep. I close the door and he still wakes us up.

He wants to be fed, but here's the situation. If you recall, I have two other young cats. Happy developed urine crystals last year. You talked to him then. He was hospitalized twice and it took me several months to get him hydrated, stable, and healthy. Because of this experience, the two younger cats are now given only wet food twice a day.

Reiki also gets a favorite wet food, but he's more of a "grazer." He doesn't eat much at a time. He's given kibble on demand, but it can't be left out as it

has been in previous years. Whenever Reiki is given kibble, the other two cats come running. I keep them away for the most part, but it's unreasonable for me to stand there and supervise Reiki every time he eats.

Please ask him to eat during the day and not to wake us up. You can also tell him he's the most important one in my life.

> It's nice to know I'm still the best and most important friend Mom has. Now that we are many in the house, it's becoming more difficult to be special, and I've often wondered what I need to do that's different so I can feel special to her.
>
> I started "calling" her at my usual awake time during the night just to see if she'd respond to me. She did. That was fantastic! I was really able to get through to her, and she understood my demand. Food was out in no time, and I was happy because I was able to get what I wanted.
>
> I decided to try it again . . . and again . . . and again. And guess what! It works every single time! She loves me and she shows it to me.

I told my client I understood perfectly well what Reiki was telling us, but somehow I needed to help him see that feeding him in the middle of the night wasn't the only way you showed affection for him.

    I explained to him that humans need to sleep more at night, which is just the opposite of what cats need. I told him sleep at night is very important for humans, and I asked him nicely on your behalf to curb his desire for attention during the time when you're in bed. In exchange, you'll make sure to give him special treats during the day and extra petting, too. I emphasized that he needs to let his humans sleep and rest for the whole night until they're up and about in the morning.

    He wasn't very happy with my nice pictures, so I had to resort to using some not-so-nice pictures to try to convince him.

    I told Reiki if he insists on waking you up at night, you'll have to set some kind of alarm to remind him that he must not interrupt your sleep. It would be a sound he really wouldn't like. I said that nothing bad would happen to him, but there would be something sitting at the entrance to your bedroom that would really startle him. (The type of alarm I'm thinking about is a motion detector that activates an air spray can.)

He's thinking about what I said and is not very happy about having to change his ways. He is *very, very* stubborn, but we already knew that, didn't we?

His mom's questions continued, followed by my notes about what Reiki was telling me:

Also, please ask him how his joints & stomach are feeling. I'm wondering if he needs a glucosamine supplement.

Yes, Reiki is telling me he's a bit more stiff than usual. I guess the cold weather is affecting him a lot, too. He tells me he loves to stay sleeping in his comfortable bed (or is it yours?) for most of the day. When he jumps off after staying there for a long time, he does feel as if his back legs are very stiff. For this reason, I think a good joint supplement is a great idea. You can use it as a treat for him.

He had teeth cleaned and blood work drawn. The vet says he's in GREAT shape. The vet did comment that he licks his belly and this can indicate bladder/ gastro upset. I have more of a feeling that it's his joints.

The vet is definitely correct. As I asked Reiki about his digestion, he tells me that the reason he grazes so much is because he can't seem to finish a big meal anymore. He says that even though the wet food is great and he loves it, sometimes when you add kibble to the mix, his tummy feels very heavy and bloated. It's as if digesting his food now takes a much longer time and he feels quite uncomfortable. You might ask your vet if Reiki could take something like Pepcid AC to help him with digestion, or maybe he can recommend something even better.

Please also ask him to be patient in the morning. He gets to go outside, but I would rather wait until 9:00 a.m. or so when the sun is bright in the sky. We

live on a canyon. I understand he's careful and usually only circles the house or visits the neighbor, but for safety, it's better if he goes out later in the morning rather than early.

I did tell him it's best to wait until the sun comes out . . . but . . . he said that if he's willing to stop waking you up during the night, then the least you can do is to make sure that when you do get up, you allow him to go outside right away so he can have some fun.

I told him I couldn't promise anything, but that if he doesn't wake you up at night anymore, then you might consider giving him a little more leniency.

As always, he's a very opinionated being and it's not easy to motivate him to change his mind, but I surely tried!

His last thought was to tell me to ask you to play with him (again?), almost as if you haven't been doing it lately.

I was surprised to hear from my client once again in 2014. By then, Reiki would have been around 16 years old.

I'd almost forgotten what a determined and strong character this stubborn little kitty has. It always takes him a while before he's ready to start talking. Once we do get started, the conversation begins to flow, but getting him started is a real challenge.

I reached out to him to begin this communication, but he ignored me, so I simply had to wait him out. Eventually, though, he came around, and I began to ask him the questions his mom sent me:

Please tell him Clark and I will be going on a trip from November 7-14. It will be a full week. Ask him if he has any questions or concerns.

> Are you leaving me? Well, it shouldn't surprise me. Just know that I'm not myself when you're not around. I don't like anybody else except you feeding me because they never do it right. Plus they don't care if I eat or not, and they won't stay around until I do. Your leaving doesn't agree with me. I need you. You're the only one who knows me. A week is a long time. If I don't eat, I might not be around when you come back!

I told his mom not to worry about this outburst. It was just an attempt to make her feel bad so she wouldn't go. It didn't sound as if it was a truly serious threat.

How are you feeling?

> Why should I explain? You'll leave me anyway.

I told him over and over that you love him very much. He's your boy and you simply want to know if anything hurts. He then replied:

> Well, I'm old. Of course everything hurts. But I manage the best I can and don't want anybody to fuss about it.

How is your energy?

> Energy? I have hardly any energy anymore. I spend a great deal of time sleeping or resting and just watching the others, or watching things happen. Before I was a doer. I was the one who was adventurous. Now I'm only a shadow of what I was. I just lie here and do nothing.

How is your body?

> Achy. Yes that's the best way to say it. My bones ache and sometimes it's painful. I can no longer go to the places I like to go. I wish I could jump like I used to. Now all I can do is look up and hope that someone will pick me up.

How are you feeling emotionally?

> Terrible! But I don't like to dwell on this. Who wants to think about how they once were but can't be any more? I'm an athlete who lost his spring, an adventurer who lost his will. That would make anybody upset. I try not to think. I just am.

Can I do anything to make you more comfortable?

I doubt it. Not because you can't do it. It's because I don't think anything will make me more comfortable or less achy. I know I'm getting old. My body is telling me so, but I'm not going to give up anytime soon.

Tell him if he wants to drink water out of the faucet, he only has to approach the vanity. Clark or I will pick him up and turn it on for him.

Thank you, I know you'd do that for me, but I refuse to be pampered like that. If I can't jump up on my own then what's the use.

I do want to say that Clark has proved he's not as bad as I once thought. He's managed to adapt to me and the others nicely. Tell him thank you for trying so hard.

Won't you please get on my lap again? We used to use this as our meditation time (your words). If you're no longer comfortable with it, that's OK.

I have such mixed feelings about this. It used to be the best time of the day for me. Now the other ones all want attention at the same time, so it's just not the same. The other point is that although I sometimes want to climb up on your lap, I don't find it as comfortable as it once was. My bones hurt.

I suggested that his mom might want to put a blanket or a pillow on top of her legs and then lift him onto her lap just to see if he liked it. If not he'd get down. At least she could offer that.

Did you like the acupuncture? I have you scheduled again in November or December.

Actually, yes. I was surprised that it did improve my overall feeling, so I'll be looking forward to that again.

I want you to know how very much I love and adore you.

I'm glad to hear this coming from you. Sometimes I feel as if we're growing apart because we can't play the way we used to. I also know that I'm getting a little more grouchy lately and I'm sorry about that. But you know me and you know this has been me all along. Thank you for your understanding and your love. I do love you very much, too, although I'm not always good at expressing it.

He'll get me up in the middle of the night to feed him. While I love him, please ask him to try to eat enough during the day so he doesn't need to wake me up. I do try to give him a little kibble before retiring. We might want to ask about his appetite. As I stated previously, he seems to be maintaining his weight, but he only eats in very small quantities.

Reiki told me he finds it very difficult to eat a lot at one sitting. He'd much rather take a couple of bites here and there and have his tummy feel half full instead of too full after a meal. This too-full feeling in his tummy makes him not feel good. He'd much rather eat less at a time and more often. He'd also much rather have soft food than hard food, because the hard food hurts his teeth lately.

He says he's sorry about waking you up, but he gets pains in his stomach in the middle of the night and he needs to eat something to help make the pains go away.

There is a way he can have food at night without having to wake you up. There are automatic feeders you can buy for this purpose. However, the feeder would have to be placed where the other cats can't get at it. If you could put it in a room with a cat door that opens only when Reiki tries to go through it, that would help. There are special collars a cat can wear so that only he will be able to make that cat door open.

I wasn't too surprised when my client contacted me in January of 2018 to let me know that Reiki had now crossed over The Rainbow Bridge. She wrote:

Reiki passed on into Spirit yesterday. Clark let him outside. He usually comes to the door to be let in. I went out to the garden looking for

> him to feed him dinner and found him under a tree and bird feeder. He must have been there at least an hour or more as he was cold. As I went toward him, a Coyote poked his head out of the bushes. I hope he had nothing to do with Reiki's passing. I would like to know. I couldn't find any wounds on him.
>
> He was 19 and woke us up meowing several times during the night. Sometimes he was a little disoriented. I mushed up his food so he'd eat more. His hearing was going a bit. I'd have to create a vibration near him to get his attention and not startle him. To say the least, he was my grumpy old man. Clark & I miss him terribly. I showed Happy & Tango his body before we took it to the vet.
>
> Please tell Reiki, we love him. He's my little boy today, tomorrow, and always. We love him and are happy he's in Spirit. Thank you Reiki for all the years we had together.

His mom hadn't had an opportunity to say goodbye to him, so she asked me to help her connect with him once again. We set up an appointment to talk with Reiki in Spirit in February, 2018.

Unlike many earlier times, when trying to start a conversation with him had been a real challenge, this time Reiki was ready to make contact with me as soon as I called his name. But, just as he and I connected, I remembered I'd sent his mom an email earlier that morning asking if she had any more questions.

I realized I didn't have an answer to that e-mail yet, so I said to him, "Maybe I'll come back to you a little later." His answer was,

> "Oh, no you won't! I'm ready now, and we will talk now. If you need to ask me any more questions later, then you can call me back again."

Well, apparently, he's still one stubborn guy!

He then went right on to say:

REIKI

I have a lot of things to share, so I'm going to start right now...

I want to tell Mom and Dad that I left exactly when I wanted to and I did it by myself because I didn't want to hear them crying around me. It was my decision and I'm proud that I was able to choose not only the right moment, but also the right spot. I loved being there before, and I picked that spot because I felt safe.

My passing was smooth. My soul came out of my body without even a jerk and it elevated. Somehow I knew I had to go up, and seeing the beautiful light shining above me, I didn't have any doubts.

There were others waiting for me at the edge of the light and they walked (actually more like floated) with me until we passed the tunnel into the full light. It was wondrous! This place is so beautiful! I've never seen anything like this before.

I saw a friend who came bouncing in to greet me and tell me how much I was missed and loved.

(This was another cat with whom he'd shared part of his earthly life.)

It took me a little while to acclimate to all the love I was receiving everywhere I turned, but in the end I began to enjoy it very much.

It's all love here. You don't hear anybody complaining or having sad moments. Everything is love and everything is beautiful. And because I don't have to worry about my body anymore, there are no more reasons to be stressed.

All I do is review my life and take note of the things I need to learn, things I need to improve, and things I need to change. Learning all of this is a big and long process and I'm doing as much as I want on any given day.

YOUR PET CALLED

Another part of my job here is also spending some time on your side and visiting the other animals in the house, and also the humans to whom we owe so much. So, I'm with you every day whenever you think of me or call my name.

I want to take this opportunity to thank you for everything you did for me, for not wanting to change me, and for accepting my ways, even though I now know there was a lot of room for improvement. But I was a student of life, and I feel confident that I was able to learn a lot of things on your side.

At the same time, I like to think that I was also a good teacher because, before me, you thought all cats were similar until I came along. Yes, I know, I had a big personality, but you learned a great many things from me, too, and I'm very proud of the Mom you became.

Know that I visit with the boys often and that they're aware I'm in Spirit now. In fact, Tango sees me often and you can tell it's me when he's looking up at seemingly nothing.

As for me, other than being able to visit with you often, and learning a great deal about me and what's ahead, I'm doing terrific.

I have a lot more friends now than I ever did before. I can travel faster than you can blink your eye, and I don't need any food or care now.

A bright, warm, and wonderful light engulfs my being constantly and it gives me all the love I could ever need.

Still, I remember you with a lot of love because you understood me, and you allowed me to be the being I needed to be on your side. Because of that, I learned a lot of things about me and about what it means to be in human experience.

I will love you forever and I promise I'll be the first one you see when it's your turn to be in Spirit. Until then, my heart is always with you.

What beautiful thoughts from a once very ornery and stubborn kitty!

It's surprising how many people don't understand that each pet truly has a different personality. Just as we adapt to each of the human personalities in our lives, we also need to adapt to the unique individuality of each pet, and accept them as they are.

They also each communicate differently. A shy and introverted pet may hardly send me any pictures at all. When I translate what they say, it may only be a sentence or a short paragraph. But at the opposite end of the personality spectrum, there are those very outgoing pets who will respond to just a single question with a whole series of pictures. That kind of translation may take me a whole page to record.

But it's those differences in personality that make our pets so unique, and often so very lovable, even when they're ornery and stubborn!

Thank you, Reiki, for just being you, and for everything you taught us!

Opus and Alex

The Yin and Yang Brothers

I always marvel at the fact that I'm able to discover so many things about animals whom I've never met before, but one of the things I truly enjoy is telling their humans how the pets reveal their personalities to me.

Just the other day I had a consultation with a client who'd adopted two siblings together at the age of four. Both were male orange cats.

They'd all shared their home together until Opus died at the age of 14. He developed a blood clot that lodged in his hind quarters. It didn't kill him instantly, but it did immobilize his back legs. His mom took him to the hospital right away, but the vet said there was no effective treatment, and the best thing at his age would be to help him make his transition into Spirit.

She now wanted to connect with Opus in Spirit, and also with Alex because he'd taken Opus's passing very hard and was very sad.

When I connected with Opus, he showed me he was a wonderfully caring and loving cat. He immediately put his mom at ease by telling her he couldn't imagine himself lying on his pillow all day long, having to be carried back and forth to his litter box, or worse yet, soiling himself. He said he was very glad he didn't have to go through all of that, and he wanted to thank his mom for everything she did for him.

Then he said:

It's true that Alex is not as doting as I was with you, but give him time. Now that he's all alone, he'll seek you out more and give you more love. I'm counting on it because I keep telling him to do that.

By the way, you survived my passing because you're strong, and you'll survive my absence, too.

Then he added:

I've had a talk with Alex already. Actually, I visit with him often to remind him that even if I'm not around anymore, he needs to continue to live his life with you, being as happy as he possibly can.

I tell him to do certain things I used to do, just so you'll know my spirit is always around. Give him time and he will come around.

Above: Opus

It was then time to shift gears and talk with Alex. As you read his answers to his mom's questions, keep in mind . . . a short-fused individual who says in a few brief sentences what others will need a whole paragraph to express. He's direct and to the point and always answers with a huff and an attitude.

Above: Alex

We began with his mom's questions:

I know you realize after all this time that your brother is not coming home, don't you?

He told me that already!! In fact, he tells me ALL the time, but I am NOT happy. It's hard not to see him all the time.

How are you feeling about that?

Sad, of course! He's been with me my whole life, and now I'm ALONE.

He paused momentarily, and I knew he was thinking about something he wanted to say. When I asked him what he was thinking about, he replied (before his mom ever asked the question) . . .

NOOOO! I do not want another friend. I want HIM back, and yet I know he's not coming back. He tells me that every single time he sees me, but I'm still sad.

Can I do anything that will help you?

I don't know. All I know is that I need SOMETHING.

Are you feeling ok physically? You seem to be doing well, eating well, and all.

Yes, my body is doing well and I don't have any problems at all. Everything is working and I don't experience any pains. Unless you count the hurt in my heart. I'm so sad. I can't find my joy.

You don't seem to want to play very much. Is there something I can do?

I know I don't want to, but you have to insist. I need a lot of convincing these days.

I love you and I'm looking forward to our relationship deepening. How about you?

Yes, of course. That's what Opus says ALL THE TIME. He says I have to give you a chance. That I have to be more "emotionally involved" in our relationship. He tells me that all the time, so I'm going to try.

What are your thoughts/feelings about bringing another cat into our home? I'm not certain that I want to do that right now, but if it will help you, it's an option.

I told you already. There's no way anyone can take the place of Opus.

Please let me know anything else you would like to say to me or tell me.

I know it's been awhile Mom, but I'm not ready to forget Opus yet. Give me time and I will try to be better about it.

I love you.

Me too. Even if I don't show it in different ways, it's true, I do love you.

As I always do when it's time for the phone call with my client, I had my consultation notes ready in front of me. Before I started relaying Opus's and Alex's messages to her, I asked her if I was correct in my assessment that Alex was a little stand-offish, and wasn't forthcoming with a lot of information.

She laughed as she told me that, indeed, he was very different from Opus.

"They were a bit like Yin and Yang," I replied, and his mom definitely agreed.

She also laughed again when I told her that, even if he was so very different from Opus, he still tried his best to come across as a "good" kitty.

She shared with me that Alex doesn't like to curl up next to her, doesn't like being petted, and in fact, sometimes he's downright mean . . . clawing, biting, and snapping at her for no apparent reason. But she was happy with his answers to her questions and looked forward to a better relationship with him in the future.

She was also very satisfied with Opus's answers, and made sure I knew he was a real sweetheart.

Opus and Alex were two very different personalities. You can just feel the difference in their responses. Alex was so sad and a bit short with his answers, while Opus sounded to me as if he was an old and wise soul. But, each pet's personality was so delightful in its own way!

Tinker

I AM the Queen!

Sometimes the personality of an animal comes through so clearly that it looks and sounds to me as if I'm communicating with a human instead with an animal.

When that happens, I like to talk directly with my client afterward to be able to "act out" that personality verbally so I can fully convey what it sounded like. I also want to know if the client experiences the pet's personality in the same way I did. And most likely, our conversation will be an opportunity for both of us to share a good laugh together!

I hoped this would be the case with Tinker. Her human e-mailed me because Tinker, her 6 ½-year-old, 10 pound Yorkie girl, was having a number of problems.

She was on a special diet to prevent calcium oxalate stones from forming in her kidneys and bladder. She'd also had a bout of pancreatitis. A third big problem involved anal gland issues that needed to be expressed at least every two weeks.

In addition to those physical problems, she'd also recently experienced losses of other pets and family members, and her mom was concerned that Tinker might be grieving.

My client couldn't find the right time to have a consultation by phone, so instead, I needed to write out Tinker's answers, and find a way to convey, in writing, the essence of the personality I experienced. This is what I said in my e-mail:

> *I'm sending you my notes, but I really wish I'd been able to share with you out loud the way I "heard" Tinker. She's sassy, sure of herself, and a little bit of a brat and a diva all rolled into one. Give her that voice as you're reading her answers, and hopefully you'll understand the tone with which she communicated everything to me.*

Then I recorded notes about our conversation, using her mom's questions:

Are you grieving?

> Me? Grieving? Why? Who's not here that I absolutely, positively need to see? Absolutely not. I have you, and you're doing just fine taking care of me. I don't need anybody else.

Are you fed up with your special diet?

> Duh! Yessss . . . it's totally devoid of any good smell, taste, or texture.

Are you going thru dogopause?

> What???? NO. Whatever problems I'm having are not the result of me being old, but rather of my body not processing things the way it should. This is nothing new, I've been having problems with this body for a long time. In fact, these things have been happening since I was very young. No one was able to see it, much less treat it, but the older I get, the more pronounced everything becomes.

Are you in pain?

> Sometimes I have an acute pain in my stomach, but other times it's not the pain. I don't even want to be close to food because the smell of it makes me feel so nauseous. Even food that has only a little smell and taste makes me feel sick, so I turn my head. If you want to make me happy, you'd better give me some medication so I don't have to suffer through all those nasty feelings.

Would you like to have your anal sacs surgically removed? It's a very, very delicate surgery, but if done correctly then there would be no more fish farts, and no more butt squeezes every two weeks or oftener.

> No. Unless this becomes something really serious, I don't want to go through surgery.

Why do you start hyperventilating in the car now? Before last summer/fall, you loved to go in the car. Now you seem to go into panic mode after 10 minutes.

> I'm just so tired of going to see doctors!

(Monica's comment: I think she's now associating going in the car with a visit to the vet, whereas before it was just for fun. Now it's become something she hates.)

Is there anything at all you need to tell me? Fire away . . . please let mom know.

I have everything I need. I really do, and I'm happy that we have such a good understanding.

Besides, I have a way of making you do just about anything I want. When I want something, I simply let you know in no uncertain terms. And the best thing is that you understand me exactly.

Do you miss ChiChi, my mother's dog who was put down recently?

I know you're joking with me now, aren't you? That spoiled little brat was never a friend of mine. I did not enjoy having to spend time in the same house with him. No, I don't miss anybody. I'm so happy now that I'm The Queen.

If a time ever comes when you need medications or more to cope with life, would you prefer to manage with meds or surgeries, or go find Bella, ChiChi, Grams, and Gramps?

I think you know me well enough to make the right decision. But I am, and always will be, *The Queen*, so it would be hard for me to be in pain. I don't like it. I'm not stoic and I *like* to complain. So, in light of this, I would say that if I have a physical problem that can't easily be fixed, it would be better for me to stop suffering, and you can help me pass in peace. I would hate to think that I'd have to be in pain, taking pills, going to see the vet so often, and feeling miserable. I wouldn't do well emotionally with something like that.

Tinker, you and I are very close. I know a lot of guardians feel the same way, but we're inseparable. The only time we've been apart is when you had pancreatitis. You're never left alone. If I ever have to go somewhere that you cannot, my fiancée watches you. However, you won't eat, drink, sleep, or play when I'm gone, even if it's only as short a time as 45 minutes to 5 hours.

Do you blame me? You made sure I was always with you from the moment we met, and we've been together ever since. When you aren't around, I'm not myself. I can't eat or sleep or rest if I don't have you. Other humans complain and tell you I'm spoiled, but they don't know the bond we have and will always have. You are my soulmate, you are half of me, and without you I'm nothing. Without you, I can't go on.

You're completely spoiled, but a bringer of joy and smiles! I'd just like to know what has made you so very cantankerous.

You! You made me this way!

After experiencing the unique personality of this feisty little "Queen," and laughing out loud several times during our communication, I then sent this information to her mom and waited for my client's response.

An hour later I received her reply . . .

> *Oh my gosh. I'm laughing hysterically and crying from sadness all at the same time!! Yes, I hear that Queenly (😊😊😊) voice and understand what you're saying, and I'm glad you heard some of her sass, too (😊). She is a piece of work!!!*
>
> *Thank you so, so much for the email and talking to her today. Wow! That clears up/verifies/validates what I thought/felt.*
>
> *Thanks again Dr. Monica, You are Pawsome!!*

Stevie

Plan B

A client came to see me with her two cats . . . Stevie, an older female around the age of 14, and the other, a new kitten around eight months old.

Recently, Stevie, the little old lady with such a personality, was very distressed to discover there was an intruder in what had always been her private domain. Ever since the new kitten arrived, Stevie had no problem letting her parents know how upsetting this new turn of events was for her.

STEVIE

But it wasn't the presence of a new kitten in the home that was the most interesting part of this conversation. It was something else Stevie said that had both of us doubling over with laughter.

Stevie always had such a strong bond with her Mom. She told me in the very beginning it was just her and her Mom, and they'd been together for many years. Dad only came later.

She thinks Dad's very nice because he allows her to do whatever she wants, but she said he's her Plan B.

"Plan B?" I asked, totally puzzled by what she meant.

"Yes," she said quickly. "Mom is always my Plan A. I go to her for everything. I cuddle with her, I sit next to her, I talk with her, and when she's home, she's my main person. But if she's not home and I have a need to be cuddled, Dad is my Plan B."

Usually animals describe their humans as: Dad, Mom, my brother, my sister, my friend, my roommate, my soulmate, or my human. Never in the more than 30 years I've been helping animals communicate with their owners, have I ever heard any pet refer to his or her dad as Plan B!

Stevie's mom and I were laughing so hard! And I think that was the moment she re-named her husband . . . Plan B!

He Never Does That!

When personalities change before their very eyes

I do consultations remotely using e-mail, phone, Skype, Facebook Chat, and even an application called Whatsapp that's very popular in South America and Europe.

Sometimes, though, I may receive a slightly better response from pets when they come to see me in person. Not always, but on occasion, I do discover things that maybe I wouldn't have picked up from a picture.

That isn't the only benefit of meeting with animals in person, though. What I really enjoy seeing is how the clients are affected by the way their pets' personalities and behaviors sometimes seem to change dramatically right before their very eyes during our visit. Often, the human's response is priceless when they see their stand-offish animals feeling so at home and comfortable with me.

I have a consultation room where I meet with clients. It has a lot of smells in it, and even if I keep it sparkling clean, the animals still notice all the various scents. But then, after checking everything out, every time animals come to visit, they always gravitate to me. They come close to me, smell me, lick me, love me, sit on my shoes, ask to be petted, and so forth. The general reaction from my clients is: He never does that!

I've been told beforehand to be careful with certain animals because they're likely to bite, only to have them become like puppies and cuddlers

HE NEVER DOES THAT!

when they meet me. They'll ask for tummy rubs, or playfully put their paws on my lap.

About 90 percent of the time, animals look as if they're asleep on the floor while I'm talking with them, but they're not. They're actively communicating with me, even from a deep state of complete relaxation. They become so relaxed because they're finally able to say what they need to.

I remember watching one personality change when a client came in with a little white dog. She said she'd rescued this dog a couple of years ago but he didn't do well around anyone except her. She was concerned, though, because he never really showed love to her. He was more of an independent being and acted as if he didn't really need her for anything. She wanted to do something to make their relationship better, so they came to visit me in person.

As soon as he came in, he did what all the animals do. He thoroughly inspected the entire room. He saw his human sitting on a sofa and me on a chair. He looked at her, looked at me, and proceeded to jump onto *my* lap and ask to be petted.

My client couldn't concentrate on anything else I was saying. She kept saying incredulously, "He never does that! He just never does that!" I replied, "I seem to have that effect on animals!"

Throughout the whole hour, I was this little guy's new best friend. He wouldn't allow me to stop touching him. He was really enjoying being so close to someone. Maybe he felt right at home with the sound of my voice and my inflection because he was part of a Spanish speaking family, and I'm originally from Argentina. Even the client felt this was true.

I could see his human becoming more and more distressed, though, because he never showed that kind of affection to her. Yet, she was happy to know that he could, in fact, accept love.

I tried to explain to the little dog how important it was for him to show this same kind of affection to his mom, but I don't know if he responded to my suggestion because I never received any follow up from the client.

This kind of affectionate reaction to me happens with all species. Cats will come out of their carriers, look around the room, and then instead of hiding under the sofa, they come right up to me and sit on my lap, or they sit on the back of my chair.

On one occasion, I remember receiving a request to go to a client's home to visit with her two indoor cats.

She'd mentioned ahead of time that she also had an outdoor cat, but he wouldn't be home during our appointment time. She said he leaves at 7:00 in the morning and doesn't return home until 8:30 at night, only to eat and go out again.

The day I was to interview her two indoor cats, I remotely spoke to the outdoor cat to tell him I'd be visiting his home later on, and if he wanted to say something to his human, this was the perfect opportunity for him to do so. I also told him his human had told me how beautiful he was and that it would be really nice if I could meet him in person.

When I arrived at my client's home, much to her surprise, the outdoor cat showed up just minutes after my arrival. He asked to come in through the sliding door. He came in, saw me, sat down, and waited for me to ask him if he had anything to say.

After he told me what to tell my client about his wishes, he simply got up, let me pet his beautiful soft fur, walked over to the sliding door again, and asked to be excused for the rest of the day.

At first, my client's mouth was wide open in awe, and then with a faint smile she said, "He never does that!"

Not long after that encounter, I had an opportunity to meet with a client who had a poodle. She was a spoiled little girl who didn't like people in general and barked ferociously at the sight of any strangers.

Her demeanor was obvious as soon as her mom opened the door for me, but when we sat down and I told her I was there to give her an open line of communication with her mom, her attitude changed. She came closer to me and gave me a good sniff. Her mom then picked her up and held her on her lap.

HE NEVER DOES THAT!

The ringing of the client's home phone interrupted our communication so that my client had to get up from her chair. She handed me the poodle so the dog wouldn't try to jump from the chair to the floor.

The poodle looked at her mom, then at me, and in an instant she laid down on my lap and curled up. She remained there and looked as if she was contentedly sleeping throughout the rest of the consultation.

My client was *so* surprised to see such a change in her dog's fiesty personality. Of course, she said, "She never does that to anyone! How did you do that?"

The only explanation I have is that pets do feel safe when they know I not only understand them, but I communicate to their parents what they want and need. That's all they need to become much more relaxed.

Meanwhile, I truly enjoy watching the reactions of all the pet parents to such delightful changes in their pets' personalities!

Chapter 10

Unique Cases

Cinco and Dion

Pretty Birds

Above: Cinco

Even if the circumstances seem very ordinary to begin with, many of the communications I have with pets bring up something very interesting, very unique, or very much out of the ordinary, as the stories in this chapter do.

Most of my conversations are with dogs and cats, but it's true that I talk with all kinds of animals, birds included.

Some people believe the smaller the animal, the smaller the brain. They think smaller animals shouldn't have as much to say, or they shouldn't be as intelligent as larger ones. Nothing could be further from the truth, as is the case with Cinco and Dion.

I've spoken with Linda's cockatiels many times. She has quite a menagerie of them and when she comes to see me, she always brings two or three with her. I love their bright colors and their very individual personalities, and we often have many good laughs about what they have to say.

Because she has so many, and we see each other only about once a year, I don't often remember what we talked about before, but fortunately, Linda remembers.

This is what she shared with me in an e-mail after one such visit:

> Dear Dr. Monica:
>
> I just wanted to take a moment to thank you for the reading. I know that working with many birds at once (especially my nuts!) must have been a challenge.
>
> The first time you read Dion, I'd rescued him just weeks before. He shared with you that he'd been living with a man. He showed you a picture of himself with his previous owner "nose to beak" to show how close he felt to him. He also talked about how sad and scared he was when his owner became sick.
>
> About two weeks later, he climbed up on me, walked up on my chest, and pressed his beak as hard as he could against my nose. Of course I started crying because I understood that his message was, "You're OK!" He was telling me that he accepted me and was once again a happy bird!
>
> Cinco talked about how she'd gotten sick riding in the car to see you because she was holding still and everything else was moving (the opposite of when she flies), and she also asked for her "blankie." You commented at the time that a "blankie" was a strange thing for a bird to ask for. Well, I can explain.

I'd done laundry at the laundromat earlier that day and it was still in the car. A friend grabbed one of my nightgowns and covered her cage when Cinco started getting sick in the car.

When she was little, I'd be wearing one of three similar nightgowns. I'd put her on my chest at night and cover her with a thin blanket. I'd pet her and kiss her and say, "Here's your blankie, Cinco, to keep you warm and safe." So, when she mentioned to you that she wanted her "blankie," after just having been covered with my nightgown in the car, I had to laugh because I clearly understood the association.

Also you told her she should get on the floor of her cage for the ride home and that I would cover her so she didn't have to see what was going on outside.

I laughed to myself when you told her that, and thought "no way is she going to do that." Everything in a bird's instinct tells them higher is safer than being on the ground!

But wouldn't you know it, as soon as I stepped outside, she hopped onto the floor of the cage and stuck her head in the corner! Such incredibly unique behavior for a bird! I laughed and thought, "You go Monica!" and covered her cage!

Well, I could go on for hours with the revelations that you've shared concerning my kids, but let me close by saying even though I understand my guys, I sometimes can't express or adequately communicate with them about what's happening or what I need them to do. For doing that, you are a priceless treasure who has helped me bridge that gap. Your communications have enriched my life, and my bird's lives as well!

Thank you,

Linda,

Horton

I am not depressed

A couple came to see me with their dog, Horton, who was named after the character in the Dr. Seuss book. He's a Cocker Spaniel/Dachshund mix, about 11 years old.

His parents were concerned because they'd moved into a new home a year ago and Horton had been hiding under their bed or under tables ever since. They thought he might be depressed and they wanted to discover the reason why.

As a translator, it's sometimes difficult for me to figure out the exact meaning of a picture an animal is sending me. This was very true when it came to some of Horton's pictures.

Not only that, but if I translated what I thought I was seeing at the moment, it would sound very "out there" to some people, and I had in front of me a man, who by all standards, was a skeptic.

Nevertheless, I started right away by asking my clients if this was a new house or an old house they'd moved into because Horton was telling me he was seeing spirits.

They replied that it was a brand new house.

My next question was, "Do you know if your house is built on a place that might have previously been used as a burial ground, because Horton is telling me he's seeing lots of spirits he doesn't know."

HORTON

Horton with Dr. Monica

I saw the husband and wife look at each other with looks of total amazement on their faces, their mouths open, and their heads shaking in disbelief.

The wife then explained that their new home is right next door to a cemetery. It's no wonder Horton was seeing so many spirits!

We decided the best course of action was to sage the whole place while asking the spirits to allow the family to have their personal space, and to refrain from coming inside the house and scaring Horton.

I also explained to Horton who these spirits are, and reassured him they didn't want to do him any harm.

What Horton sent me was an *amazing* piece of information that neither I nor my clients could possibly have thought about ahead of time. Who would have ever guessed that seeing spirits would have been the reason he'd been hiding under beds and tables?

Horton's story is an excellent example of how incredibly well some animals are able to describe even the most unique situations so clearly in picture form. The pictures he was sending were almost beyond real to me, but they did enable me to accurately translate why he'd been hiding.

His mom and dad were relieved to know the real cause of their dog's distress, and to discover that it was something they'd be able to resolve. And Horton was very happy to have had this opportunity to finally express what had been bothering him for so long.

Later, his mom sent me an e-mail saying, "After using the sage in our home, he was back to being his usual self and we thank you for giving him his smile back."

Kismet

180 "First Dates"

At the end of August, a couple came to see me with two of their dogs. One was a female Coonhound mix and the other a small breed mix. As is my custom, I didn't ask my clients for information about their pets ahead of time. That way, they can be sure all the answers to their questions are coming directly from their pets.

In the beginning, I told them Kismet was very slow about sending me her pictures. It seemed as if there was something very unusual about that. It didn't feel to me as if we were having a regular conversation. The couple didn't make any comment about that information, so I continued.

I mentioned that Kismet didn't like her name at all. It just didn't make sense to her, and therefore she wasn't responding to it. They agreed with that statement. She'd been a rescue who'd come to them with that name about six months before.

I also said it felt to me as if some "wires" in her brain were not really connecting. They nodded their heads in agreement, which confirmed what I was sensing.

Next, one of them asked me to ask Kismet about her past to see if she remembered anything about the time before they rescued her.

Above: Kismet with Reily in the background

Her answers had been so slow in coming during the first part of our conversation, but as soon as I posed the question about her past, her pictures came in very fast and very clear.

She showed me how she'd been badly mistreated at the hands of a man, and how she was punched and kicked with heavy boots. One of those times, the kick was so intense that she ended up lying on her side. Her new family confirmed that she'd suffered a broken tooth and a broken jaw.

Everything about her past came in so fast in comparison with how slowly she gave me information about the present, that I knew, right then and there, in the present, she was suffering from short term memory loss caused, either directly or indirectly, by the intense punches and kicks she'd endured.

Her mom and dad then told me that, **every** morning for the past 180 days, she'd acted as if she'd never met or known her loving daddy, yet by the end of the day she was once again Daddy's Little Girl and couldn't get enough of him, only to forget who he was by the next morning.

KISMET

Every single morning had been a struggle just to let him feed her. She'd cower and try to escape because she didn't remember that this was her new dad. She wouldn't come to him in the morning, but later on when he arrived home, she'd recognize him, want to play, and even ask to be petted.

My clients were familiar with the Adam Sandler movie *50 First Dates*, so they immediately understood what Kismet was going through.

The information Kismet gave us during our conversation helped to clarify everything about her short term memory loss for her mom and dad. Together we then created a plan to deal with the situation.

I was able to tell Kismet many helpful things, although we didn't know if she'd be able to remember any of that new information. But, for her humans, the communication was successful because they were now able to understand her so much better.

In a follow up e-mail, quite some time later, her mom shared this information with me:

> *Kiszy is doing very well. She's so happy and quite comfortable in our home. She has her spot on the sofa. Larry has one end and she has the other.*

> *She's okay if I'm sitting alone on the sofa as long as she can be up there, too. But if I'm on the sofa sitting next to Larry, and if Reily (our other dog) is on the other end, she bugs me until I move off the sofa. The rub is, she doesn't want to sit there. She just wants me to move away from Larry. She's so sweet and so gentle, but he's **her** guy!*

> *When he wears a hat, I don't know if she recognizes him or not, but she's totally in love with whomever the hat person is. When she's looking at him, it's as if she's seeing a whole different person.*

> *He'll take the hat off and her look is like, "Oh. It's you. Did you see the hat guy? Can you slip him my digits?" She's very cute about that whole thing!*

Larry was playing music one night, wearing one of his hats and singing to Kiszy. I thought she was going to give herself a seizure because her eyes were going in different directions and blinking in different patterns. She was smiling so big, and she was so in love with him.

He stopped and took off the hat, and she was like, "Oh, Daddy. When did you get here? Where's the hat guy?" He put the hat back on and she was back to smiling and having a good time.

I'm sure you remember the issues we were having with Kiszy when we went to see you. She only wanted to pee in the front yard, wouldn't go in the backyard, was scared to go in the car, didn't recognize Larry in the morning, and was having seizures.

After you talked with her, she jumped right in the car, smiling.

When we got home, she went straight to the backyard, did her business, and came in looking so proud and relieved. She'd then watch Reily and wherever he went, or whatever he did, she'd observe and learn.

She does recognize Larry in the morning now. Sometimes she wants him to pet her right away, but sometimes it takes time for her to warm up to him.

She still has seizures maybe once every other month, and when she does, something changes in her personality, but not in a bad way.

Dr. Monica, you were so spot on with helping her be comfortable in our home and become part of the family. She's done quite well since our consultation with you and we've been thinking about bringing her back to find out what she thinks about the hat guy and how she's feeling about her home now. We really love her.

Many times, clients come to see me thinking their pets have behavioral issues. Sometimes we discover it's not a behavioral issue at all. Instead it's a neurological condition.

Having a consult with an animal communicator might not solve the problem, but it can at least help identify the cause and give you some peace of mind about what's going on in your pet's brain. You'll still need to work with your veterinarian, or a specialist, in order to treat the problem, if treatment is necessary, or if it's even an option.

Other times, as Kismet's story shows, with time, love, and effective animal communication, some things will improve on their own. You just need to be super patient and develop a steady routine for your pet. Good routines can help pets learn new ways to deal with life.

For Kiszy and her family, their story was very unique, but it definitely has a happily ever after ending!

Chapter 11

CHANGING A BEHAVIOR
. . . OR NOT!

Changing Pet Behaviors

Many times my clients ask me if I can change an undesirable behavior their animals are engaging in. My answer is always NO. I can't change anything.

What I CAN do is to translate for the pet, telling you why they think it's necessary for them to do what they're doing, and explaining to them why it's important for them to do things in a different way.

Granted, many times, when the explanation makes sense to them, they'll stop the bad behavior immediately. Other times, they'll at least be somewhat better for awhile, but then forget about our original conversation.

And then there are always those few, no matter how many times I ask them to do or to stop doing something, they just won't. They seem to think their behavior is absolutely necessary, and no explanation is ever motivation enough to encourage them to change.

But for those who are willing to change, how do we go about helping them correct their unwanted behaviors?

We need to listen to our pets first and try to understand why they're doing what they're doing. Is there anything we can learn from their answers that would help us do something to make the situation better?

Often when we respond to their requests to change their food, change the litter more often, take longer walks, provide more attention or play time, or meet whatever need they have, their unwanted behaviors will change in response.

Other times, clearly explaining why they no longer need to act a certain way, or how changing their behavior will help their human, is all it takes to effect a positive change.

And then, there are those moments when pets are just doing something because they feel like it. There's no serious reason. They just feel like it. Sometimes motivation works with those pets, and sometimes it doesn't.

Let's look at a few specific cases to see what's worked and what hasn't...

Plato

This is your forever home

Plato is a very good example of an animal who just needed to understand what was happening.

He was rescued by a kind woman who finds strays from the street and gives them a home. Sometimes she ends up placing them with other families, but at other times she keeps them herself.

Evangelina e-mailed me from South Africa to tell me she'd just picked up an adult stray. He was having problems adjusting to life with her other six dogs. Plato would growl and raise his lips at some of them, especially at Sebastian, a big dog who rules the house.

I had a very productive conversation with Plato. I started by telling him about his new name. Then I explained that this would be his forever home, but only if he was willing to share. He would have to share the wonderful woman who rescued him with all the other dogs, who like him, had also been found wandering the streets and didn't have a home.

I told him he could be himself, but in order to stay in this new home, he would have to be nice to everyone and let everyone else just be themselves, too.

This was all news to Plato. He didn't know about his new name, and he hadn't understood that this was a forever home. Much less could he even imagine that he'd ever be living in a family with so many dogs, but never have to fight for food, water, or love.

He understood everything I told him, and I felt comfortable that he'd give himself a good chance to integrate with this new group.

It wasn't until I received a follow up e-mail from Evangelina that I realized how effective my communication with Plato had been.

She wrote:

> Dear Dr. Monica,
>
> First, I send you my warmest regards. I hope you're keeping well. Second, I send you my sincerest thanks. You've been a wonderful help.
>
> As I write this e-mail, I have all seven of my "children" sleeping on or around my feet . . . from the largest to the smallest, from the oldest to the newest, including Plato!
>
> I write to you to tell you how amazingly well Plato has adjusted. He's right now lying down next to Sebastian, sound asleep, without any problems.
>
> I was amazed when I noticed an almost immediate change in his attitude towards Tala (the puppy), but I'm thrilled to see how readily he has accepted Sebastian as well. He hasn't lifted a lip or raised his neck hair to anybody, even once, since you spoke to him, except on one acceptable occasion.
>
> Plato was lying on his back with Tala licking his leg. She's currently teething. At one point she decided his leg looked like a munchy, juicy thing to bite into. Well . . . Plato did not think that was funny. But no harm done. He just told her his legs are off limits!

The difference it has made in my life, and in our household, cannot adequately be described with words. To be honest . . . I never thought it was possible. But here we are. All thanks to you.

Warmest regards

Evangelina from South Africa

This was truly a success story when it comes to a pet changing his behavior.

Lucy
No more diapers

One of my clients had a small dog named Lucy. She was going potty all over the house while the client was at work. Not only that, she'd even been known to do this when her mom was at home. What was even worse, Lucy would potty in the house immediately upon coming back from a long walk.

We scheduled a date for our talk and they both came to see me.

For some time, it was just Lucy and Mom, but then her mom had adopted Grayson. That was very upsetting to Lucy. She'd been distressed about such a major change for quite awhile. She'd decided that Mom didn't love her enough, so Mom had gone out and found herself another friend to bring home.

Lucy was one of those dogs who paid little attention to her human. Grayson was just the opposite. He was a love bug who'd be beside Mom all the time, while Lucy would lie on her pillow just watching them.

Mom mistook Lucy's standoffish behavior to mean that Lucy didn't love her, when in fact, Lucy was very jealous of Grayson. He'd been a good boy and the two dogs had never had an argument, but seeing Grayson have such a good relationship with Mom was actually hurting Lucy's feelings very much. She needed some way to express all that hurt. Ergo, peeing all over the house.

Above: Jealous Lucy

Mom wanted me to reassure Lucy she'd always be loved as the first dog in the house. I also explained that Mom had enough love in her heart for everybody. She loved Lucy with Lucy love, and she loved Grayson with Grayson love. Grayson would come to Mom all the time whenever he wanted petting, and I reminded Lucy that she could also do the same.

We went back and forth for awhile, continually reassuring Lucy that she was very loved, and always would be.

Once Lucy felt that her mom truly understood her concerns and still loved her, then we were ready to start working on the potty problem.

I asked Lucy to stop peeing around the house and I told her that Mom would clean all the areas really well so she wouldn't smell her urine scent any more. I asked her if she'd remember from now on not to pee inside the house.

She told me she might need a reminder for a few days so that she wouldn't mess up again, and I agreed to send her those reminders.

Her mom and I decided that putting a diaper on Lucy might help, at least temporarily, while Mom was away at work for four or five hours. This would be a momentary reminder for Lucy to "hold it," and she agreed to doing this.

The next step, without the diaper, was to put puppy pads by the back and front doors because these were areas she gravitated to.

Finally, when we could trust her again, her mom was able to remove even the puppy pads.

A couple of days later, I received this e-mail:

> *Thank you! Lucy is tolerating the diapers although she's still uncomfortable walking while wearing them. She hasn't had accidents today, and she even went five hours between potty breaks. She's also loving the string cheese treats. She seems more at peace. Thank you so much for your help!*

Five days later, I received another e-mail:

> *Lucy is insecure, so all the praise and encouragement goes a long way with her. Puppy pad was actually dry when I got home from work yesterday and no accidents last night, even without the diaper on to remind her to wait. Cannot tell you the relief to not have to clean the carpet every day, and the best part is the relationship with Lucy has already improved. You are a godsend!*

And after a whole week, a final e-mail message:

LUCY

I can't thank you enough! As of this morning she has not peed in the house one time, including on the puppy pad. Thank you again for all your help!

When Lucy's concerns were recognized and taken care of, it was then much easier to help her make the necessary behavioral changes. She also began to love cuddles and sitting on laps. And when a grandbaby joined the family, Lucy was full of affection.

Definitely a success story!

Luna

Blind Kitty

Another e-mail I received had a subject line that read: *I am desperate!* I opened that one very quickly!

Robin was writing to tell me she'd adopted two blind cats in December 2017. One of them, Luna, kept peeing in multiple places around the house... in the kitty sunroom, on her mom's bed, on a rug in the bedroom, and near the front door.

My client had done absolutely everything she could think of to fix the problem, but nothing worked. When Luna finally peed on top of Robin's head, that made her reach out to me for help.

"The cat is sweet and beautiful," she wrote. "She's had a rough start, but I won't abandon her. She's been abandoned before. Instead, I'm praying you'll be able to help us."

We scheduled an appointment and met via Skype.

When I reached out to Luna, she was very sweet and gracious. She told me she'd be happy to talk with me and that I could ask her anything I wanted. She seemed aware that we were going to be meeting like this, and it didn't come as a surprise when I spoke to her.

Luna told me she likes the name her mom gave her, and she also likes her mom's scent very much. She says she's still getting used to her new home, but can tell where she's going by the smells. She's very smart and, maybe because she doesn't have her eyesight, her sense of smell is heightened.

I then told Luna her mom loves her very much, but isn't happy that she's peeing outside the litter box.

"I'm really sorry about that," Luna said. "But she just didn't understand how frustrated I was with my litter box, so one day, I decided to just pee in the playroom and see if that would get me the attention I needed. I'm so glad she's talking to me about this now.

"I'm a very petite cat, and climbing up so high over the sides of the litter box is not my favorite thing to do. I'd like something that I can easily walk in and out of.

"I do like the smell of the litter, but I don't like the location of the box. It's hidden away, and I just don't like the idea of having to go to that place.

Above: litter box when it was hidden

"Could she put a box for me in the corner of my playroom? That way I wouldn't have to leave my sun room if I need to go. That would be lovely.

"I'm happy here. I have a lot of room to move about, and as long as things don't get moved too far out of place, I can tell where I am, and know where I'm going.

"I also think my human is very nice and she's trying hard to please me.

"I like Quincy. He's my seeing-eye cat. If I follow him, I know what to do and where I am."

Above: Luna (black fur) with her seeing eye cat Quincy

After listening to Luna's requests, I suggested that Robin use uncovered, shallow boxes, with the same litter, and put two more boxes where Luna can easily smell them. It was important to put them in the right locations, because as a blind kitty, she always needs to have easy access.

It was going to take a little patience, though, because it would take Luna some time to adjust to anything new. This was a case of don't stress, clean up the mess, and wait a few more days for improvement.

A few weeks later I received this e-mail message from Robin:

So far, so good, no peeing! Quincy is being so sweet and being Luna's guardian angel. Thank you for your help, patience, and kindness.

And then came a more recent e-mail update:

Just a short note to say that Luna has not had any mistakes since I wrote to you last. She's been staying close to me and kissing tons! We have 4 litter boxes ☺ but it's working, and she seems happy, so that's the only thing that matters ☺ We hope you have a very merry, joyful and loving Christmas holiday 🎄🎄🎄 The entire family appreciates all you have done for us.

YOUR PET CALLED

Finally, a January 2019 e-mail update said:

Luna has been perfect!!!! She seems so much happier in general and is even more affectionate. I'm forever grateful to you!

Another success story!

Gaby

Not just one, but three behaviors

Gaby is a lovable little 10 ½ year-old Shih Poo who can go from being a snugly sweet cuddler almost all the time, to abruptly trying to take absolute charge when *she* thinks the occasion demands it.

She's very healthy, and she's had a very good life from the first moment she was adopted at a local pet store. She had a very loving mom, as well as many loving aunties, who helped care for her from the very beginning.

There was, however, one major sadness in her life. When Gaby was 7½, her first mom was diagnosed with cancer. She then passed away just a few months later.

Gaby's a good little diagnostician who likes to check everybody's breath, so even before other humans knew how sick her mom was, she already knew. She also had the opportunity to regularly observe her mom's rapidly declining health while her mom was in hospice care, so she clearly understood what was happening.

There was no gap in Gaby's care, though, because her mom had a Pet Protection Agreement. This agreement named someone to take over her care immediately. Gaby's new mom was one of her favorite aunties who had known and dearly loved her, and spent time with her almost every day, ever since she was 11 weeks old.

Her Auntie Colleen's house had always been Gaby's second home. For the first five years of her life, until her mom retired from work, she'd stayed there for several hours every day. Because she knew this home so well, her permanent transition from her first home, just across the walkway, to her Auntie's home was very easy.

When her mom passed on, everything in Gaby's life stayed the same except for her first house and her first mom . . . same neighborhood, same pack of doggy friends to walk and play with, the love of all the doggy moms in the neighborhood, a home she was already totally comfortable in, and the love of her Auntie Colleen who'd always been such a special person in her life from the very beginning.

As sweet and wonderful as Gaby is, she did come with three pesky problems, so her new mom (or Auntie as she's always been called) asked for my help with each problem at different times.

THE FIRST BEHAVIORAL PROBLEM

We addressed the first problem of peeing on the carpet when Gaby was around 8 years old. She'd always been very good about using her doggy door to go outside at both her first and second homes, so more training didn't seem to be the issue.

Were fears and anxieties causing her unwanted behavior? She'd lost her mom, and she did have some significant separation anxiety issues. Also, big dogs next door, who barked ferociously and lunged against the fence, were potentially scaring her. Were these the reasons she wasn't going outside to pee? My consultation with Gaby in July 2017 provided some very interesting insights.

These were her auntie's questions followed by my translations of the answers Gaby gave me:

Can she give you any clue at all as to why she continues to pee in the house when she has access to the yard 24/7?

It's a comfort thing, and it's a Gaby thing. She tells me she's simply too lazy to go look for the doggy door, or to go outside. She'd much rather just pee on the carpet, so it's also a carpet thing.

Is she trying to give me a message?

Nope, no message. She simply chooses to go there sometimes when she's lazy.

Is she not getting the attention she wants at the time?

She says she thinks she's getting plenty of attention.

Does it hurt when she pees (wanting to rule out any infection)?

Nope.

Is it separation anxiety?

Nope.

When I showed her the spot in the den, did she understand that I was showing her the spot where she'd just peed only a moment ago?

She says she did understand because she could smell her pee.

Does she understand that it's difficult for me to have to soak it all up and then treat it, and that every time I find yet another new spot it makes me very sad and discouraged? (It doesn't really, but I'm just trying to appeal to Gaby's caring nature to try to motivate her to stop.)

She understands, but to put it bluntly, she doesn't care. She doesn't think about what needs to happen after she does it. She simply goes where she wants without stopping to think that you'll have to clean up after her.

Does she understand that it's very, very important to me that she pees only outdoors?

She gets it. She understood how important it was from the very beginning when she was first trained to go outside as a puppy, but she just doesn't stop to think about how important it is to you.

If there were no carpet, would she pee on a wood or tile floor, or does she only like to pee on the softness of carpet? (I've never seen any evidence of pee on any of the tile floors in the house.)

She says she doesn't know if she'd do it or not, but she does know she's very partial to all kinds of soft things under her toes, like carpet.

Is there anything I can do to stop this behavior? Is it just a Gaby thing, or is it a Shih Poo thing?

It's definitely a Gaby thing.

So much for the cause of the peeing problem being fear or anxiety! This was one very willful little girl doing exactly as she pleased, when she pleased, and where she pleased!

I then gave her a major pep talk about using only the grass for pee and using the carpet just to enjoy the feel of it. I encouraged her to help her auntie by always going outside to do her business. And I continued to send her occasional reminders.

Apparently, that encouragement helped, at least somewhat at first, because not long after our conversation, her auntie confirmed there were fewer and fewer wet spots. There'd be an occasional spot once in a great while, but it was no longer the almost every day problem it had been.

It's now been more than two years since Gaby and I talked about always going outdoors to pee. Her auntie still feels a little wary, and she checks every so often, but for more than two years now, there've been no new spots at all! Considering Gaby's attitude when we first talked, she does seem to have decided to make the requested change. Thank you, Gaby!

THE SECOND BEHAVIORAL PROBLEM

The next problem we addressed, when she was 9 years old, was a little more serious. When she'd meet certain dogs, large or small, this sweet little 15-pound ball of fur could go into the red zone in a flash, barking hysterically, and trying to lunge toward the other dog. This happened even if she'd met the same dog before. They weren't friends, but at least they'd already met previously.

Her auntie wanted to know if Gaby could explain why some dogs make her go absolutely ballistic for a few minutes whenever she sees them approaching.

She replied, "This is something I've done all my life. It's the way I deal with surprise encounters, sudden noises, and various other things that bother me. It's the only way I know how to cope. Once I can process what my brain needs to know about a situation, then I'm fine and I no longer need to remind everybody that I'm in charge and I won't back down.

"Auntie can tell me to stop, pull on the leash, talk with me, show me great treats, and nothing will make me change my mind. I know I'm stubborn and I realize I have to work on this. So far, I haven't been successful, and I can't promise I will change either."

Her auntie confirmed that even if she's put on a sit-stay well ahead of time, and offered a high-value treat when the temptation to bark has passed, it still isn't always enough to keep her focused during the worst of those times.

What's interesting is, after finally settling down from her moment of hysteria, usually Gaby and the other dog end up sniffing each other and settling down quietly while their humans visit, or sometimes they'll all do a pack walk together.

Apparently, it's just very important for her to let certain dogs know, beyond a shadow of a doubt, that she's in charge. Sort of "the best defense is a good offense" attitude.

More importantly, her auntie tuned in to the fact that Gaby talked about "being in charge and not backing down." This meant she really needed a big reminder about who was, in fact, in charge.

At her auntie's request, I talked with Gaby again and explained to her that she's not the one who's in charge; her auntie is. Auntie will be the one to take action if action is needed. If she's calm and happy to meet other dogs, then Gaby needs to be calm, too.

Gaby did listen to me attentively, but she definitely wasn't convinced that her auntie could deal with certain situations without Gaby's help. She said she'd try, but she couldn't promise she'd always do it.

Her auntie, who's successfully trained three tough-to-train terriers, has her work cut out for her with this usually sweet little Shih Poo, but she's up to the task.

In this case, the communication was clear, and Gaby has made some improvement, but she hasn't yet made a consistent behavioral change. Maybe with some extra strong leadership, my talk with her will eventually have some good results, but only time will tell.

This is a typical example showing how I can encourage, but only the animal can decide whether or not to make the change.

The Third Behavioral Problem

A fearful behavior Gaby frequently exhibited really tugged at her auntie's heartstrings, so this was her question:

When I clear my throat, cough slightly, or sometimes sneeze, Gaby will immediately get up from wherever she is and slink off fearfully to a place she considers safe, usually under the bed.

Even when I call out in a happy voice to say it's ok, she still leaves the area to go hide. She can be in one room and I'll be in another, and she'll still go looking for a safer place.

Over the past two years, I've practiced coughing or clearing my throat at times when I've been in a good position to pet her gently and talk quietly to reassure her, or even give her a treat. My hope is that she'd associate positive things like love, petting, and treats with those sounds.

Sometimes in those circumstances, she'll stay for a few moments, especially when there's a treat, but what she really wants to do is to move away, so she still leaves to find a safe space as soon as she can.

What makes her so fearful about those sounds?

Gaby replied, "When I was very young, many people had coughs and sneezes. Both sounds were loud to my ears and because they were usually cleaning my cage, I became worried about it. Sometimes there was water involved and I didn't like that feel. Combined with the noise, it made me worry about what was coming next."

Her auntie confirmed that this fear could easily have started at the kennel where she was raised for the first eight weeks of her life, or at the pet store where she spent a couple of weeks.

Was she scared the same way when her mom, Chris, coughed, sneezed or cleared her throat?

Gaby's response . . . "Well, absolutely! After she started feeling bad, and her breath smelled worse, I realized that those sounds are the beginning of something bad. I feel it, and I can't shake the thought that something is about to change. It makes me sad and I hide."

I tried hard to explain to Gaby that these sounds had nothing to do with the breeder cleaning her cage, or her mom getting sick and going away. I told her that her auntie is just fine and isn't going to go anywhere. I wasn't sure she got it, but I know she was listening. However, when an animal is so afraid of something, the fear reaction is almost automatic and hard to change.

Her auntie replied by e-mail:

This answer about her mom getting worse and Gaby thinking it was the beginning of something bad really helps to explain why she also runs from me. She doesn't always run when someone else in the house makes the same sounds, so maybe she's just really concerned when the person who's caring for her is coughing or clearing her throat.

The good news is that today, I was in the recliner in the living room for a quick power nap and Gaby was just a few feet away from me in her bed. I had an irritating tickle in my throat and had to cough several times to clear it.

I looked over and there she was, still in her bed, looking straight at me, with no indication that she was even thinking about moving!

This may be a one-time thing, or maybe now she does understand these sounds are not such a bad thing. Any time in the past, she would have been out of sight before I even finished getting rid of the irritation and could look to see if she was still there. The fact that she hadn't slunk away this time was amazing!

Would you please ask her if the reason she stayed in her bed today when I cleared my throat was because she now understands that I'm ok? I keep telling her in a happy voice that I'm just scratching an itch in my throat, and it's perfectly normal for me to do that.

> *If she does understand now that she doesn't have to run and hide when I make any of those sounds, please tell her that will make me very happy!*

When I checked in with Gaby again, I told her that her auntie was very, very happy that she didn't move from her bed when she heard the throat clearing sound. Gaby said she was happy with herself, too! She told me it was because I'd explained things and she understood.

I had this conversation with Gaby just in the nick of time. Her auntie had a very bad reaction to some exceptionally strong oil-based primer fumes that brought on a case of sinusitis and bronchitis just about a week later. Now Gaby was hearing some really serious and prolonged coughing.

Did she run and hide while her auntie was recovering? Her auntie said she might skitter off once in a great while if the sound really startled her, but in general, she was continuing to stay right where she was.

More than a year later, she now stays put where she is about 98% of the time when she hears a potentially triggering sound. This happens even when she and her auntie are super close together snuggling on the bed or cuddling in the chair, or when Gaby is lounging just two or three feet away. Sometimes she looks up to observe. Other times, she actually goes right on sleeping without even bothering to look up.

This has truly been a success story!

When it comes to behavioral issues, only the pet can decide whether to make the necessary changes. I can explain what's happening, and suggest what they should do instead, but the outcome is always totally the result of their free will choice. And Gaby has definitely begun to make some new choices!

Lily Mae

It didn't hurt!

Just the other day, I had a consultation in my home office with Renee and her female Italian Mastiff, Lily Mae. She's a very impressive Mastiff, not only because of her height, but because the girth of her body makes her look more like a male. Her weight is around 150 pounds.

One of the first things she told me is that she needs to wear some bling on her collar to help identify her as a female to strangers on the street so she won't be mistaken for a male.

But the main reason Renee had come to see me was that Lily Mae had had an unusual experience the other day. She was attacked on the street by another dog and suffered a gash on the inside of her leg.

It was deep enough that she had to have it kept "open" with a drain stitched in until it healed enough to allow the vet to suture it closed. She also had several bite wounds elsewhere on her legs and body.

Renee complained that Lily Mae is sometimes very hard to control on a walk. She herself had fallen down several times because she just couldn't hold onto such a powerful dog when Lily Mae decided to just take off.

This was particularly true when other big dogs were walking near her. Lily would sometimes go ballistic around them. Immediately, I had a picture in my mind of a big dog attacking Lily.

Imagine my surprise when Renee told me that the attacker was . . . wait for it . . . a tiny 10 pound Pug!!

As it turned out, Lily did not defend herself. Instead, she allowed the Pug to come running out of his house and attack her while she was walking down the street with her mom. And this was not the first time it happened. I later learned that it was the third time! The first two times Renee had been able to shoo the little dog away.

Amazed by this event, I went ahead and talked with Lily about it. She said, " You need to tell Mom it didn't hurt at all. He's just a puppy and was playing with me. I can't possibly do him harm. I love puppies and my job is to protect them, not to bite them."

Renee told me that Lily wouldn't bite the Pug at all, but instead, when she'd had enough of him biting her, she'd simply sit on top of him, and that stopped the little one from doing any more harm to Lily.

Lily continued to talk and told me she could have been a great mother. She said she loves puppies, kittens, little humans, and anything that resembles small or young beings. She couldn't possibly harm any of them.

I told Lily she was a very good girl, but she needed to find a better way to prevent attacks by giving small dogs a warning, just as she'd do with babies when they were trying to do something wrong.

She thought about it and told me she could put her paw on the top of small dogs' heads to give them a warning. I said that would be a very good solution.

What a lesson in love and patience it was for Renee and for me! And Lily was happy that she wouldn't have to harm anybody in the process of teaching them a lesson. She was even the one who came up with her own way to change her behavior in this case.

During my conversation with Lily Mae, we'd also talked about how important it was for her not to lunge at big dogs. I explained to her that when she moved so suddenly she could cause her mom to fall and be badly hurt. I told her that she could keep her mom safer if she'd just stay close to her side whenever a big dog passed by.

Apparently she *really* listened to what I said because her mom sent me this e-mail message later on:

> In August, we were hiking in Mammoth and a bear walked by us about 12 feet away. Lily Mae stopped and watched – with NO barking, NO pulling, nothing!! Such a Good Girl!!

It was truly an amazing change in her behavior that she wouldn't lunge even when a bear was so very close! If the bear had been threatening in any way, I have no doubt, however, that Lily Mae would have seriously challenged such a threat.

Maybe, though, she was remembering my suggestion to change her behavior in order to keep her mom safe from falling and being hurt. If so, this was definitely another success story.

Leo

Remembering a past life

When an animal has a persistent behavioral problem, it can sometimes be fixed only if the human is able to discover the root cause. In some cases, though, the root cause is known *only* to the animal.

However, during a consultation with an animal communicator, not only might the pet be able to reveal the root cause, but he may also be able to tell his human about the lessons that can be learned, just as Leo did for his mom in this case.

My client, Brittanie, had two German shepherds. When the older dog died, she'd been very sad for a long time, even though she still had Leo for company.

A friend then told her about a litter of puppies that would have to be taken to the pound if they couldn't find homes for them. Against her better judgement, she decided to "just go see them."

There were nine puppies. As she came into their pen, all but one of them started playing and doing their own thing. Only one of them sat down quietly on top of her shoe and stared at her. Interestingly, she felt as if she knew him already and needed to take him home. Needless to say, this is exactly what she did!

When the puppy was first introduced to Leo, the little nine-week-old immediately tried to growl and bark at the bigger dog, but Brittanie provided the right kind of training, and today the two dogs are the best of friends. In fact, this now-grown-up canine is the only dog that Leo accepts.

Leo has a major problem of his own. He cannot be close to *any* dog, other than his friend, without immediately going into the red zone. He lunges, barks, growls, snarls, and carries on ferociously. Corrections don't help, treats don't help, and a pinch collar has no effect. He simply remains in the red zone until the other dog is out of sight.

Brittanie is a dog trainer so she's familiar with all types of training techniques, but so far, she's never been able to get Leo to modify his negative behavior.

They worked with a dog behaviorist and she used master training techniques, but nothing brought about a positive change. It was at this point that she decided to see if I could help with Leo's negative behavior.

LEO

Five-year-old Leo looked around my consultation room and studied every exit. He made sure his mom was sitting down and was relaxed, then he came to me for some "hello" petting.

He said he didn't need to sit down. Instead, he stood and put his head between my knees and started communicating right away.

He told me he knew he'd come into this lifetime with a mission to educate his mom. When he first saw her, he recognized her soul right away, even though he was very young. Intuitively, he knew his job was to be with her, and only with her.

Leo then explained that Mom didn't understand the intensity of his fear. He said she needs to know the history of any dog's fear before she'll be able to fix the behavior. His mission is to help her understand that.

He then told me that in a previous lifetime he'd been a pit bull who'd been used as bait in the ring to entice others to fight. The experience of always having to defend himself left a very deep impression on his psyche that was causing him to react in a similar way in this lifetime. He could remember very clearly what his job had been in that previous lifetime, so now he expected that every dog he came in contact with would try to attack him.

Interestingly enough, he said he didn't feel he was damaged by what had happened to him in the past. Instead, he wanted to use his past life experience to help his mom understand how important it is to know and understand the triggers behind unwanted behaviors.

Leo also told his mom what he needed from her: speak in a calm voice, don't scream, make sure you're in control of every situation we're in, and always love me because I'm your teacher.

Before we finished our communication, I then gave Leo a number of explanations and suggestions that might help him decide to change his behavior. However, because his previous life experience had affected him so profoundly in this lifetime, this was a case where I couldn't be sure if anything I told him would help that much, but it's always worth a try.

One of the things that's so fascinating about this consultation is, when Leo was telling me he was a pit bull in a previous lifetime, I had no idea during our conversation that Brittanie's other dog . . . who is now Leo's best friend . . . is a pit bull!

After our communication, his mom now understood the root cause of the problem Leo has whenever he meets unfamiliar dogs. She also now understood why maybe her two dogs had such an affinity for each other.

When Leo helped us identify the reason for his behavior, only then were he and Brittanie able to work together so they could both learn the lessons they were meant to learn with each other.

His mom says that Leo now seems to calm down faster and not stay in the red zone for as long. Knowing that his behavior is fear based has definitely enabled her to take a more calm and patient approach when working with him, which seems to have made him feel more secure.

While there hasn't been any major change in his behavior, Leo's experience does show us that, while some pets with problem behaviors need only a little extra guidance from an animal communicator, or some extra training in order to learn to behave, others have problems that are so deep-seated that no change is readily going to take place.

Nonetheless, it's always imperative to identify the underlying cause. And sometimes, only when we hear the story from the pet's point of view are we able to do that.

Ace

Training to become a champion

I've had the opportunity over the years to work with several animal trainers who've had trouble getting through to some of their trainees.

These highly specialized clients have years of experience when it comes to training, but occasionally, even with all their knowledge and expertise, they encounter some dogs who just don't seem to respond. Those animals may display a certain dislike for a particular activity, or they may even be totally uncooperative. Ace, a three-year-old German Shepherd, seemed to be one of those dogs.

Getting to know Ace

Ace had been with Chris for a little more than a year. Genetically, he was an extremely gifted animal. Chris believed, though, that some mistakes made by Ace's first owner had allowed Ace to develop some habits and behaviors that were very difficult to overcome.

Ace was also very different from other dogs Chris had trained in the past. He was a high-drive, strong, and somewhat edgy dog. This made him prone to show, and use, his natural aggression, which unfortunately meant he wasn't well-suited to simply be a pet. He came from a long line of champions, and he was destined to work.

Chris had already identified two key problems that were affecting their work and their relationship:

1) Ace seemed to be very selfish and aloof. He only tried hard or put in a genuine effort when he felt like doing it. Chris had struggled for two years to teach and encourage him to actively engage and work as a team, but he'd had only marginal success.

2) Ace was easily distracted and, in general, lacked focus. When he was "on," he was capable of doing fantastic work with great energy and enthusiasm. However, when his mind or attention wandered, he'd make mistakes. This led to conflict and stress between the two of them.

Specialized training

Chris had been training Ace for competition in the sport of Schutzhund, a German word loosely meaning "protection dog." While Schutzhund Training has now morphed into a sport that various dog breeds participate in, it was originally designed by the founder of the breed as a very systematic method for training and testing German Shepherds. It was used to see if they had the genetic traits desired, and to showcase their abilities, not only as a shepherd's companion, but also for use in what was at that time the newly developing field of police and security work.

This training, as well as the sport, involves the skills of tracking and obedience, but it also adds a third element — protection. Both the training and the sports competition involve active aggression, high levels of drive, and physical and mental conflict that test the dog's soundness, strength, ability to handle stress, and willingness to work.

A dog in Schutzhund must be able to respond to commands reliably, precisely, and quickly, as well as be able to act independently, even when no command is given.

The commands that must be mastered include the basics: Sit, Stay, Come, Down, Stop, Stand, Heel, Leave it, Out/Drop it, and Fetch.

But a Schutzhund-trained dog must also master the commands of: Go, Search, Track, Guard, Follow, Jump, Hold, and, most importantly, Release (meaning to disengage or let go).

Notice, there is no command to attack because Schutzhund training is based on the principle of protection. The dogs are trained to engage or bite and hold *only* when they recognize a threat, and they're further trained that they must stop immediately when the threat is neutralized.

As you can see, this training and testing is very rigorous and demanding because the dog must *consistently* demonstrate the willingness to work. It also measures his or her ability to pick up a scent and track, as well as measuring a dog's *consistent* initiative, endurance, courage, perseverance, mental stability, and focus.

Chris e-mailed me in July 2018 to see if I might be able to help him with Ace who was in training for an upcoming Schutzhund competition. He knew I couldn't actually change the dog's behavior, but he wanted to better understand the reasons behind his dog's resistance to training.

After we corresponded back and forth in July, Chris decided not to schedule a consultation right away. He e-mailed me again at the end of August to say they were doing a little better with their training now. He felt that maybe they'd just been having a rough patch when he wrote to me in July.

However, over several more months, the problems he and Ace were having just never seemed to completely resolve. Chris felt he hadn't been as successful with the training as he should have been by now. He also wanted to do something to create a better working relationship between the two of them, so finally, in February 2019, he decided to go ahead with the consultation.

My initial work with Ace

Chris shared the following information with me in his February e-mail:

> *In the two years I've had Ace, we've struggled at various times with our relationship and our training. While we've come a long way and made many improvements, there are recurring issues that have continued to plague our working together, and our relationship as a whole.*
>
> *I accept that many issues have been my fault because of a lack of understanding or a lack of patience. I've tried very hard the way I approach our relationship and training partnership and feel there's been much improvement on my part.*
>
> *However, the continued occurrence of these issues with Ace makes me feel discouraged, and I'm at a point where I must decide if it's in both of our interests to continue, or if Ace would be better off going to live with someone else.*
>
> *I care about him a great deal, but also admit to getting very frustrated by him at times. I've also faced the possibility that I may just not be a good enough trainer, or the right trainer for him.*

I could feel the frustration Chris was experiencing, and I was ready to do everything I could to help him identify the cause of the problems.

When I spoke with Ace, my first impression was that he was very smart and personable, but way too active. He reminded me of someone with ADD or ADHD because he lacked focus, even when I was simply trying to convey the reason for this communication. He understood my images, but he told me to hurry up because he didn't have time for this nonsense. He said, "I am who I am, and no one and nothing will change that."

I told him his dad was reaching out to him to try to understand him better, and all Ace had to do was be honest with his answers. I also asked him to explain what he needed in order to become great with his training.

Ace told me he can be great if he wants to . . . but apparently he didn't want to. He did, however, accept the fact that his dad was once again asking him for more information.

(Later on, Chris told me that he'd worked with another animal communicator in the past and that his dog was well aware of this type of conversation. No wonder Ace was somewhat temperamental when I, as yet another animal communicator, first approached him!)

We then went back and forth as Ace answered his dad's many questions. His responses to all the questions are summarized here, and they were very informative:

> We both have quick tempers so it's hard for us to work together at times.

> Many times I feel as if you don't know, or are not sure, exactly what you want me to do. Your body is saying one thing while your mind is busy making different images. It's not that I'm not understanding. It's that you're sending me conflicting messages. That kind of information is very confusing for me.

> I just follow what's in your mind. If you're worried that I won't do something, then I won't.

> I love to run, but not to jump. I definitely don't like to jump when I can't get a really good running start. And when I'm running fast and have to stop suddenly, I'm not happy about that.

> Tracking is so very difficult for me. When I put my nose to the ground, I can smell hundreds of possibilities, not just the one and only thing you

want me to track. I easily forget the smell I'm supposed to be tracking because my mind often goes in different directions. I have a good sense of smell, maybe too good, so I can be tracking several things at the same time. I don't know how to focus on just one scent. It's not natural for me to do that.

If there's something you know I don't want to do, then try to make it fun. We should definitely have fun. I'm all for fun. Having to do something because you have to is no fun at all.

I love you and I want to do things that will make both of us happy, not stressed, not upset. If happiness is not in the picture, I'd rather not do something at all.

I enjoy life when life doesn't have so many of your rules attached to it. This is not supposed to be work. It's supposed to be fun for both of us. You never have fun because you have to follow the rules, and I'm not like that.

When I do a job really well, you don't always show that you appreciate the effort. It's almost as if you expect certain things from me every single time. I want to make you happy, but I want to feel appreciated and loved by you. That's all I want.

I see no reason why we can't improve together as long as you understand that we're having fun and that you don't need to get so upset or stressed.

I love you more than anything, more than anyone. When I look at you, there is no one else I see as my human, just you. But that doesn't mean that I live for competition. No. I live to be with you, to share experiences, to learn about unconditional love. To always be together.

From all of these answers, Chris was then much better able to understand some of the reasons for the various problems they'd been having.

Next Chris said, "I want Ace to know that I truly love him and want him to be happy, but in return, I also expect some things from him. I'd love nothing more than to be able to come to an understanding and bridge these divides so that our relationship can deepen. He's an amazing animal and I want to enjoy our life together. The thought of giving up on him is heartbreaking and it would be a bit demoralizing to me as a trainer, so I desperately want to avoid that if possible."

I conveyed that information to Ace, and his reply blew both of us away:

Did it ever occur to you that we were put on this path together so you could learn a very important lesson?

Yes, that's right. I just know you're my life's mission. I came to you with a lot of hangups. You might have thought you could fix everyone or train everyone, but then I came along.

I'm here to show you the other side of things. I'm here to show you that all beings have this amazing ability to exercise their free will and make choices, no matter how much they love and enjoy each other.

Yes, we make choices every day, and although training is a very good thing, there are those of us who are here to show you that we're thinking beings and that we make decisions based on how we feel, not necessarily on our training.

We can be loud without speaking, we can be tough without biting, we can be stubborn without complaining, but what you can't do is change our instincts, change our choices, or change who we are inside.

I'm just here to remind you that we're all different, we're all individual. We're able to reason things out and act according to what we feel at that moment, regardless of training.

It doesn't mean you're a bad trainer. It means we (those who are the same as me) are here to train *you*.

Chris and I were both speechless, but we both agreed, Ace understood a whole lot more than we'd been giving him credit for.

After the consultation, Chris wrote to me saying:

> *I was very moved by Ace's comments for a couple of reasons. First, it showed a depth of emotion and understanding that we often do not attribute to our animal companions. Second, it confirmed what part of me knew, but had struggled to bring into practice or accept — that the emotional and mental piece is just as important (if not more important) than the physical actions. It truly made me stop and think about my mental place whenever I'm working with him. I try to focus on the positives and appreciate the being that he is, rather than attempting to change him.*
>
> *I now have a better understanding of how he views our training, our communication, and our relationship overall. While it's not perfect, our relationship has improved. And I acknowledge that a big part of that is me changing my attitude toward some situations, and making a better effort to differentiate between Ace being disobedient and Ace just being Ace.*
>
> *We still have some issues from time to time, but overall, the working relationship has improved drastically. Some of the issues (I believe) are residual from the past and will simply take more time to overcome. Others are just things that Ace may struggle with, and it's up to me to find ways to work through them. Like he said — he is who he is, and he's here to teach me some things, too.*

PREPARING ACE FOR COMPETITION

A couple of days later, Chris wrote again. He was going to try to get a title for Ace in next weekend's Schutzhund competition, but he had some concerns. He explained:

ACE

We had a little incident in training last night that has me concerned about this weekend. Not sure if there's anything that can be done, but I'd appreciate your advice if possible.

First, a little background about the competition . . .

Ace and I have been disqualified three times so far for "lack of control" in the protection phase. This has happened because Ace comes up so high in his drive that he's either unable to think or listen clearly, or he gets so amped up and feeling strong and free that he doesn't listen.

The first time we failed, he didn't let go of the helper's padded sleeve when I gave the command. The second time, he left my side and went back to guarding (barking) in front of the helper. The third time he bit the helper on the leg when we came beside him for the final transport to the judge to complete the exercise.

It's extremely difficult to simulate this level of drive/energy in training, but we need to test those exercises with Ace being in the same state of mind that he may have to be in on trial day. Last night we got the closest we've ever been during training and testing, but he still almost left me to bite the helper. I corrected him, but I'm not sure the correction was enough to make it clear to him.

I'm extremely nervous that we may have the same issue as we've had in previous attempts. If so, then all the training we've been doing will be for nothing, and we'll have to start all over to prepare for this same Level 1 test again instead of being able to move on to the higher levels. This would be extremely disheartening and frustrating.

I don't know if Ace would be capable of understanding, or how one would even attempt to make him understand, but is there anything we can do to try to convey to him how important it is for him to listen to me, to stay totally focused, and absolutely, positively NOT bite the helper when it is not allowed?

Above: Ace in protection mode

Thank you so much for your help. I feel like we've come a very long way and desperately want to avoid another setback.

I replied right away with an e-mail to Chris saying:

I received your email and I'm so sorry you're having such a big problem with Ace, but I do need to be his advocate and tell you that he's all in. I mean when he thinks he's doing a good job, he won't stop, he won't let go. He doesn't understand that the helper is not a real threat. This is not just an exercise for him. It's real.

However, this is what I propose to do: I'm booked, so I can't really give you a formal consultation time, but I will talk with Ace tonight and tomorrow night about the problem and see if I can correct it with my pictures.

I can tell you it will be hard for him and he might not perform perfectly. I know what he needs to do, and my personal goal is to get him to perform so he doesn't get disqualified, although I won't tell him that.

Please let me know how the training is going. In between the training exercises, if he's having any problems, send me a quick email before the next exercise, and I'll get right on it. I'll do my very best!

Above: Chris and Ace during competition

Chris responded right away:

I admire that he commits himself so fully, but I need to help him understand that in the end, it is a sport, and so following the rules is what is most important on the field. His genetic tendencies are what make him a great representative of his breed, and perhaps a great stud dog some day. But we must pass the titles first! I appreciate any help you can offer. Thank you!

I sent Chris a couple of follow-up e-mails telling him I'd already spoken with Ace many times, and he was definitely receiving my images.

The next day, Chris then wrote:

> Just an update to let you know we had a very good training session tonight. Only a couple of mistakes, but I think our plan is a good plan.
>
> We'll compete for the Obedience and Protection portions on Friday afternoon/evening and Tracking on Saturday.
>
> I don't know if it's possible to communicate this to Ace, but if you talk to him again . . . the time will come when we start competing at a higher level that I'll need to have him give his maximum effort in all phases of the competition. Tomorrow, though, in protection, it would be better for him to give only 90% effort and be correct than to give 100% effort and risk losing control. I want him to do a good job, but this trial is just a stepping stone.
>
> Once we complete this title, we'll continue to work together to find the perfect balance of his power and abilities within the rules. But for this one event, we just need to get through.
>
> He's a good dog. I love him, and I'm proud of our progress.
>
> Thank you for all of your help.

My reply on the same day:

> I'm so happy Ace is doing well during the last couple of days of training. I'm continuing to send him images so he'll know what to do, and I also told him how very proud you are of him. But there's something I do have to tell you.
>
> When I told him that this is only the beginning, and he'll need to apply himself even more consistently for future certifications, he wasn't that happy. I think he doesn't want to continue. I know it's hard to hear

after all the time you've invested in him. We might be able to work around it, but I needed to let you know what his response was right now.

The very next morning (Friday), Chris wrote:

Interesting. Well, let's get through this weekend and then we can see what happens. We've been training six to seven days a week for a couple of months, so I'm also tired. We'll take some time off either way.

And then on Friday night, I received this message from him:

Just wanted to let you know that Ace got 94 points in Obedience and 98 points in Protection tonight! I'm very happy and proud of him. We had a couple of close calls, but he kept his cool and listened, and we were able to get through it. I'll let you know how tracking goes tomorrow, but I'm very proud of Ace and appreciative of your help.

And on Saturday night, Chris sent an e-mail saying: *98 points in Tracking!*

Above: Ace with both his trophies

Way to go, Ace! What an amazing and successful ending to this part of their story.

Sometimes, when I have a conversation with an animal, I may be able to help him understand the reasons why he *should* decide to change a certain behavior. However, in this case, Ace identified some changes that his *human* had to make first before he was able to make any changes in his behavior.

In my work as an animal communicator, I've always known that I can't change an animal's behavior, and Ace clearly and eloquently explained why this was so in his case. But . . . he listened to me, and *he* decided to make changes . . . even some very big ones.

Ace is indeed an amazing animal. He's taught all of us so much about animal behavior and feelings, why they do certain things, and what an uncanny understanding they have about the reasons why.

I can't begin to tell you how happy I am with the incredible progress Ace has made. Although Chris waited three months before he still reluctantly decided to ask for my help, he now wants me to work with him and Ace every time they compete. It will be my joy and honor to do so!

DJ

Help with training his human, too!

Because I have such an affinity for both dogs and cats, my communication with those two animal species feels more fluent than it does with any other types of animals. That's no doubt because I've talked with so many dogs and cats professionally for more than 30 years, and cared for so many of them as my own pets for my entire life.

Nonetheless, I often communicate very effectively with a variety of other types of animals that I'm not nearly as familiar with. This includes horses. I don't know their quirks, I don't know what they want or don't want, and I certainly don't know anything about their training.

But . . . I can still accurately translate their images.

It was the winter of 2016 when I received an e-mail request to do this particular consultation. My client wanted to better understand the reason for her new horse's seemingly unruly behaviors, and she also hoped I could encourage him to make some changes. He was about nine or ten years old, and she'd just acquired him about six months ago.

His original name was Michael Jackson because the barn owner had insisted on giving all his horses celebrity names. That name just didn't feel right for this horse, so she'd renamed him Diggity Jones and called him DJ.

He was quite trustworthy when both she and the horse were on the ground, but when she was in the saddle, it was quite a different story.

Above: DJ riding with his new owner

Observing some of his behaviors in the beginning, she had reason to wonder if he was scared, or if maybe he'd been abused in the past, so it was important to her to reassure him that she'd never hurt him.

As soon as I connected with DJ, I realized he wasn't scared at all. I immediately understood his fiery personality. He can be pretty tame when he's inside the barn, but his true personality emerges when he's outside, particularly when he's ready to be ridden.

He LOVES to go fast, and like a Porsche, he can go from zero to 60 in three seconds.

He also knows what he wants, and he doesn't take direction well unless he's really familiar with his rider.

The first picture he sent me was that of his previous owner, a man.

DJ told me the man was very sure of himself and he'd ask DJ to start his routine right away. In fact, this rider enjoyed having him sprint, almost as if he was starting with a jump from his rear legs. Since I'm not all that familiar with horse behavior, I didn't know exactly what he meant, but I could at least convey what he was showing me in the pictures he sent.

Now that I knew he wasn't scared, and probably hadn't been mistreated in the past, my mission was to explain his new home and his new person to DJ.

I began:

Your new rider has different preferences. She wants you to go slow at first and then speed up gradually, instead of starting off so incredibly fast. She can't ride you until you slow down.

DJ was having none of that. "I LOVE to run and go fast," he said. "She just doesn't follow the right protocol with the lead, so I can't understand her."

When I asked him to explain, he said, "She either pulls too much on the reins, or too little. Her hands need to be softer on the reins for me to understand her better, not tight. Her feet need to work softly, too. Other riders sometimes guide me only with their feet instead of with the reins. Clicking of the tongue should also be very subtle."

She just wants you to feel safe with her. She doesn't want you to be nervous and scared and take off running.

DJ replied, "I'm not nervous. I get excited!!! I really enjoy going fast!"

What else can she do to make things better?

DJ then explained things this way: "Apparently I'm different from others she's experienced before. I need to know how she moves, how her hands signal, the strength of her legs, and particularly her feet. We're just not communicating. I'm a runner, a sprinter, and if she doesn't like that, I need to know what she wants instead. We can work with each other. I enjoy learning new things, but I need to understand her.

"We should try exercising together first in a small area so I can understand her reins commands better. We can move to the arena after I get it. Also she needs to mount, relax, and then walk, just walk for three paces and stop. I just need to feel her directions first. I need to understand many things about what she's doing. I agree, we can't go riding yet. She's not ready for me."

Is there anything else you want her to know?

DJ replied, "Please know that the problem we're having has nothing to do with me not liking her. I *do* like her. She's gentle and very nice to me. I enjoy her hugs and treats. But as a rider she's just not connecting with me. She wants to go slow, I want to go fast. She wants easy, I want full blast. I love to feel the wind in my face and run with abandon. I enjoy life!"

After I shared this conversation in an e-mail with my client, she replied:

> Dr. Monica, thank you so much for this information. Actually, I was very distressed to hear it (even though it makes perfect sense) because at 68, I don't have time to become the trained rider DJ is used to having.
>
> I know what he wants, but I get scared when I'm on him, so it will take quite awhile to get there. I don't have the confidence he needs. I have to decide if I'm the right owner for him. I've already signed up for riding lessons starting tomorrow to improve my skills, but I'll take them on my other horse so DJ doesn't have to endure my mistakes.
>
> I also love to run, but only when I feel safe on my horse. I have another horse I run on all the time because she listens to me and will stop or slow down on command. Because DJ doesn't do that, I don't trust him.
>
> It takes a long time to learn the cues a horse is used to when you don't have the previous owner to talk to, so we're trying to figure it out. I now understand the trust issue is mine, not his. That was very enlightening! I'm glad to hear he was not abused, so he isn't nervous or scared, just excited.
>
> If you could follow up with him to find out how to get him to slow down when he starts speeding up so I don't panic and pull tight on the reins, we would both be a lot happier! I've made a plan for our training together. Please let him know what it is and see if that works for him.

DJ

> *Each day we train, I'll let him run and run in the arena (it's quite large) until he doesn't want to run anymore. Then I'll put the saddle on and we'll work together in the smaller round pen. If he could just slow down and stop on command (and what is the slow down command!!; usually it's "easy" with other horses, but that doesn't work for him). If we can find the right command, then I'll build my confidence and trust in him.*
>
> *Please let me know if any of this needs clarification. He's so gentle and calm when I'm not on him that I trust him totally on the ground. I would love to have that feeling while on his back. Thank you so much for your help.*

After reading what she wrote, I talked with DJ again about each of the ideas in her e-mail. Then I recounted for her, in writing, my second conversation with him:

> *The first thing I did was to explain the new plan to DJ. He was very happy when I showed him that you'd allow him to run as much as he wanted in the large open pen.*
>
> *But . . . when my picture turned to the smaller pen, he wasn't nearly as excited about it. Not because it's small, but because he couldn't put the idea of that small pen together with learning. Apparently, he'd learned to sprint in a long narrow space. The picture he sent me reminded me of a lane where horses train to compete.*
>
> *I then explained that the small pen is the only place you have available for him to feel secure and to learn to slow down. He didn't make another comment, so I then continued with your other questions.*

What command does he need to slow down, and will he stop if I say stop? (I've tried it and it doesn't always work).

When I told him that whoa means stop, he said, "No. Stop means stop." I felt as if he meant the man used specific words to describe what he was supposed to do, rather than using just sounds. From the images and feelings of his next picture, it seems to me that the commands were in another language, possibly Spanish. He doesn't understand any of the words you're using.

He doesn't even get your reins commands, because he says they're all over the place. He added that he's very sensitive to the right pulls, but you aren't doing them.

Would he be happier with an owner who knew how to ride him better already?

He enjoys riding and doing his dance so much, that yes, he would be happy being partnered with someone who knew exactly what to ask of him. Please realize the word he used. He didn't say owner because he feels he doesn't belong to anyone. He's in need of a good partner.

Will my new training plan work for him?

He said he'd give it a try, and hopefully be patient with you while you learn. But he added that he can be a challenge because he knows so much, and you know so little.

Can he give you any other words that he's used to responding to?

Since I don't usually get words, I really can't help you here. But as he continues to send me the feelings of the words, I really believe they aren't in English.

I hope this information helps you somehow. He's a magnificent horse, but you might not be the right match.

Please let me know how things go.

The very next day my client sent me another email, saying:

DJ

A friend where I board DJ knows Pasos (Paso Fino, DJ's breed) and rode him today in his special gait. Then I had a beer to relax and I, too, rode him. I also used the Spanish word for stop (alto) and it worked beautifully! Everything DJ described to you is exactly how Pasos are trained for competition. That's exactly what I needed to know. I will never be able to thank you enough.

Sincerely, GG

At first, DJ's story seemed to be about an apparently unruly horse who needed to change some of his behaviors, but it ended up being the human who needed to change some of her behaviors instead!

This wonderful story illustrates very clearly how startling and enlightening the information I receive can be, not only for me as a translator, but also for the human.

It shows not only the unique personality and temperament of this horse, but also the effort a human must put into understanding what an animal needs.

If for any reason animals don't feel fulfilled, or if they don't think you can provide what they need, they'll let you know. The information they provide may even be a little distressing because animals do have a tendency to "tell it like it is." Often though, what they have to say is quite an awakening for us humans, and very accurate.

Many people give up too easily, and too soon, when the going gets tough. But this story is proof that some problems can be resolved with the help of an animal communicator who can identify what the animal needs, and also convey to the animal what the human needs.

DJ was very intelligent and very sensitive. He was just taking much longer to bond with his new person when she was riding him because they weren't communicating in the same language. The truth, as he conveyed it, did hurt at times, but with patience, compromise, and some new understandings, this horse and rider were soon able to build a fulfilling relationship together.

Chapter 12

GIVING SUGGESTIONS AND GETTING RESULTS

Spence and Harold

What a difference simple changes can make

I'm very fulfilled being an Animal Communicator and translating what your animals want and need from you, but at the same time, my job isn't always complete unless I'm also able to give you some specific suggestions about how to make changes when your pet needs them.

Take for instance the situation Lori found herself in. She has an older cat named Spence, the love of her life. She thought he needed a friend and companion, so she decided to rescue Harold, a younger cat about two or three years of age.

Spence, however, was not at all happy with this new addition to the family. He was hiding under the bed most of the day, and even skipping some meals. This broke Lori's heart because Spence was her first love, and she wanted him to still feel as if he was the most important cat in the house.

Harold was also having some problems adapting to his new home, so he wasn't all that happy either.

Lori wasn't willing to give up on Harold, though, so she decided to give me a try, to see if I could help.

When I visited their home, I talked with Spence about coming out of hiding. I also talked with Harold about not interfering with Spence since he was the older resident of the household.

I then offered Lori some suggestions about things she could do differently around the house. We came up with a plan of action, and I left feeling confident that both cats "heard" me, and that some simple changes might make a difference.

Just a couple of days later, I received a follow up e-mail from Lori saying:

> *I wanted to thank you so much for making the long trip and coming over so quickly! It was so great to meet you!*
>
> *I thought you might be interested to know the results of your work. For two hours after you left, I really seriously reflected on what to do.*
>
> *Every time I looked at that sweet Harold, I just couldn't imagine letting him go. But then my love, Spence — I would never want to make him unhappy!*
>
> *In short order, I decided that I must keep Harold and give him at least six months, with no pressure, to just acclimate at his own pace.*
>
> *I also decided to shower Spence with much more love and affection. I'm talking to him, explaining to him that he's No. 1 and always will be, but that Harold needs a safe home, too.*
>
> *I'm bringing Spence on the bed every night where he's snuggling up with me, while Harold is happy to sleep in his room (my office).*
>
> *Also, I immediately went out and bought Harold a four foot tower. I moved the fax machine over as you suggested and put the tower in front of the window in my office.*
>
> *Well, these changes have produced amazing results in just two days!*
>
> *I spent some time with Harold on Friday night lying on the couch in my office. He crawled up on me and purred at high volume. He was so relaxed and happy! I really believe he was thanking me for everything I'd just done for him, and for having you come over!*

SPENCE AND HAROLD

By the next day, Spence started gradually coming out from under the bed. By last night, he was with me in my master bath and closet, hanging out!

He was on my bed this morning, and he's hanging out regularly in my bedroom window checking everything out! And it's only been two days!!!!!!

So thanks again... you made the difference for me and the two beauties!

Lori, Spence, and Harold

Our animals need to know we still love them and that we aren't trying to replace them when we bring someone new into the family. Sometimes a little conversation helps everyone understand why we're doing things differently. Also, making some effective adaptations will often help pets adjust more quickly to their new housemates or to their new living accommodations.

Lori followed my suggestions and needed to make only some simple changes, but it was those very changes that brought about immediate and satisfying results for both Lori and her beloved cats.

Sneakers and Georgie

Once terrorized, she now rules the roost

Lana called me from British Columbia, Canada to talk about her cat Sneakers who'd been terrorized for years by the other resident cats.

Sneakers was a very shy female. She was continually running away from the others to hide in a safe place, usually in the closet. Consequently, she could never enjoy living in her home as a regular cat would.

After talking with Sneakers, I realized that we needed more than just a conversation. I gave Lana a number of suggestions about changes she could make around her home that would give Sneakers the opportunity to begin to feel brave around the other cats.

Before we finished our consultation, I also talked with one of Lana's other cats, Georgie, who'd been ill for a long time.

Because I had so many clients back-to-back at that time, I'd forgotten about my conversations with Sneakers and Georgie until Lana e-mailed me a few days later saying:

> *I just wanted to give you an update about two of my cats for whom you did consultations shortly after Christmas.*
>
> *Sneakers, my lovely long haired tabby, was being attacked for years by all of the other cats in the house, and we had no idea why.*

SNEAKERS AND GEORGIE

You told me you sensed that she was giving off an odor that the other cats didn't recognize, and they didn't even accept her as a cat.

You also mentioned that she smelled the same way a diabetic person does, and that she may have an underlying health condition which could need attention.

We haven't taken her to the vet yet because all of our funds have gone towards Georgie's care, but we did follow your suggestion of trying to mask the scent with another.

I went to a health food store and picked up some lavender oil. I confirmed with the store that it was safe for cats providing it was diluted with water. I put about 15 drops in a spray bottle of water, spritzed some on a towel, and then rubbed her down with it.

It was the most amazing thing! From that moment on, she's never been attacked by a single cat in our house. It was so stressful before. The attacks had been daily and repetitive, so we're all thrilled with the results.

The other thing you mentioned was that Sneakers had indicated that she liked high places, and she hoped we could create a place for her that was high up and safe from the other cats.

The same day I spoke with you, I made a soft bed on top of one of our china hutches in the living room. It's very tall, and we have to help her up there a few times a day, but she loves it!

Only a moment after I put her up there for the very first time, she curled up and went to sleep as if it had always been her favorite spot.

I'm not sure if it's the combination of both the high up space that's all her own, and the new lavender scent (which we no longer have to use), but she now rules the roost.

Above: Sneakers in her favorite place

On a daily basis she gives chase to every cat in the house, but in a playful way. They aren't exactly sure what to make of her new actions, but some of them are starting to play with her a bit, and it's wonderful. Thank you!!

I also wanted to let you know about our Georgie. He's our short haired tabby cat who was struggling to get air through his nose.

Before calling you for the consultation, I'd taken him to numerous vets and no one had been able to help him, or determine the cause of this mysterious problem.

You told me that he was indeed having trouble breathing and that he sometimes would wake up in the middle of the night worried that he couldn't get enough air.

You also told me that you could sense that he had a tremendous headache along with the breathing problem, kind of like a sinus headache.

You thought that it might be a growth, but whatever it was it would take some real investigating by veterinarians to get to the bottom of it. The investigating part has proved to be so true! Instead of my "Curious George," he's my "Mysterious George!"

Another thing you mentioned in our conversation was that I should find a diet with no preservatives for him.

We're moving to a nicer climate in a few months and into a house that we can all live in together, so no cats will have to be in a barn or a garage. They seem to be listening when I tell them that things are about to get a lot better for all of us.

It's really neat to be able to communicate with them. Sometimes I try to send them images I'm thinking about, but I'm not sure I'm doing it right, so I end up speaking out loud to them. Seems to be working!

Thank you again for the consultations with my cats. I look at them in such a different way now and I also try to explain things to them hoping they'll understand.

A good communication, accompanied by some helpful suggestions, made life so much easier for everyone in this family. This is yet another story with a happy ending, and it's the kind that makes my work so rewarding!

Chapter 13

PETS AS DIAGNOSTICIANS FOR THEMSELVES AND OTHERS

Sully

This is how I feel

Sometimes pets can be their own best diagnosticians. They can tell me exactly what their symptoms are, where it hurts, and how it makes them feel.

Because I'm not a veterinarian, I can't offer a medical diagnosis, but I can tell you where to start looking, based on what your pet has told me. All you have to do then is to share this information with your veterinarian.

True, some doctors will think you're crazy at first . . . until their own tests reveal the accuracy of what your pet has said.

Here, in her own words, is what happened to my client Carol after she came to see me with her dog, Sully.

YOUR PET CALLED

My black lab's name is Sully and we came to your home for a session about a month or so ago. He told you that he was having a pinching sensation in his throat, and you were also concerned about his kidneys.

About a week later, he had some blood in his saliva, so we took him to a vet whom we really like and trust. He ran tests and found out Sully was going into kidney failure. He recommended we hospitalize him immediately. We did, and after three days he looked so much better!

He has to be on blood pressure medication, he's on a special (and expensive!) low protein diet, and he receives sub-q fluids daily.

He also has paralysis in his larynx, which worries me a lot. He can't get overly excited or pant too hard or his airway will close up. I assume it can get worse over time. I'll have to ask the doctor about that. But he's doing so much better!! He seems more like his old self this week, and we are so happy!!

Both of these problems came up in your reading. Thank you so much for translating them! I knew something was wrong because Sully was weak and had low energy. His fur was awful and his appetite was really strange, not like him at all, but we didn't know why. The vets we took him to before, simply thought he was old and arthritic.

Just wanted to thank you and to let you know how much your reading helped us in case you come across a similar situation in the future.

Peace, and God Bless,

Carol

This is the first good example of how just a little bit of information coming from a pet can really help to pinpoint one or more problems. All we have to do is really listen to what our pets are describing, and then act on it.

Rocky

I have a pain in my neck

When pets are able to identify something that's causing them pain or discomfort, it's important for pet parents to take action. Rocky's family is a good example.

Rocky is one of three Pugs in the family. He's about eight years old. When his previous owners moved out of the country, they gifted him to my clients who already had two Pugs.

Rocky is quite a character. He's smart and quirky, and loves his new family. When they first adopted him, Rocky told me his neck was hurting. He said he couldn't lie down with his face straight on top of his front paws. Instead, he needed to put just one cheek on top of his paws. That way one side of his neck would be higher and not pull, so it wouldn't hurt as much.

My clients promptly took him to see the doctor. An x-ray showed that, sure enough, the first few bones of his neck were completely out of place. Fortunately, all it took was an effective chiropractic adjustment to relieve his considerable discomfort. The chiropractor told my clients that Rocky had no doubt been in pain for a long time, most likely from having worn a collar in the past and tugging hard on the attached leash.

After the adjustment was made, followed by a few more months of treatment, my clients came back to see me again. Rocky wanted to thank them for fixing his neck. He told them his neck was doing very well, but this time, he complained about feeling pain inside his mouth. It seemed to me as if the problem was with a tooth.

Again, they took him to the doctor who found a deep cavity in one tooth, and two other teeth that needed to be removed altogether.

When the family came to see me after all that dental work had been completed, Rocky told me he didn't understand why he drooled more from his mouth. He didn't know what had happened while he was under anesthesia, so I explained to him that the doctor had to remove a couple of his teeth that were no good. That's why he now felt a gap where the teeth had been, and why he drooled more. He was just happy that he no longer felt any pain.

During this current visit, he also wondered why he found it difficult to get enough air into his lungs through his nose. He was also often making snorting noises. It's not unusual for Pugs to have very narrow and short nasal passages, so this wasn't particularly concerning.

His mom told me he's always done that. If he gets really nervous, he snorts. She frequently puts her hand on top of his body to calm him, and this usually stops the episode.

I want to commend these clients for always listening to what their pets tell them, and for taking such quick action to follow up with veterinary care whenever it's necessary. They truly know their pets, and they're quick to recognize the difference between usual behavior and behavior that requires professional assistance.

Bacardi

It's not cancer!

Denise came to visit me with her dog Bacardi, a 9-year-old Weimaraner. She's had several dogs for as long as she's been my client. Jewel, a German Shorthaired Pointer, passed last year at the age of 12, and Brandy, a mixed Weimaraner/Pointer passed twelve years ago at the age of 13. Denise lives close to me so she's often here asking me to find out how her pets feel, and she makes sure I see them if there's anything major.

On this occasion, Denise reminded me that she'd brought Bacardi to see me eight months ago because she was concerned about her dog's rear legs. Bacardi has had a few scares throughout her life when a number of small carcinomas had to be removed, so her mom was concerned that this might be another cancerous episode.

During that prior visit, Bacardi told me one of her back knees was hurting so much that she couldn't put any weight on it. Denise told me now that, when we were having that consultation many months ago, I said then I didn't think the cause of the problem was cancer.

At the time, she wanted to investigate Bacardi's discomfort further so she went to her animal hospital, which had a good reputation.

As many of my clients are, Denise was afraid to tell the vet she had information from an animal communicator that might be helpful, but in the back of her mind she remembered every word I said.

Above: Bacardi on the left with her sister Jewel on the right

Her regular vet was on vacation so she and her dog were seen by another vet. They took x-rays first and she was told Bacardi had a slight fissure on her hip. Denise didn't believe this was the cause of the problem with Bacardi's leg, so she waited for her own vet to return from vacation to make a follow-up appointment.

Her own vet looked at the x-ray and said she didn't think the problem was in the dog's hip either. The x-ray simply wasn't clear enough.

Remembering everything I'd said during our previous consultation, Denise then asked her vet to check out Bacardi's back knee. After examining the knee, the vet told her Bacardi had a torn ACL (Anterior Cruciate Ligament), or in laymen's terms, a torn ligament of the knee. Bingo! Bacardi was right, and so was I. It wasn't cancer. It was Bacardi's back knee.

BACARDI

Today, our conversation covered not only medical aspects, but other points of interest as well. As I began my conversation with Bacardi, before her mom started asking any questions, I did as I always do. I opened our conversation by telling her it was her turn to say or ask about anything she wants.

One of the first things she told me was that she did not want another dog. She said this was her time to be number one. Throughout her life, she'd had to play second fiddle to Jewel who'd always been the boss. Bacardi always acted the way the boss wanted her to act, but now that Jewel was gone, she didn't want to share her mom with another dog.

Denise told me that asking about getting another dog had been the number one question on her list, and she was disappointed by the answer. She couldn't believe Bacardi would say that because she really loves other dogs.

Bacardi, who was listening to our conversation, jumped in and said, "Yes, I love other dogs. I love to play with them and spend time with them. I just don't want any of them to live with us at home!"

When it was Denise's turn to begin asking questions, she wanted to know how Bacardi was doing since she'd had to have three different operations in the past year.

Bacardi didn't complain about the operations or how she felt now, but she did bring up an important consideration. She said she had a big problem as she was waking up after one of the operations, and she wanted her mom to make sure that didn't happen again.

Denise then explained to me that Bacardi always has trouble coming out of anesthesia, so they've tried various types. After one of them, instead of being groggy, she was hyper and she couldn't stay still. She bumped against everything and injured herself. Denise reassured Bacardi she'd definitely talk with their vet about the best anesthesia to use if there had to be any additional surgeries.

Bacardi continued providing more information . . .

She said that although it had been three months since she'd torn her ACL, she was still not back to being 100%. Denise told me the vet had warned her that Bacardi might never fully recover movement in that knee.

Bacardi mentioned that she couldn't stand on that leg and showed me how she only stands on the very tips of her toes. Again, Denise confirmed this was true.

Even though her knee problem was still bothering her somewhat, Bacardi had important work to do, and she began sending me images about that.

One of the first images was what I call a split image. One picture was of her sitting and then lying down with a big X superimposed on it meaning "no." The other picture showed her standing and being a great therapy dog, which she is. This was one of those split pictures I wasn't really sure how to interpret.

When I described the two pictures to Denise, she was the one who provided the translation. She said Bacardi never sits down or lies down on the job when she's visiting sick people at the hospital. She always stands, even though her knee continues to bother her. Now, that's a good translation of a split picture!

The last picture Bacardi sent me was of a small room, but it didn't seem to be in her home. I asked Denise if they had a motor home. No, they didn't. I asked her if they had a cabin. No, they didn't. But then Denise said that when she takes Bacardi with her to work, they're usually in a small room.

Once I correctly understood the place, I could continue translating the picture. Bacardi then said she's always the greeter and she loves her job because it gives her purpose.

Just before leaving, Denise also reminded me that I'd had a consultation with her first dog Brandy many, many years ago. On that occasion, Brandy told me exactly where it hurt and what she needed. When her mom took Brandy to see the vet, the problem was exactly as Brandy had described it to me.

When dogs tell me about a medical problem, and provide information during a consultation that helps with their diagnosis, it's always rewarding every time a client gives me the kind of feedback Denise provided about both Bacardi's and Brandy's actual diagnoses.

Although Denise didn't feel comfortable directly sharing Bacardi's information with her veterinarians, she was able to use that information herself to guide the veterinarian to look at Bacardi's knee when the time was right.

Wouldn't it be wonderful, though, if clients could openly share, with their veterinarians, the results of their consultations with animal communicators, without the fear of being ridiculed.

In some instances, that's already happening as you'll see in some of the stories that follow.

MacKenzy

She needs to tell us where the pain is

Occasionally, clients who see me somewhat regularly become not just clients, but friends. This is what happened with Nancy and Kay whom I first met 15 years ago with their dog Troy, whose story appears in Chapter 1 of this book.

They have many animals, so it's not at all unusual for me to receive an urgent e-mail request from them. This time, it was about their female Shetland Sheepdog, MacKenzy.

MACKENZY

They wrote:

A month ago, MacKenzy woke up paralyzed-like. She could barely move. We took her directly to Dr. Jacquie (their chiropractor) and then to Dr. Sig (their vet). After x-rays, Jacquie determined that MacKenzy had sustained a severe neck injury requiring a mild tranquilizer, an initial adjustment, and then four follow-up visits. After a couple of days of rest she was back to normal.

A week later we mentioned to our regular vet that Mac, although eager to eat, would hesitate. She'd then eat as if her teeth or throat hurt her. He couldn't see or feel anything wrong with her teeth and surmised that she may have a sore throat. At that time we started to blend her food and warm it for her, and she gobbled it up.

A week later she developed an eye infection in her left eye and was treated with eye drops by our vet.

A few days after that, during Mac's final visit with her chiropractor, Dr. Jacquie noticed a large thickening on the left side of her neck that extended from her ear down her throat. Very concerned that it had appeared in such a short time, she sent us to Dr. Sig who performed a needle biopsy. The biopsy came back as a "hyperactive lymph node" with no cancer. The recommendation was to just watch it.

After a round of antibiotics, and now a second round, the mass has almost completely disappeared, but Jacquie is still concerned about what caused it to appear so quickly. We, too, continue to be concerned because Mac still acts as if she has problems eating. We still think it might be a tooth or something in her mouth or throat. Jacquie surmises that either the eye infection caused the mass, or something else caused both.

What we need from Mac is for her to try to pinpoint the problem . . .

- *Is it a tooth?*
- *Is your throat sore?*
- *Is it something else we're missing?*
- *Do you prefer your food blended and warmed because it eliminates pain or discomfort?*
- *We put your dish up on a stool so it's easier for you to eat, but sometimes you act as if you want it on the ground. Is there a reason?*

Next Thursday we'll be leaving for two weeks, so we need to know if we need to address something before we leave.

As an empath, I can actually temporarily feel a pet's pain or discomfort, so it's very important for me to check myself for any pain or discomfort that I may be experiencing before I attempt to understand what the pain level and location is in the animal I'm working with.

Unfortunately, when Nancy and Kay requested my help, I was dealing with neck pain and tingling on the left side of my face. For that reason, I was very explicit about telling them that I didn't know whether or not I'd be able to translate Mac's pain accurately. However, because we're good friends, they wanted me to try anyway. I told them I'd do the very best I could.

When I write up my notes for a client, I don't consciously choose the color I type in, but I'll usually use blue, or maybe green or purple. When I unconsciously type in red, it means my subconscious mind definitely picked up a problem. I noticed, when I finished writing up my notes for Nancy and Kay this time, that I'd typed them in red.

This was my reply to them after my conversation with MacKenzy:

Is it a tooth? Is your throat sore? Is it something else we're missing?

I grouped the first three questions as one because I needed to feel everything she was feeling.

I've given this a lot of thought and will try to describe it as best I can. However, please bear in mind that I'm having to separate the feelings coming from my own problems from the feelings Mac is sending me about what's bothering her.

As I approached Mac, it was obvious that she wasn't well. Something is there, or is brewing, and she knows it.

When she sends me what she feels, I don't feel it on the left side but on the right. The reason for this could be twofold: 1) it could be that my own pain on the left is too strong, so I'm getting MacKenzy's pain on the opposite side just to be able to describe it, or 2) I'm mirroring her pain and therefore it's appearing on the opposite side. I'll need to leave it up to you to figure out which side her problem is on.

If you touch her jaw on the outside at the point where the jaw opens and closes, and put your finger at the same point inside her mouth where her tongue is, that's the area where she tells me something is going on.

Then she says the pain or mild discomfort goes down a bit into the throat/neck area and suddenly stops. It doesn't go any farther than that.

Additionally, I feel a pressure in my head that I'd describe as a headache, but it's more concentrated behind the eyes. I have no idea if this is related or not.

Then I continued with the rest of their questions . . .

Do you prefer your food blended and warmed because it eliminates pain or discomfort?

She says it's easier to eat the food when it's prepared this way because she doesn't have to work her mouth so much, and she does like it warm.

We put your dish up on a stool so it's easier for you to eat, but sometimes you act as if you want it on the ground. Is there a reason?

She gives me no specific reason. She just says she likes to have the option and it depends on how she feels at that time. This is so very Mac!

Next Thursday, we'll be leaving for two weeks, so we need to know if we need to address something before we leave.

You will need to address this because I feel that although she's feeling better, and she isn't complaining that much, the discomfort is always still there.

Let me know if you have any other questions you want me to ask Mac. The next day they sent me this update:

We took her to see her chiropractor yesterday after we read your notes, and we're taking her to see Jacquie again on Saturday. Mac was tranquilized yesterday and is still out of it today, so Jacquie doesn't think she'll be able to tell if there was any relief until tomorrow.

Jacquie said what she saw on the x-ray was something she <u>never</u> considered with dogs. Mac's TMJ was out of whack, and that's what was causing her pain. Because Jacquie hasn't worked with TMJ in dogs before, she's concerned whether or not what she did was actually what needed to be done. Only Mac will be able to tell us that.

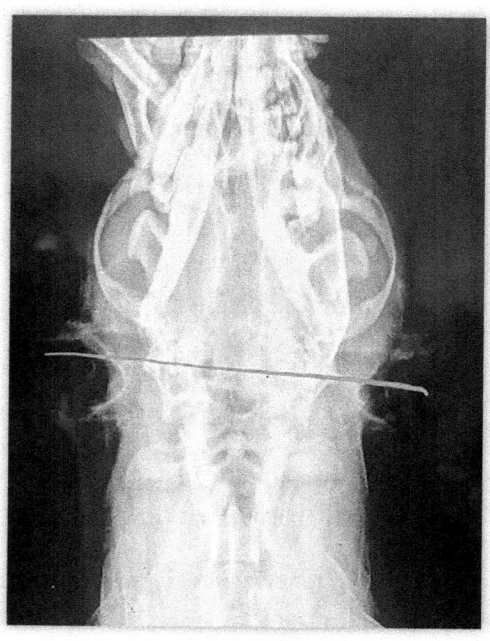

I was speechless. I'd felt Mac's pain so clearly that I knew exactly where it was, although I had to feel it on the opposite side because of my own pain. But the problem is clearly evident on the x-ray. The line should be straight.

TMJ is the acronym for Temporomandibular Joint. It's a joint on each side of the jaw that acts as a sliding hinge, connecting the jawbone to the skull. Because TMJ can cause severe pain in the jaw joint, and in the muscles that control jaw movement, it was no wonder Mac was experiencing such pain.

The chiropractor, who's also a member of our circle of friends, said she wouldn't even have considered the TMJ if it hadn't been for what I experienced when I communicated with Mac because it just isn't something you see in dogs.

What I love about all these friends of mine is that they never question what I say, ever. Nancy and Kay immediately take their dogs to the vet or the chiropractor, then Dr. Sig and Dr. Jacquie consider all the possibilities based on what the pets have told me. Everyone's confidence in me amazes me every single time.

Even though our pets aren't able to provide us with a diagnosis, we do need to recognize that they know when something hurts, and they can also identify the location for us, just as MacKenzy so effectively did this time.

As an animal communicator, my role is to help them by being willing to share in their pain for a few moments so I can translate that information for their owners.

This is definitely an example that shows how beneficial it can be for veterinarians and chiropractors to work collaboratively with pet parents and animal communicators.

Ideally, there will come a time when animal communicators will regularly work hand-in-hand with veterinarians all across the world to help them make the most accurate diagnosis for all the pets they treat. That's my vision for the future.

Sweet Pea

I'm not fat!

Above: Sweet Pea

Sweet Pea is a 10-year-old Silky Terrier who's both a little diva and a very effective protector. She first appeared in a story earlier in the book along with her brothers, Sandy and Bear.

Her case is another good example of how the information a pet provides, even when it's not very specific, can be used to help a veterinarian make a more precise diagnosis.

Sweet Pea had a malignant tumor removed back in 2016, but her dad and the vet soon brought her back to good health again. She'd just been diagnosed with cancer for a second time in June 2018, although they didn't yet know exactly what part of her body was affected.

During her visit with me in June, she made a poignant statement that ultimately helped her dad and their vet identify where the new cancer was hiding. She told me she wasn't fat because she eats too much, but that something inside her body was making her look fat.

That statement prompted her dad to ask the vet to perform an ultrasound. The test showed that her liver and pancreas were enlarged, and she appeared to have a tumor developing on her adrenal gland.

This kind of substantive information enabled the vet to provide the right treatments to eliminate her cancer for a second time in just a few months, and also to treat her liver and pancreas problems.

During a follow-up visit with the vet, it was very encouraging to know that her blood levels for her liver were reduced dramatically from five times higher than normal down to only two times higher than normal. She was eating better, climbing up and down the stairs more easily, and enjoying her walks again.

Sweet Pea also had an issue with going potty in the house, even though she knew very well how to use her doggy door. She'd done it many times before, just because she was willful (I'd told her dad at our very first meeting that he "had a diva on his hands"), but sometimes, that behavior can also be a dog's way of telling us she's sick. Since the vet began treating her liver issues and her cancer, she's virtually stopped peeing in the house. Another problem solved!

In spite of any health issues she was experiencing, she seemed to also have a mission in life to be a protector.

Her dad would take the dogs to the local park for walks every morning and evening. There was a dog with whom Sweet Pea's brother Bear desperately wanted to play, but that dog was mean-spirited and a bit of a bully. She'd bark at Bear in a mean tone and then walk away.

One day, even though the other dog was twice her size, Sweet Pea had enough of this. She got up in the other dog's face, snarling and barking at her in a way her dad had never seen her do with any dog before. The bully dog was so scared and upset by whatever Sweet Pea said to her that she ran cowering behind her owner.

After that incident, whenever she met Sweet Pea and Bear in the park again, she'd always seek out a safe place behind her owner. Now, apparently, Sweet Pea's very presence as a protector was all that was needed to keep the bully dog in her place!

When it came to her other health issues, more recently, Sweet Pea told me she was having trouble seeing, especially when she was going up and down the stairs. Her dad left lights on for her, but that didn't seem to be enough.

Her dad then mentioned to their vet what she'd said to me about her vision. This new information led her vet to discover there was a problem with her tear ducts, so for a second time, she'd been the one to provide information that would help with an accurate diagnosis.

Many animals can tell me they're sick, even if they can't tell me exactly what's wrong. This little girl was able to guide us just enough so that her dad would know he should ask their vet do the appropriate testing to determine where her pain was coming from in one case, and to check her eyes in another.

She's now recovered, so she can continue her work of being a protector ... and a little diva!

Cali

The bigger story

Pet parents often find themselves feeling totally helpless when a pet has an illness for which there seems to be no effective treatment. But . . . with the aid of an animal communicator, the pet herself may be able to reveal some helpful information.

This is exactly what happened for Chris and Sarah when their dog Cali became critically ill. It was something Cali told them during my communication with her that would help change the course of her near death illness.

In October 2018, their 10-year-old Beagle suddenly began vomiting up both food and water. At first they didn't think it was too serious because it's not uncommon for Beagle noses to sniff out something that gets them into trouble. Chris and Sarah wisely gave the problem a little time to see if it would work itself out, but they soon realized the severity of the situation and quickly sought veterinary help.

The doctor determined that Cali was suffering from acute pancreatitis and immediately put her into intensive care. He offered three possible options. One was a risky, expensive surgery with a high probability that she wouldn't make it. A second was keeping her hospitalized using what little medical treatment was available, hoping against hope that she'd respond. The third option was euthanasia.

Chris and Sarah were absolutely devastated by this news because Cali seemed to be so healthy just a week ago. She'd already been through a major operation just nine months earlier and was about to turn 11, so another surgery, and a risky one at that, was not the best choice. Neither was euthanasia.

It seemed their only option was to keep her hospitalized with medication and pain management. If she became stable enough, maybe her pancreas, liver, and gallbladder would begin to settle down.

Over the next few days, all they could do was pray that she'd pull through, but also prepare themselves for the worst possible outcome.

After three days of treatment, Cali still wasn't showing any signs of improvement, and her biomarker levels continued to rise at an alarming rate.

Chris and Sarah have a close friend who loves both of their dogs (Cali and Rocco) and has a wonderful relationship with them. He suggested they contact me to see if Cali could tell them how she feels, and possibly point them in the right direction.

They'd never worked with an animal communicator before, but they were very open to the idea. They were willing to do anything to help their precious girl, especially since time was not on Cali's side. When they explained the severity of the situation, I immediately put them on the schedule for an emergency consultation.

I helped them understand how I communicate with animals, and they provided me with a list of their questions. They wanted to find out how she was feeling, whether or not she felt she could fight this, and if not, what her wishes would be. They were hoping she'd want to fight for her life as much as they did, but they didn't know if she had the strength and the will to do so.

Cali responded to all of their questions.

First, she said she felt awful. Even the very *thought* of eating made her feel so sick. But . . . she said she did want to fight this illness as long as she could. She felt deep down that this was not supposed to be her time to leave her body. She agreed to cooperate with the doctors as long as there wouldn't have to be any more surgery.

Her response to their final question wasn't a direct answer to what they'd asked, but it really caught their attention.

She said, "Mom and Dad, I thank you so much for giving me such a wonderful life and for trying your very best to save my life now. I love you so much. I don't know what the outcome of this will be, but I want you both to know that there's a bigger story we aren't seeing that could change everything. I know this because of the visitors from Spirit who've been helping me cope with my pain."

After hearing such a thought provoking statement from Cali, Chris and Sarah spent hours on the internet in search of what the bigger story might be. Could there be another form of treatment that the hospital didn't have available?

Their diligent research did, in fact, reveal that acupuncture can sometimes be a very effective treatment for certain patients with acute pancreatitis. That's because it improves the flow of energy throughout the body.

It's true that both human and animal bodies require movement energetically to be healthy. Lying in a cage all day hooked up to feeding tubes and intravenous medications can only help so much. They now wondered if what Cali needed was something to help get her internal energy moving again.

The hospital was definitely keeping Cali alive and stable, but that was about as much as they *could* do. Meanwhile, her biomarkers were continuing to rise alarmingly instead of showing any signs of improvement.

So . . . armed with this new information about an entirely different treatment modality, Chris and Sarah then asked the hospital to allow them to bring in a western veterinary doctor who'd been using acupuncture to help her patients. They wanted to see if there was any way that acupuncture could help Cali.

The new vet said if she couldn't get her to eat after two treatments it meant the prognosis was very poor. Although it didn't stimulate her interest in food, fortunately, Cali did respond very well to the needles during the first treatment.

The next day when they re-tested her blood work, her biomarker levels had gone down significantly. This was thrilling information, and it was a step in the right direction. However, after not having eaten for 10 days, Cali definitely needed to begin eating again if she was ever going to have a real chance at surviving this illness.

The veterinary acupuncturist then gave her another treatment 48 hours later. This treatment seemed to be even more powerful than the first, and it was evident that Cali was working some serious trauma out of her body.

Afterward, as Chris described it, "She crashed out about as hard as we'd ever seen. We laid on the floor of the treatment room with her for three hours while she slept. We played meditation music and prayed that there'd be an even better outcome from this second treatment."

Once Cali woke up, they took her outdoors to do her business. While they were outside, Cali used her tongue to express an interest in something that was on the curb. Sarah quickly ran inside to get the food they'd prepared in the hope that she'd eventually develop an appetite.

Putting a small amount of food on her fingers, Sarah offered it to Cali. This sweet Beagle girl then happily licked all the food off her mom's fingers. Not only did she do it once, but she did it several more times! It was the first food she'd eaten in 10 days. They quickly ran back into the hospital to share the wonderful news with everyone. Knowing what a significant breakthrough this was for Cali, there was rejoicing all around!

Chris and Sarah left her at the hospital for a couple of more days just to be sure her blood work remained consistently good enough that she'd be able to safely continue her recovery under their care, but they left her that night feeling much more confident that their precious little girl would hopefully be coming home soon.

The very next day, they received a phone call from the doctor at the hospital saying that Cali's biomarkers had gone down drastically once again, and if things kept moving in this direction, she'd be able to leave the hospital within 48 hours.

Sure enough, she slowly began eating small meals, and her biomarkers continued to move closer and closer to normal. Chris and Sarah were then able to check her out of the hospital just a couple of days later to finish her recovery in the loving care of her family.

She'd received two acupuncture treatments while she was in the hospital, and she received two more treatments once she was home just to solidify the progress she'd already made. She's now fully recovered from her near death illness.

In an e-mail to me later on, Chris said:

Looking back on this incredible experience, we firmly believe that acupuncture treatment was the bigger story we hadn't been seeing, which Cali had said could change everything.

True, it was the collective effort of everyone involved in helping Cali, as well as the result of our extensive research, and the persistence of my wife to fight for her life. But it was only after she received the acupuncture treatments, provided by Dr. Renae Johnson, that we saw any positive change.

Your communication with her helped us significantly to be able to navigate and conquer this. We're forever grateful to have met you, and to have you share your invaluable gift with us to help save Cali's life.

You've been instrumental in our lives ever since then, communicating with all of our animals. I can't say I was a skeptic before, but I was always unsure about how this kind of ability worked. After experiencing it first hand, though, we're now firm believers in the gift you came to this earth to share with all of us. Thank you Dr. Monica. We love you!

This is an excellent example of how our pets can sometimes provide the guidance we need in order to persevere, even when the situation seems to be virtually hopeless.

It was Cali who kept their hopes alive with what she told them. The profound message she shared inspired Chris and Sarah, motivating them to do the kind of diligent research needed to reveal what the bigger story might be that Cali was talking about.

Their research uncovered the treatment that would change the course of events and effectively save Cali's life.

This was also another example of an effective collaboration among pet parents, an animal communicator, and veterinary professionals.

Without a doubt, another significant part of the bigger story is that others, too, will now be helped by the important information Chris and Sarah discovered.

Bear

The diagnostician, healer, and comforter

Bear's real name is Oliver, but during our first meeting in 2011, he told his dad he'd much rather be called by his nickname, so Bear then became his everyday name. He'd wag his tail in approval whenever he heard it!

He had the unique ability to be empathic . . . to be able to actually *feel* another's pain. That special ability enabled him to be quite the diagnostician, healer, and comforter for both humans and dogs.

He first demonstrated this ability when his mom, Janine, became ill with cancer. He identified exactly where her cancer started, and the locations to which it had spread, by putting his paw on the spots and licking her in those very places in an attempt to make it better. Sadly, he wasn't able to bring about her healing, and his mom eventually passed on. You may remember reading about this part of Bear's story in the chapter *"Pets as Bridges to Humans in Spirit."*

There were three dogs in the family at that time (Sandy, Bear, and Sweet Pea), but Bear probably had the most difficulty coping with the loss of their mom. He'd actually been lying on the bed just after she passed, but because her scent was still so strong in the house, he hadn't yet fully realized she was gone and wouldn't be coming back.

When he couldn't find her for a very long time, he began to experience separation anxiety, and that led him to become an escape artist. He tried to leave his house and yard numerous times to go looking for her.

During our first visit, I helped him understand that his mom wasn't coming back, but he still continued to escape for awhile after that, although now he had a different reason.

His dad finally brought him back to see me a second time after one escape attempt landed him in the hospital with cuts and bruises all over his paws and face from trying to dig out of the yard. Turns out, his dad had gone back to work and Bear was afraid that *he* wouldn't come home either, so now he was trying to search for *him*.

Fortunately, visits and walks by a pet sitter helped to break up the boredom of his day, and once Bear realized that Dad was coming home every day, he eventually calmed down and stopped trying to escape.

It was during our next visit, almost a year later, that Bear exercised his diagnostic capabilities a second time. He let me know his older brother Sandy was in pain and needed attention because something was definitely wrong.

Since I'd given so much accurate information to Jeff during our first meeting, he immediately paid attention to what Bear was saying and took Sandy to see the vet right after our visit.

Above: Sandy

The vet discovered a bad infection in his jaw that was caused by a couple of teeth that needed to be extracted. Sandy's health improved immediately after that. Had Bear not spoken up, his dad might not have seen that Sandy was in pain because he hid it so well, but Bear knew, and he saved the day.

When they arrived for a visit in June 2018, Bear, who's usually very friendly and animated, hid on the floor by the far side of the sofa, seemingly out of our sight. That was unusual because he'd always been on my lap or in plain view during our previous visits. But even though he was more comfortable hiding away this time, he was still attentive and willing to respond when I talked with him.

He first confessed that he felt as if he was losing his hearing. His dad had suspected this for awhile but he'd never mentioned it to me, so he was amazed when Bear revealed that fact through my translation.

Bear told me he also felt as if he might be going a little crazy. He was forgetting things and feeling lost. This might have helped explain why he preferred to hide out this time, but as he was about to show us, there was an even more serious reason.

He then shared a mind-blowing revelation with me, showing just how far he was willing to go to help someone he loved who wasn't well. He told me he knew his dad was sick, so he'd "been taking the sick from him."

My jaw positively dropped when Jeff then told me that, for more than five years, he himself had been suffering from cancer during each of the times he'd brought the dogs to visit. All that time, I had no idea. And now, just a few days before this June visit, Bear had been diagnosed with the same type of cancer.

Bear had said he felt as if he might be going a little crazy, but this wasn't so at all. His dad explained that the "dementia" Bear thought he was experiencing was really due to the cancer lowering his hemoglobin & red blood cell levels. This was causing his energy, physical dexterity, and mental acuity to suffer.

What didn't surprise me, though, was Bear's desire to try to help heal his dad. He was both a diagnostician and a healer. But . . . I needed to show him that "taking the sick from his dad" was not the way to make his dad better. First, he needed to help himself get well again.

I was able to communicate successfully to Bear that he wasn't going crazy. I explained that he needed to eat all his food so he'd receive all the medicine that was in it that would make him better. He absolutely *loved* the chicken pieces his dad would give him as a treat after each meal, so we made a deal with him that if he ate all his food, his dad would give him some extra chicken each time.

He went into remission by September, but unfortunately he had a setback in October and almost died right after Thanksgiving. In December, his dad and veterinarian then decided to start him on chemotherapy to see if that would help.

Even when Bear had to be an in-patient at the hospital, he'd spend most of his time caring for the other patients. The hospital became his "workplace." He'd make his "rounds" with the doctors and would always go to the most critical patient first. Cat, dog, rabbit, bird . . . it didn't matter. Whoever was sick or sad was going to receive Bear's love and attention. He would also always find the person in the lobby who was in the most distress and comfort that person as well.

When it was time for his own chemo treatment, he'd practically run to see his doctor, and he went willingly into the infusion room. As soon as his treatment was completed, he'd snuggle with the other animals who were also receiving treatments, spending the most time with the sickest ones.

Once again, he was using his empathic ability to actually feel the pain others were experiencing, and then he was living up to his job of being a healer and a comforter. His oncologist said she'd never seen this kind of behavior from any dog before . . . especially not from one who, based on his lab tests, was as sick as Bear seemed to be.

The treatments did help for awhile. Then in June 2019, Jeff and Bear came to see me for an emergency consultation when Bear was having a very difficult time.

He looked fine as he was walking around my consultation room, and he was wagging his tail when he saw me. He also paid good attention during our communication. That's why it was so hard for Jeff to accept what I had to translate.

Bear said right away that he was done fighting, that he wanted to leave on his own terms, and that he was happy with everything Jeff had done for him throughout his life.

As all clients do, who love their pets and don't want to see them go just yet, Jeff tried to bargain with Bear about eating a special soup he'd made just for him. I tried to tell Bear what his dad wanted him to do, but he said he wasn't sure he could do it. The thought of food, even with important medicine in it, was not pleasing to him. This was a feeling that had just started a couple of days earlier.

Bear did listen to his dad's requests, but he then made it very clear that it was now his time to go. He said his work was done and he'd accomplished what he needed to do.

Jeff then told Bear he had his blessing and permission to go if that was what he needed to do. Then he had one last question for Bear. He simply asked if there was anything else Bear wanted to say. And Bear definitely did!

He told his dad he wanted his body cremated and his ashes put in a box next to his brother Sandy's box.

Then Bear said he wanted some sign of affection along with his name on the box, but he didn't want to be remembered as just Bear. Instead, he wanted a two-word name that Jeff often used when calling him. It was a name that was very endearing to him, and *that* was the name he wanted to have put on the engraved plate.

Next, he said he wanted Jeff to put both boxes, his and Sandy's, next to each other in a special place of remembrance. He also told his dad that he must add a specific picture of both Bear and Sandy together. Bear said this would be a nice reminder of two of the special beings Jeff had had in his life.

We had a very good session and Jeff left, still half confident and half hoping that Bear would eat his soup, which contained a lot of good medication. I wasn't so sure he'd be able to do that, but I asked Jeff to keep me informed and text me if Bear was able to eat.

Two hours later Jeff texted me saying that Bear had experienced soiling problems in the car on the way back home. He then vomited at home while sitting on his favorite chair. When Jeff tried to take him out for his favorite walk, he stopped walking and had to be carried back home in his dad's arms because he'd become so very limp.

He didn't want anything to do with his soup and simply walked away from it. He then started going downhill very fast.

The very next morning, Jeff sent me an e-mail saying:

> *Good morning, Dr. Monica. Although you've probably already felt it, Bear went to Heaven last night at 11:30 p.m. He had a great last day thanks to you. However at 4:30 p.m., he started to shut down. By 8:30 p.m. he was showing signs of pain, so after trying some pain medication and letting it take a little time to work, I apologized to him for trying to make it better one last time and took him to the hospital.*

During the 90 minute drive to his specialty hospital and "workplace," Bear (whom I'd placed on the passenger seat) summoned his last bit of energy as if nothing was wrong and walked over to sit on my lap, pressing his face into the crook of my arm as I was driving. His heartbeat was as strong and sure as ever. But . . . when we arrived at the hospital, he didn't even look up to see any of his friends and "coworkers."

He was my little boy with a huge heart, and he was an amazing little angel. He lived life on his terms. He was unstoppable, unflappable, and as selfless a being as I've ever met. He will be missed by many as he had friends and fans all over the world. His journey has also been very impactful to many.

Both his oncologist and his primary doctor at the hospital were crying on the phone when they called after they each heard he'd passed. It was the same at the hospital that night when Bear made his transition . . . the entire staff was in tears.

Bear's sister, Sweet Pea, came with us to the hospital, so I hope she's aware and was able to say goodbye in her own way.

I think our visit with you yesterday was exactly what Bear needed in order to let go. He understood that he had my blessing and that it was ok to stop fighting.

Thank you as always for enabling Bear and me to have that quality discussion.

During our last consultation, Bear did have some very specific requests about what should be done with his remains, and his dad has lovingly fulfilled all of his requests.

The plaque on the box containing his ashes reads *"In loving memory"* above his name, according to his wish for a sign of affection.

His name reads "Ollie Bear," just as it did on his ID tag, and just as his dad often called him. It's a way of keeping the connection with his original name, Oliver, before he himself made the request to always be called by his nickname, Bear.

Jeff definitely included the picture of him with his brother Sandy, and he also decided to include some other precious pictures that show Bear's amazing smile and beautiful deep eyes (see pictures below).

Bear is a perfect example of a dog who always wants to help others. He was able to detect his Mom's cancer, he helped his dad discover that his brother had a severe tooth infection, and he even went so far in his efforts to help his dad by trying to take on his dad's cancer. He also loved and comforted all the other sick animals who were at the hospital when he himself was there.

When he was diagnosed, three different vets had given him only one more month to live, but it wasn't until exactly one year after being diagnosed that his time finally came, and his mind was made up with certainty.

It always amazes me that our pets absolutely "know" when the time has finally come that they must leave, and yet they still try to ease their humans' pain by listening to their requests and accepting any attempts at bargaining.

After having a good conversation with Bear, his dad lovingly honored his request to let him go, and I'm absolutely certain that Bear is now smiling down on his dad with a big grin on his oh-so-cute face!

Chapter 14

REMOTE HEALING

Kintaro

Can you help me, please?

After I've done a reading for an animal who's very sick, and there's nothing else I can do, I often send healing energy to them remotely. Remote Healing can be done over great distances. The healing light I send travels at the speed of thought, instantly finding it's target. When I send it with intention, the healing light goes wherever it's supposed to go.

I received a request for remote healing from one of my clients in Japan to help her cat, Kintaro. I'd talked with him a year ago, but this was a new request that nicely illustrates the positive effects of remote healing.

I was going to convert my client's original e-mails into regular English, but I've made only the most subtle changes so you can also experience the heartfelt feelings she expressed in the same way I received them.

> Dr. Monica,
>
> I am Emiko. I live in Japan.
>
> I received your consultation about my cats last year. Thanks to your consultation, I became more closer than before with my cats. I am so happy every day.
>
> Then I ask you a question. Although I couldn't find it on HP, I think that you are doing healing maybe.
>
> If possible, can I get to your healing for my cat? Because Kintaro has little stone in his bladder, and it causes bleeding. I wish his pain should just disappear.
>
> If it is my misapprehension then I am sorry.
>
> All my love.
>
> Emiko

My answer went like this:

> Dear Emiko:
>
> Thank you for e-mailing me and thinking about me.
>
> It's true I offer to send healing light to all those animals who are sick.
>
> There is no fee required for this. I simply do it for my clients because I want to see your animals healthy.

> I do need a recent picture of Kintaro and I will start sending him healing light right away.
>
> Love and light,
>
> Dr. M.

I also e-mailed her two days later and said:

> I've been sending Kintaro some healing light and I believe the stone is getting smaller but I'm a little concerned because I think he might have some other smaller stones, too. Can you confirm that?

She said she'd seen one big stone on the x-ray, but she didn't remember seeing smaller ones.

Then 22 days later I received this e-mail from her:

> Dr. Monica,
>
> Today I have a very good news.
>
> I send to you an echo photograph of Kintaro before and after your healing.
>
> His bladder stone became small!!
>
> Doctor said, "I think that's the effect of the therapy food," but I don't think so, because Kintaro does not like new food and ate regular food almost.
>
> I am deeply indebted to you.
>
> Thank you so much Dr. Monica!!
>
> I pray to God Kintaro will be fine and you will be more happiness.
>
> I wish you the very best New Year filled with love, family, friends, fun.
>
> Emiko

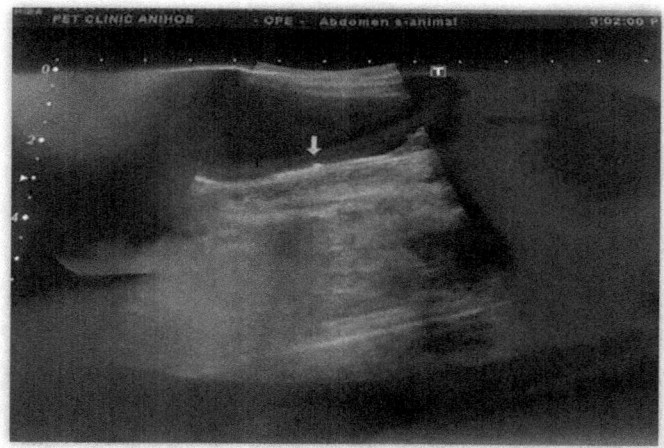

Above: Kintaro's bladder stone before remote healing

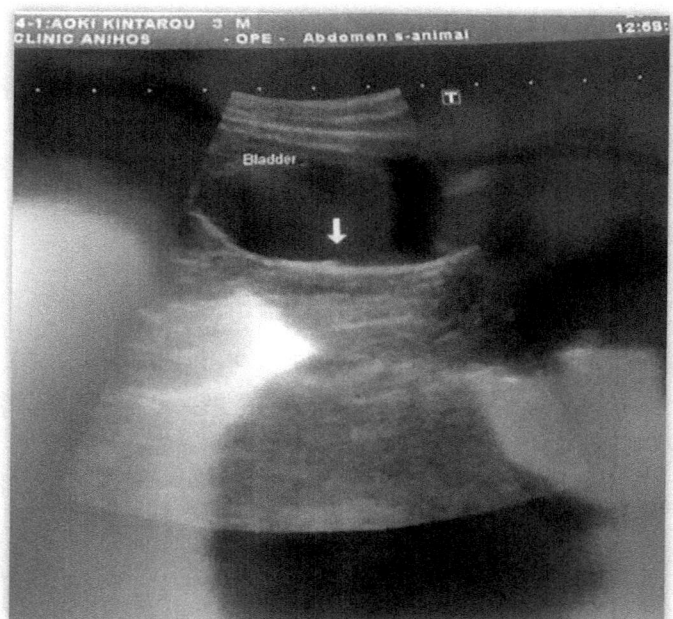

Above: Kintaro's bladder stone after remote healing

Since Kintaro didn't like the new food and he was still eating mostly his regular food, it's very likely the healing light energy I sent him helped reduce the size of the large stone.

You, too, can send healing light energy remotely all the time, any time. Simply become quiet in mind and body, and let the healing energy flow through you into the body of the person or pet you're trying to help.

What exactly are you doing when you send healing energy to someone, human or animal?

You're harnessing the energy of the Universal Life Force and sending it to the place where the intended receiver is. It's not you, or your own energy.

This energy is flowing through you as a person, but it's not from you. It's the energy that comes from the Source of your Being that does the healing.

This healing energy then flows through the energy centers of the recipient. These energy centers are called chakras. Both humans and animals have basically the same seven major chakras, as well as a number of minor chakras, throughout the body.

Since we're not just a physical body, illness doesn't always start in the physical body. It can start in our emotions or in our mental state. The same is true for our animals. Therefore when nothing else seems to work, it's important to send universal healing energy to try to correct the problem at its source.

Will this healing light energy always work?

The healing energy itself is always working, but there's no guarantee that it will be used by the recipient with the intention you sent it. That's because the recipient always has the freedom to either accept or reject healing, whether they do so consciously or unconsciously.

The beauty of remote healing, though, is that we're always free to send out loving, healing light energy with a pure intention. You can express the purity of your intention by concluding with the words: For the highest good of all.

If the recipient is open to healing, the energy will then do its work. If it's not used by the intended recipient, you've still blessed that being with Universal loving energy.

Chapter 15

Lost, Stolen, or Presumed Dead

Why Lost Pet Cases Are So Difficult

Of all the various types of pet communication I'm asked to do, there's one that's much more difficult than any other . . . helping to find lost pets. There are a number of important reasons why this is so.

It's a very emotional situation for everyone . . . the client, the lost pet, and me.

Sometimes, I'm receiving a very good picture, but since I can communicate with pets who are living on earth, and also with pets who are now in Spirit, *those pictures don't always tell me if the animal is still alive or has already made his or her transition into Spirit*. Not knowing for sure makes it very difficult for me as well as for the pet's owners.

This is not a one-time communication. It's very time-consuming. Unlike one-time regular consultations, or communications with dying pets, or communications with pets in Spirit, helping find a lost pet requires communicating with them . . . and with their humans . . . many, many times per day, usually for several days in a row.

As clients are searching, many questions arise. They may ask: Can he hear me calling his name? Can he catch my scent so he knows I'm close by? Does he smell the open can of food I'm carrying? Does she see any other animals around? Is she near any water? Is she hiding under or inside of something? Does she see any people?

As the search progresses, even more new questions arise, so the client and I spend the better part of entire days e-mailing or calling back and forth.

If clients contact me right away when a pet is missing, these communications often do have better results. But all too often, **people wait too long to ask for my help.** They do many good things. They search on their own, they post flyers, and they put notices online. But some people simply wait for their pet to come home. Some clients even wait for weeks and months before asking for my help.

Actually, if we want to have the best outcome, it's imperative that I start my communication with lost pets within the first 24 to 48 hours.

Otherwise, a lost pet may move farther and farther away from home and end up in very unfamiliar territory, or in predatory or otherwise dangerous situations.

Pet parents usually ask me to tell their pets to please come home. This is the first thing I almost always do even before I formally start our conversation, and some pets do return on their own because of my request that they do so.

Sometimes I'll ask pets to let themselves be seen by other people, wherever they are, so those people can tell their humans where to find them. That's why it's important for pet parents to post signs up to a dozen blocks away so other people will be on the lookout, too.

But some pets may be so terrified that their fear doesn't allow them to move, or they may have run too far into unfamiliar territory to know how to go back.

For that reason, it can't be left up to the pet to find his or her way back home. It's mainly up to the humans to find the pet using all of the clues they have, as well as using all of the clues I can provide from what the lost pet is able to tell me.

If there are houses, buildings, streets, people, and other specific objects the pet can tell me about, that makes being able to find them much more likely, but . . . *when they're lost in rural or wooded areas, pets can't identify clear landmarks in their surroundings.*

Even if they see many trees, clumps of bushes, or certain items on the ground, everything looks so much the same. There are no people, houses, streets, or very specific objects they can use to describe their location in unpopulated areas.

Additionally, the pictures that lost pets send me don't have any date or time stamp on them. When I'm communicating with a pet, it's logical to translate those pictures as if they're happening right now. But the pictures they're sending could be from right now, or they could be about something they saw or where they were yesterday, a week ago, or even longer. The pet's humans and I definitely have to keep this in mind when we're working with any clues the pet is sending us.

Many animals, especially dogs, are walking or running most of the time, so I may receive a picture that's current at the time the animal and I are directly communicating, but within just a few minutes, they've run somewhere else, so where they are next is different from where they were when we talked just a few minutes ago.

What's more important is to use those pictures the pet sends to identify the *places* the pet talks about. We may not know the exact time in which those pictured events take place, but those messages may tell us something about *where* the pet has been. Many times, we can obtain valuable clues about one of their locations, even if they've already moved on to some place else. Those clues can then be a very productive place to start.

One time it was an old shed in the middle of a forest. Another time, it was an electricity pole, one of those big gray ones. Sometimes it's dogs barking nearby. It could be a pool or a body of water, or a pipe, or something specific that we can actually find.

Once we have something identifiable like that, I can ask the pet to stay there and wait, or to go back to that place and wait if they've already wandered away.

I remember one time I explained to my client where her dog said he'd been after being lost for several days. She found the house, knocked on the door, and the lady who answered confirmed that a strange dog had been seen roaming around her front yard for a couple of days.

My client then stayed in her car with her other dog and waited by this lady's front yard all night long to see if her dog would come by again.

All this time I was in contact with the dog and told him to go back to the house where he had been seen for two days straight.

It was dawn the next morning when he finally and cautiously approached the house. My client quickly but quietly jumped out of the car with her other dog. They sat on the sidewalk as I'd suggested she do, and she called her dog in a loving, welcoming voice. It was a perfect reunion!

I also remember another dog who was by a brook. He said the water was nice and fresh and then he showed me a cave or a big hole in the ground where he'd spent the last two nights.

My client knew exactly where the brook was, and with the help of the fire department and some friends, they combed the entire area, but with no luck. She was so disappointed that none of them could find him, even with all of that extra help.

I told her he didn't seem to be injured and that I would tell him again to go back home if he could. She was awakened the next morning by her beloved dog slobbering all over her face! He had come home on his own, maybe because of our conversation!

Many of my lost pet stories do have happy endings, but as you can see by re-reading the items in bold type above, and by reading all of the stories that follow, communicating with lost pets and helping to find them is much, much more difficult than any ordinary communication. But . . . if I have enough information to work with, I still do it because my heart melts every time, and my life's purpose is to help those who need me.

Now, on to the stories about some of the lost pets I've worked with . . .

Maggie's Mexican Adventure

A heartwarming reunion

On a Monday afternoon in July 2015, a former client left me a voice mail message. She reminded me that I'd helped her so much when her beloved older dog was dying of cancer. Now, she told me she desperately needed my help right away. Her sister's dog, Maggie, had been lost since July 4th during a camping trip from San Diego to Ensenada, Mexico.

Family and friends had already done an extensive search of the area before they'd had to return home to San Diego on the evening of the 5th. They were heartbroken because they'd still found no sign of their precious dog.

They very effectively continued to use social media, as well as many flyers, to spread the word about Maggie all the way from Rosarito Beach to Ensenada. As a result, an incredible number of concerned people from veterinary offices, rescue groups, groomers, shelters, businesses, resorts, restaurants, and networking groups continued to be on the lookout. Although none of them found Maggie, their warm and caring responses were a tremendous support.

Nellie had just flown into San Diego on Monday night, not long after leaving her voice mail message for me. Then, together with her brother-in-law, Marc, she'd driven south early Tuesday morning, back to the Ensenada campground to continue the search for Maggie.

When Nellie and I connected by phone on Tuesday morning around 9:00 a.m., she and Marc were just about to leave the campground to start searching nearby areas on foot again. They were prepared with food and pieces of her sister's T-shirt in hopes that Maggie would recognize and respond to the familiar scents.

When I'm communicating with most pets, I don't want to have a lot of information ahead of time. However, when I'm going to communicate with a lost pet, I need to know as much as possible ahead of time. For that reason, Nellie handed the phone to Marc so that I could gather some additional information directly from him.

He told me that on July 4th, they'd gone from their campground to a nearby beach with Maggie. She'd been doing just fine until a boy, about 20 feet away from them, set off a bottle rocket before the fireworks actually started.

Maggie was so spooked that she took off suddenly with a mighty pull on her leash. The retractable leash handle slid out of Marc's grasp, and Maggie started racing away from the beach with the retractable leash handle bouncing along behind her. It seemed as if her life depended on getting as far away as fast as she could.

This was not a stretch of sandy beach, but rather it was an area with large volcanic rocks, and Maggie was racing along a sort of pathway. Marc said he ran after her for about a half mile, but then he lost track of her.

Later, he met a boy who was walking with a dog of his own. The boy told Marc that he'd seen Maggie all right. She went sprinting up the hill, right past him.

Maggie had run off a little after 8:00 p.m. on Saturday and wasn't spotted at all during the weekend search. It was now Tuesday, so it was going on around 60 hours since Maggie had first disappeared.

Nellie sent me some e-mail pictures of Maggie . . . the kind of pictures, clearly showing me her face and eyes, that are so helpful when I have to communicate remotely with a pet. She also sent pictures of the camp area where they'd been staying, and of the path Maggie had run up. But Maggie had not been seen again in either of those areas.

I promised to get back to them within 15-20 minutes, but it took a full half hour before I was able to call them back. That's because, when I did connect with Maggie, she was so scared that it took me a very long time to get her to show me some things around her that might help pinpoint her location.

People think that, because I communicate with animals all the time, I should easily be able to find out where they are. The fact is, it's very hard to get pets to communicate when they're lost, upset, cold, hungry, and scared. When they feel that way, it's harder still to get them to focus on showing me details about where they are. If they're lost in an unpopulated, wilderness, or rural area, then there's not much they *can* tell me about their surroundings because in those cases, all they usually have to show me are bushes, trees, grass, and dirt.

Sometimes I'm able to help their owners locate them, but sometimes not. For this reason, I don't look forward to having to communicate with lost pets. On the other hand, I experience such joy on those occasions when I am able to help their owners find them that it makes all the effort very worthwhile.

MAGGIE'S MEXICAN ADVENTURE

I explained to Marc why there could be no guarantees that my work would be successful, but that I was willing to attempt to find Maggie, and that I'd do the very best I could. Maggie meant so much to Marc and his wife (Nellie's sister) that he wanted me to at least try.

After I connected with Maggie, I wrote up, and e-mailed, the information to Marc, but in the interests of time, I also called and read my notes to him over the phone:

Maggie was/is very, very upset. She's tired and completely lost. She doesn't know which way to go anymore. She showed me that she went up a hill and then had to double back. I believe she might still be in the same neighborhood near where you met the boy who had seen her.

This is a small area with not too many houses. The interesting thing is that she takes a street that seems to go in a circle, or a half circle, so she continues to be in the same general area.

She didn't cross the high-speed toll road, so she's still on the ocean side, although she hasn't gone back toward the ocean. She doesn't want to. She says she never wants to see the ocean again.

Our conversation is a little difficult because she's so scared. She definitely hears me, but she's too scared to give me a lot of information. At least I know I'm getting through to her, and that she's still alive.

She told me her leash became tangled at one point, but she was able to pull loose and managed to free herself from where she was initially.

She's in the bushes and hiding a lot, especially during the day because it's hot and humid, but she's not in a wilderness area because she's always showing me some houses.

She's showing me a house that's white. The roof appears to be made of red Spanish tiles. There's no movement around there, and she likes that.

> *I told her to be sure to listen for anyone calling her name, and to come out a little bit if she hears anyone so they can see her. Again, she told me how scared she was, but I told her to be patient and that she'd be home soon.*

I asked Marc if any of this made sense, and he said yes, actually it did. There was a small private community up the hill where they'd been searching on the weekend. The roads in that community were sort of like circles within other circles. Because of what Maggie had shown me when she pictured herself walking around the streets of the community, this realization gave Marc and Nellie renewed hope that she might still be in that area.

While I was on the phone relaying the above information to Marc, I asked him to let me know right away if anyone had seen her, or if any other information surfaced. I then hung up the phone, but I was too preoccupied to start working on anything else, so instead, I paced up and down for awhile trying to tell Maggie that help was on the way.

Meanwhile, Nellie and Marc were again focusing their search in that private community with the gracious permission of one of the homeowners. Based also on what Maggie had told me, they were particularly watching for white or light colored houses with red Spanish tile roofs. They walked for several hours, sometimes retracing their steps.

Once again, they passed a house on the hill near the top of the outer loop. It was under construction, but it was quiet because there were no workers around at the moment. It was only half painted, but it was mostly white, and it did have a red tile roof. This house seemed to match the white house with a Spanish tile roof, without movement around it, that Maggie had shown me, but was it the same one?

Marc went to check the brush across the street, while Nellie walked down a small side street that they hadn't yet checked. They met up again, but without finding any sign of Maggie.

Marc spotted more thick and tall brush that was farther down and across the street from the house under construction. The thicket was beyond a barbed wire fence in a large field where they'd actually searched on the weekend. If Maggie had been hiding over there, then from that vantage point, it's true she would have been able to see the house that she'd shown me.

Marc searched to the left while Nellie searched the area to the right. Neither of them heard or saw or found anything. Marc turned around to leave, but a gut feeling strongly drew him back again. He decided to make his way even deeper into that exceedingly dense thicket. And that was when he finally saw her precious face!

Suddenly, Nellie heard Mark yell at the top of his lungs that he'd found Maggie, so Nellie came running! Marc offered food, but Maggie seemed to be very spooked and fearful, and she would only come out so far and no farther. The third time, he tossed a piece of T-shirt closer to Maggie, but still she wouldn't come to him.

At Marc's suggestion, Nellie then moved up to a place on the other side of the barbed wire fence so that she'd be ready if for some reason Maggie did bolt and head in that direction.

From where she was standing, Nellie could sometimes see Maggie trying to move inside the brush. Observing the stretched out position of Maggie's hind legs, it looked as if she might be trying to move forward, but couldn't.

Marc soon discovered that her leash was once again wrapped around something that was partially holding her back. This was great news because now they knew they could approach her gently without the risk of Maggie running off again.

Nellie climbed back over the barbed wire fence and made her way back down to where Marc and Maggie were. She actually had somewhat of a hard time finding the two of them again because the thicket was so tall and so very dense.

If she was having trouble finding the two of them, even though she now knew approximately where they were, just imagine how much more difficult it had been for Marc to find someone as small as Maggie who was hidden so deep inside all that brush.

As soon as she knew Maggie was safe and secure, Nellie immediately called her pregnant sister, who was at home in San Diego, to share the exciting news with her.

Around 1:30 p.m. Tuesday afternoon, I then received this e-mail from Nellie:

> *We found her Dr. Monica! And everything you said helped us!!!! You were right. She was in a deep thicket of brush. Leash was still on (minus the handle), and over the little hill there was a house, half white (and half gray as it is still under construction) with a red Spanish tile roof! Marc felt something that told him she was in that thicket. He checked and she was! She was a little stuck and was pulling on the leash. Thank you, thank you, thank you!!!*

It's truly a wonder that Marc ever spotted Maggie so deep inside a thicket of brush that was so incredibly dense, but he did so because, in spite of any feelings of fear or hopelessness, he listened very attentively to his intuition.

Another wonder of it all was that, at one point during their search, they realized the partially painted white house with the Spanish tile roof was in direct sight of the thicket of brush where Maggie was hiding. The house and brush were there, just as Maggie had shown them to me.

It had been 64 hours since Maggie had gone missing and she'd had to spend all that time by herself out in the open. But, with Marc's diligence, and his keen attention to his intuition about searching even deeper inside that incredibly dense thicket, Maggie was found unharmed and well.

After getting some food and water, and being exposed again to familiar scents, she seemed to be returning to her regular self. Soon, she was safely home in San Diego, relaxing in her very own bed, and enjoying all the comforts of home sweet home.

MAGGIE'S MEXICAN ADVENTURE

In the aerial picture above, you can see a white circle around the house and another white circle around the thicket where they found Maggie.

In this aerial picture, you can see the path Maggie took from the ocean all the way up to the thicket of brush.

Vinny

Working without a picture

A picture is often the only way I'm able to locate and communicate with an animal who needs my help. Therefore, it's the one item I most need to have before I can have a conversation with a pet.

It should be as current as possible, and I need to be able to clearly see the pet's eyes. The substitution of a picture that looks like the pet just doesn't work. Vinny's story is a good example.

On a Sunday in late December, I received an emergency request to help locate a lost cat. Vinny lived in Delaware and had not been seen since December 23rd when he didn't answer the call for dinner. His human was so concerned that she sent both an e-mail and a voice mail request for help.

I was taking a short vacation between Christmas and New Year's, but I couldn't ignore this request, so I read the e-mail to obtain more information.

Vinny, an outside kitty, who was all black with long hair, was 13 years old. His mom said he never wanders out of their backyard, is a sweet kitty who loves other pets, enjoys being brushed, and comes when called for dinner every night.

His mom also said she didn't have a picture of Vinny, so instead, she sent me a look-a-like picture of another cat she'd found on the internet who looked very similar to Vinny. While this did give me a general idea of what Vinny looked like, I couldn't look into Vinny's eyes in that picture.

VINNY

When I received the look-a-like picture, I knew my client was trying to do the best she could under the circumstances, but it wasn't a picture of the pet I needed to communicate with. It was as if she wanted me to call someone but didn't have their phone number, so she gave me a similar one. If I called that similar number, there would be no Vinny there, and no one would know who he was.

However, I don't give up easily, especially in the case of a lost pet. Without a picture, it took much longer to connect with him, and I could only hope it was truly Vinny.

This is how I explained the conversation to his mom:

I'm hopeful that it's Vinny I've connected with, and I'll describe the picture information the best I can.

The first picture he sent me showed him lying down under something, and then he showed me that there's a beam of sunlight. He was so happy to see it, almost as if it had been a few days since he'd seen the sun.

He'd decided to walk away from wherever he originally was, probably toward your neighbors.

He showed me that he was stepping on something white. I thought it was snow at first because it was not gray, not brown, but white. I don't know if he means to say it's fresh snow, or if this is a place where everything is bright and clean, either on earth or in Spirit.

I asked him if he reached the neighbors where he always goes. He replied that he didn't.

I asked him what happened. He said he was attacked.

I asked him if it was an animal or a person. He said it was some kind of an animal.

I asked him if he could describe the animal. I waited but he said nothing.

I asked him if he was alive. He took such a long time to answer me that I was just about to give up.

Finally, he said he didn't think so because he was surrounded by light. He said it's never dark.

His answer certainly made it seem as if he was no longer with us, but I still can't be absolutely certain because the connection we had was definitely not the best.

His mom then replied:

Oh, Monica, I'm so sorry I made it more difficult by sending a picture of a Vinny look-alike. Thank you for not giving up. Is there anything else I can do, or information I can provide to help you connect with him?

What you've told me also coincides with the concerns I've had about him being hurt and not able to get home; also that he may no longer be with us. Please let him know that I love him wherever he may be.

As a result of what you've said about the importance of having a picture, my husband is going to get pictures of all of our cats over the next few days so that we have them on file, with maybe an information sheet also. I know that doesn't help with Vinny, but it will be helpful for the other cats we have.

Talk to you on Monday.

Because the next communication I had with his mom was by phone instead of e-mail, I don't have any notes or recollections in order to confirm the outcome of Vinny's situation one way or the other.

However, later on, before the phone call, I tried again to connect with Vinny to see if he'd send me any new information. I received no response

VINNY

from him at all. This is often an indication that a pet has made his transition into Spirit, and that may well be what happened to Vinny, especially if he'd been attacked and seriously injured by another animal.

Once again, I can't stress enough the importance of always having a good picture showing the pet's eyes because that kind of a picture is so necessary for our communication. That's why you should always have a *recent* picture available.

So take a picture of each of your pets and have a folder on hand, or keep it on your computer or cell phone. Update it often, and know that if you need it, someone like me will be able to use it to connect with your pet immediately in an emergency situation.

Soxsie

Mortally afraid of fireworks

It was just after the 4th of July when I received an e-mail about a lost dog. Soxie, a Jack Russell/Terrier mix, small and female, black with white paws, was one year old.

The client, who lives in a rural area in Pharr, Texas, said she sent the message to the wrong e-mail address the day before, so we'd lost a whole day of working together. Since it's very important that I be able to contact the lost animal within the first 24 to 48 hours, she was worried that her window of opportunity was fast closing up.

SOXSIE

She wrote:

> *My son went outside to watch fireworks. Soxie never runs away, but she must have heard the noise, bolted out the door after him, and started running. She's mortally afraid of anything like gunshots or fireworks so we'd already made sure she was safe inside. I thought she'd gone to bed with my granddaughter as she always does. We didn't realize she was missing for about two or three hours.*

The client's e-mail provided me with some important information, but one of the questions I always ask when I work with a lost pet is if there have been any changes in the animal's environment or within the household.

My client replied:

> *Her continuous barking set off one of my sons and he tried using a cap gun just once to scare her so she'd stop barking. We don't allow that, and I was shocked to learn what he'd done. But she must have other fear issues also to be so afraid of loud noises.*

In response to my other question about any sightings of the animal, the client said:

> *Yes, my son said he saw a little black dog running down Jackson Road at about 11.30 p.m. on his way home. We didn't know she was missing at that time.*

> *He didn't know who it was, but he followed her in his pickup using blinking lights to protect her from getting hit on the five-lane highway. The dog was running north toward Moore Road, and just before the road there's an open field just south of an enclosed levy. She went through the open field.*

> *I e-mailed you the map separately and you can even see it in satellite view if you go to MapQuest.*

> We went to the area and spoke with a man living there. There were many bales of hay and trailers. He said he did see a little black dog, but thought it belonged in that neighborhood.

I replied to my client with a return e-mail:

> I've been looking at the map and reading your information. I also looked at the pictures, and Soxsie came to talk to me right away.
>
> She's telling me she's with a young child. She probably felt at ease around children because of your granddaughter.
>
> Is there a school close by? Is it possible some kids are in school, even though it's summer time?
>
> Just in case, you need to put up some signs in and around any area where you think children might be.
>
> She tells me she's still a little scared but she's not hungry or thirsty, at least not at the moment.
>
> After I've talked with lost pets, it's possible they might want to move on from where they are if they're able to leave the area. She knows you're looking for her and she might try to find her way back home.
>
> I told her she's far away from home and in a place where the houses are very far apart. She said she knows she's a long way from home because she was so scared she couldn't stop running. She mentioned that the lights behind her made her very upset but when she turned into the small road she felt a little better. She said she hid in a low dark place (under something) until the next day when she ventured out a little.
>
> It's 9:25 a.m. here in California, and you can call me until 10:00 a.m. because I'll be at the computer. Otherwise tell me when to call you.

The client then e-mailed me back saying:

Sorry, I had a problem here at work and couldn't e-mail right back. If she's in the same area and did not venture very far from where she hid the first night, then there are lots of small travel trailers about one block from where she turned in, and another house that's close by, but back off the highway. There are lots of young children in the park because it's home to young poor families.

After work I'll go back to that area and go door to door and call her. I've driven through the park twice and called her name, but if they have her inside, I don't know if she could hear me.

I put flyers up on fences and mail boxes in the park. Don't know if she can tell you if she's still in the same area or not. Please tell me what to do, Monica. Thanks!

I replied:

In looking at the map, I'm seeing there's a structure on the left of SK Ctr that's attracting me for some reason. Is it a school, a shopping center? Check around there as well. It's only about a block or two more than where she was last seen. Please reply to me this evening, and we'll continue.

In the meantime I'm talking with Soxsie to tell her you're looking for her, and to tell her to allow herself to be seen or heard if at all possible, also to go toward home if she can. I'm telling her she's very loved and her whole family is missing her. I'll do whatever I can from my end to guide her.

Part of my message was a little confusing for the client, so she wrote back:

What are you referring to (SK Ctr)? There are two schools within a half mile from where she turned in. I'm attempting to send you a map by text, pinpointing where the two schools are in relation to where she hid. Around the one school on Moore Rd, there are very high-end, extra large homes.

I wanted to find out what SK Ctr was to give her a clue, but I couldn't, so I wrote:

> Sorry about the SK Ctr, but that's what I saw on the map the first time. When I enlarged the view, that name didn't even appear, so ignore that.
>
> I'm looking at Moore Dr, and then to the left of the screen it turns into Yuma Ave. I know you said she was spotted at the trailer park to the right of Jackson and she might still be around there.
>
> For some reason, my eyes keep trying to go towards Yuma Ave to the Country Club. I don't know if this is coming from her, or if it's just my imagination. But just because we don't want to leave any stone unturned, I would suggest you also put some flyers in that area.

I'd been talking with Soxie frequently, and her mom and I had been e-mailing or texting back and forth all day long. The last thing I wrote said:

> I received your text about rain/lightning/thunder. I'm telling Soxsie to hide and not to worry about the rain. I'm telling her it's safer for her to stay put and hide somewhere until the storm passes.
>
> She's so scared that she's unable to tell me exactly what she sees. I do know she's upset and trembling, but I can't get her to tell me much more. I will keep on trying. I have to leave today at 5:00 p.m. but will check the computer when I get back. Good luck!

Because I had good maps to work with, I knew that Soxie had traveled about five miles away from her house on the road going north. This is when my client's son saw her running down the road without having any idea that it was Soxie.

SOXSIE

She was in that area for awhile and then she crossed to the other side of the highway. That's where she saw children and the trailer homes, and where she was when I talked with her for the first time.

It seems that she then left that area and continued to walk south toward her home through a rural subdivision where the houses were as much as half a mile apart. She was still a good two to three miles away from her house when the thunderstorm began.

Then on Sunday night, as I was going out to dinner, I received this e-mail on my phone:

> *We found her! She was rescued several miles from our house by a family with small children.*
>
> *When it started thunder storming she must have bolted as you suspected, running toward home. The route you described, ie: Old Ridge Road, then SK Cntr, then Yuma was almost a straight line back home.*
>
> *She apparently hid in a curbside gutter during the storm and was stuck. The neighbor in the nearby subdivision who found her said she was wedged in the under-street drainage below the curb. When he pulled her out he discovered she'd been prevented from going down into the city drain system by one of the kid's toys.*
>
> *I've bathed her and fed her. She hid under a chair for a while but now she's asleep in her bed.*
>
> *I didn't tell you this before, but my 4-year-old granddaughter has some extraordinary gifts also. We gave her two three-mile radius Google Earth maps and asked her to circle where she thought Soxsie could be. She circled Yuma area and SK Center.*
>
> *She doesn't know she's different and we don't want to discourage her, rather we would like to find someone to help develop her gifts. I didn't want to tell you any earlier lest it might have interfered with your concentration!*

> *I do want you to work with Soxsie to try and get control over her loud, intense, uncontrollable barking. We've tried everything including the horrible vet approved bark collars. Talk with you tomorrow about that, and all of the other stuff. Thanks a million!!!*

I was so happy to receive this e-mail and to know that Soxie was now safely reunited with her family!

It was also heartwarming to learn about her granddaughter's gift. This 4-year-old girl pointed out the exact same streets as I did. That's remarkable for such a young girl to do!

We have to remember that some of us are born with this gift and it comes naturally, but when we start school and people laugh at us or ridicule us, we simply "lose" our gift, at least temporarily, because we want to fit in. But if this young girl's gift is nurtured from the very beginning, she too may someday become an accomplished animal communicator who can help find lost pets.

Murphy

Not lost after all

My husband laughs because he says I'm like a doctor of old, always on call.

While I was visiting one of my sons in Nevada, I received an e-mail about a lost cat named Murphy. I wasn't going to be headed home to California until the next day, though.

In her e-mail message to me, the client, who lives in Michigan, explained how Murphy disappeared approximately two days ago:

YOUR PET CALLED

Due to the unseasonably warm weather, we were enjoying a bonfire in the backyard. All three kitties were hanging out in the backyard with us – and going in and out of the house via their cat door. We put out the fire and came into the house around 9:30 p.m.

About a half hour or so later, we called the cats to come in because we lock their cat door so they stay in at night. Murphy didn't come right away. Sometimes he does like to stay outside a bit longer, but he didn't come home at all last night. The last time we saw him, he was sitting on the deck in the dark about 10-15 yards from where we were sitting. This was around 8:00 to 8:45 p.m.

Jim searched the backyard and under the deck where Murphy likes to go. He also searched the surrounding yards and in the car.

We thought he might have become trapped in a neighbor's garage. Today, we noted surrounding homes opening their garages – but no Murphy. We've enlisted some neighbors to help look also.

We live two houses back from a main road and thought he might have been hit by a car – but there's no sign of this.

It's now more than 24 hours later and he still has not appeared, despite searching and calling. He always comes in and does not stray far from the house. He's very attached to our other two kitties.

Whenever pets are lost and I receive a call or an e-mail about them, I immediately connect with them to try to find out what happened. The sooner they talk with me, the better the chances we have of finding them, or of giving them guidance so they can find their own way home.

First I sent Diane an e-mail reply right away:

Just a quick note to let you know that I'm not in my office today Sunday, but will be traveling back to California tomorrow Monday.

I will, however, start communicating with Murphy right away. I'll tell him you're looking for him and ask him to come home on his own if possible.

I'll also remind him how much he's loved by the whole family. I'll send you an e-mail with all of his comments as soon as I'm back in my office, hopefully Monday evening.

In the meantime, if you have a back porch light, keep it on for him because I'll explain to him this light is there to guide him back home.

If you'd also like to communicate with Murphy, just sit quietly for five minutes, see him in your mind, and guide him home through the backyard into the cat door. This is important coming from you because your animals are able to receive your thoughts if they're sent clearly and with emotional content.

I'll be back in touch with you soon.

Monday night I received this email from Diane:

Murphy's home! He came running in through his cat door just before midnight. He ate right away (after much loving up) and seems fine. He's snuggling up next to our cat, Bailey, who was looking for him as much as we were.

I'd like to know what you can tell us about his experience, how he managed to get lost, anything, when you have an opportunity.

This was my e-mail reply:

I knew it! I just knew he was close by and all we needed to do was to remind him he was loved and missed and give him a way to come home. I'm so relieved! Almost as much as you are!

YOUR PET CALLED

I talked with him during my trip back to California from Nevada. Thankfully I wasn't driving because I usually "talk" with my eyes closed! Anyway, he shared some information with me that I know you'll find interesting . . .

*He had quite the adventure! Truly exciting for him! I really had to curb his enthusiasm because he said he might want to do it again, which I definitely cautioned him **not** to do!*

He said he realized his "friend" cat was nearby on the night of the bonfire. He simply went close to him to say hi. He said his friend told him he usually goes out at that time of night to do his "rounds," and the friend asked him if he wanted to go along.

Murphy thought it would be a great idea to follow him around for a couple of hours and then come home, but the adventure took much longer than he'd planned.

From the pictures he started to send me, I can tell you they went to the left of your property (looking out the backyard door) and they traveled in that direction but did not cross the street.

In fact, he said they didn't cross any street but simply stayed around the neighbors' homes.

Murphy told me they visited a shed. His friend showed him how to go in, but then they couldn't find a way out for a long time. A long time here means around a day. That makes sense because he said it was already nighttime when they finally did make it out.

Or, I should say he made it out, because in the picture he sent me he was alone at that moment.

His friend must have joined him shortly because he said on the way back, they stopped to see a beautiful cat. She was inside her home and they were outside. In his pictures, this girl cat had a lot of white in her fur, and he thought she was gorgeous!

Murphy then said he stopped at a sand box??? I don't know exactly what he's talking about except to say that it feels like sand or very fine dirt under his feet. He enjoyed that tremendously because he said it was the first time he'd felt something so soft.

He didn't tell me where he spent the second night, but he did say he heard me loud and clear when I told him he was loved by his whole family (sisters included), and that they were all waiting for him to come home.

Then, when he heard you, Diane (because of the pictures you sent him), he knew he HAD to make it back home. Although at first he was a little confused as to where home really was, the light and the love coming from his house made it very clear.

He said he's extremely happy to be back home and although his adventure was a success, he realizes he's not as good a "hunter" as you are. He discovered he can't provide all the good food for himself that you find for him!

I made sure to repeat the fact that he is not to go out on long adventures any more. A day outing will be OK as long as he remembers to come in at dusk. (Hope this is OK with you, but if not just let me know and I'll tell Murphy your preference.)

Well Diane, that's everything I learned from Murphy. Please give him a little kiss from me.

I was delighted when she emailed me back with some validations:

Thanks so much for talking to Murphy. I'm glad to hear he didn't cross the street – we had a strong feeling that he followed his friend and got lost. A very dense fog settled in not long after we went in the house – which may have caused them to lose track of where they were. When he came home, his fur smelled of cut grass. Since it's too early in the season for anyone to cut the grass yet in Michigan – we figured he must have been in a shed or garage around lawn equipment.

What you told him is fine. We prefer him to stay close by the house all the time, and to come in at "bedtime" when we call him.

We're so happy to have our baby back. My husband was in tears of joy when I brought Murphy to him last night (he was already sleeping when the little guy showed up). Lots of kitty hugs.

It's nice to know, in times of uncertainty, that you're available to communicate with our "furry children." What a special gift you possess.

I love what I do, especially when Lost Pet cases have a happy ending.

But in every case, happy or sad, it's very important for me to receive feedback from my clients. Only then can I really close a case and concentrate on *my* next "adventure."

Moe

Her choice to leave

One of the most difficult things I have to do is to tell clients that their lost pets have died. I always remain hopeful and wait as long as possible because I want to be as sure as I can that any pet has really passed on before I convey that information to them.

Moe's story is a good illustration of a case where I was able to talk with her for awhile when she was first lost, but at some point, she did pass into Spirit.

With my client's permission, I'm going to share her e-mails with you, almost exactly as she wrote them in English as her second language, so you'll be able to experience all that she was feeling in her own words.

I received this e-mail from her first:

Hello. My name is Yukiko.

I live in JAPAN.

I have a favor to beg of you.

My cat is missing from last night, and she has heavy kidney disease.

She is 19 years old and female cat.

Our family love her so much.

YOUR PET CALLED

Above: Moe and her best dog friend Nana

She need drip infusion at regular intervals (2 days).

Today, heat wave attack Japan, and temperature is 38 degrees Celsius (100 degrees Farenheit).

I really worry about her because she often tend to dehydrate.

I think she teeters on the brink of die of thirst.

Our family search for her all day. But we couldn't find her unfortunately.

So, please help us to find her. We need your help.

I can't speak English well, but I can understand English by e-mail.

I appreciate your reply.

Moe had already been missing for two days when I received this e-mail message.

When Yukiko filled out the lost pet form, she said Moe usually stays around her yard and would come home after thirty minutes of being outside, but not this time.

I replied to Yukiko right away, and then the very next day, I wrote to her again saying:

It's Monday morning and I'm at the computer early to talk with Moe again.

She's still communicating with me so I know she's still alive.

She did see a stream, and she says she's very familiar with it because she sees it all the time when she's outside.

She's a little lost now and doesn't really know how to find her way back home.

I also sense that she's not feeling very well. She's upset because she doesn't like to feel that way. When I experience what she's feeling, I feel very tired, very thirsty, and I don't have the strength to move around as much as I should.

I do believe she's not too far away from your home, but she will be difficult to find. Yesterday, I described how she was under a tree, but now as I ask her again, it looks more like thick bushes. It could be a tree, but underneath there are many branches all together. If that's where she's hiding, it will be difficult to see her.

> Also she might have crossed a big road. I'm seeing a bunch of trees and a building that looks as if it's been empty or abandoned for a long time.
>
> Yesterday, before I went to sleep, I was talking with Moe and telling her how much she's loved and missed by the family. I told her to try to make it back home on her own, or at least to let someone see her if she can't. I'm repeating the same thing to her now.
>
> She knows you're looking for her, but she probably won't make a sound, so don't expect her to call out to you. Instead, look under every bush and take a flash light even if it's daytime. Some places are too dark to be able to see well inside of them, even in daylight.
>
> Because she's in an abandoned place I doubt that anybody has seen her.
>
> I'll continue to talk to her throughout the day to make sure she knows we're looking for her.

Yukiko then replied:

> Thank you for trying hard to let her know I'm searching for her and that she needs to make the effort of going out in the open so someone can see her. I hope she will do so truly.
>
> I got additional information about her. I'm sorry to be late to tell you about it. 08/08 15:30, when I was searching for her along stream, a neighbor told me her husband saw her early morning near to little bridge over stream at 5:00 am of 08/07.
>
> At that time the husband walked with his dogs (Labradors), and he saw her sitting nearby the small bridge over stream. He said to me at that time her appearance looked clearly strange. She looked very weak. She had no usual response when she saw the dogs. She loves dogs and runs to them, but this time she run away to farm road.

And the abandoned place is really adjacent to the bridge, so I guess maybe she is in the abandoned place, and I already have searched for her last night about 2.5 hours, and early this morning about 2 hours. I focused under bush, and call her name many times, and took flash light when I look in bush so many times. Nevertheless I have not found her yet.

It really hard to work, but I don't know what should I do.

You told me that, "I even told her to cross the road back to the stream and look for her house. Make sure you can leave a window open for her just in case." We will do that.

If she really stay in the abandoned place, your direction is really right.

I hope to find her so much. Please keep contact with me and Moe, and if possible please tell her if my guess is right or not and can she hear my call. And give me hint to rescue her.

My next reply said:

I continue to talk with Moe and to tell her you're still searching for her. She's not telling me if she hears you or not. She's very weak and I don't think she can walk that much anymore.

She says she's hiding in a dark place, so I don't think she's in the bush anymore. She might have found a place under the abandoned building. She doesn't need a lot of room to be able to get inside.

I'm truly sorry. I have tried as much as I can but she doesn't have the energy to move and she's close to making her transition into Spirit.

I will not give up but will continue to be in contact with Moe.

As I do with all pets who are lost, I continue to send them information during the day whenever I'm not in consultation with another animal, as well as every night before I go to sleep.

When they don't send any information back, and when I no longer feel their presence, as was now the case with Moe, it's a pretty good sign that they're probably not with us any more and that they've made their transition into Spirit. Only then will I tell my clients their pet has most likely passed on, although sometimes they tell me first, as Yukiko did.

She wrote:

> *I think she had already died in the dark place.*
>
> *I would like to express to you my deepest gratitude for your kindness.*
>
> *You have been keeping contact with her every day, every night.*
>
> *And you keep encouraging her all time. I'm most grateful to you for telling her about how much we love her.*
>
> *Evening of yesterday we have found a small abandoned house along the stream. There was an abandoned car, too. We searched to find her around there, and inside of the car with flashlight.*
>
> *Also this morning my father went there to search her again, but finally we couldn't find her. It was really difficult.*
>
> *But I will try to go there again even if she's dead. I hope to find her body.*

I then confirmed for Yukiko that what she was feeling was most likely correct . . . that Moe had passed on. The family was never able to find Moe's body, but they did honor her memory with a funeral service.

Yukiko then wrote:

MOE

We did the funeral for Moe at the night of 08/11. It was very sad funeral to us, but I think it was solace that you let me know about her transition back into Spirit.

I found a picture. And I would like to share the picture with you. The picture was taken 19 years ago. Moe was kitten. She is my precious cat.

I'm appreciate for all what you did for Moe and us. I think you may have tired because of hard work for us. And I feel sorry to ask you additional request. But we would like to know about her spirit after the terrible tragic death.

Could you possibly communicate with Moe again? We have been worrying about her so much still, also we have urgent questions to Moe. Because each of my family have been feeling very serious remorse for her, we need to tell her about our feelings and tell her how much we love her.

Several weeks later, after Moe had time to adjust to her new experience in Spirit, I had the conversation with her that Yukiko had requested.

Since Yukiko was most comfortable e-mailing back and forth, that's how we had our communication with Moe. She would send me some questions and I would reply with Moe's answers. Then she would send me another e-mail with her comments and additional questions until all the questions she and her family wanted to ask had been answered.

What follows are the most important questions and comments that went back and forth between us.

I began by telling Yukiko that Moe was very pleased to talk with us again, and this time she was able to speak without a problem. She was no longer stressed or worried. She was happy and said she would love to answer all of Yukiko's questions, so our conversation began . . .

When did you make your transition back into Spirit?

> I don't know what day it was because it's always difficult for us animals to understand the days and times humans have. But now there's something important that I must tell you, and I hope you understand me.
>
> My life was always so happy and I had the best family. I knew that if they knew I was sick they were going to try to fix whatever was wrong with me and I didn't want that.
>
> I knew my time to die had come and I needed to do it by myself. I found a time to leave my home so they wouldn't see me or find me, and I went to a place where I knew nobody could see me. It was my decision to go. I needed to die by myself.
>
> I know I have caused all the family a lot of pain because of my decision, but I also know that I would have been very unhappy if I had to go to the doctor and get a lot of medication. It would have prolonged my life, but I would have been truly unhappy.
>
> At that time, I thought it was the best thing for me. I'm not sad I made that decision. I am sad I made you worry so much about me and that you spent so much time trying to find me.

It came as an awful shock to know your disappearance at that time, and your death is great sorrow to us still now. But now I want tell you that I want to respect you for your decision. My mother said same thing, too. And I admire your dignity a lot. And we promise you that everyone in our family forgive you for your decision, even so we're sad, because we love you truly.

Thank you for this. My heart is glad.

Could you go back to our house safely and meet us after you died?

I can assure you I've been here at your home every moment of your day. I visit with all the family as much as I can. I'm sending all of you little messages to tell you I'm free of pain now. I can see you and feel you and I'm very happy.

We are very happy to hear that. Thank you very much Moe. What kind of little messages are you sending for us? Can we know it?

I do what I can for each of you. Sometimes it's a feeling that I'm there watching one of you. Sometimes I send you a bird so you know I'm free. Sometimes a song.

We will continue if you want to have the offering of cat food in front of your photograph, and we keep your bed in same place. Do you know it?

I do, and it makes me happy to see that. Thank you.

What are you doing now? What can you see?

I was able to be with you during the ceremony you had. It was beautiful and even through all the sorrow I could feel the love you had for me. Thank you for the flowers, thank you for my favorite things.

How do you feel now? Are you fine?

I'm doing great now. I no longer wear a body that gives me trouble. I'm no longer sick or in pain. I'm free because I'm a being of light. I enjoy it here. There's a warm light that covers me and makes me feel loved and cared for. This is heaven.

Did you meet someone who you lived together in your life, for example Nana (dog) in the heaven? (Nana was Moe's favorite dog.)

Yes, Nana is here with me now. But also I have many others that have been a part of the family and still others that I had never met but they have a certain attachment to the family. We have a big group here and everyone sends you their love.

I asked Nana to take care of you. Also I asked Daisuke (dog), and Miki, Teio, Ru (cats) to help you when you started new living in heaven. I believe they help you a lot. Thank you for sending us their love.

Everyone here is happy and loves you.

We tried to search you as much as we can, but we could not find you, also we gave up to find your body after you died. Because abandoned place is too large to find you. What do you think about it? Are you sad about it?

I'm not sad. A body is like a used shirt that has many holes in it and you just have to throw it away and forget about it. My soul does not live inside the body. My soul is free and is here, and it's there where you are. I see you, I hear you, and I continue to love you.

I love your beautiful eyes and body so much. but I understood what you said.

Good, I tried to explain it simply so that all of you can understand.

This is other question. You had to be put on a drip at regular intervals every 2 days because of kidney disease. I know you dislike it. So I often feel sorry about it. But I had continued it for your health for long time. What did you think about it? How did you feel it?

I hated every minute of it. I didn't feel right. I can tell you that not only was the drip uncomfortable, but I was also in pain all the time. Yes, the drip helped me to cope, but it didn't take away the pain. I couldn't take it anymore and that's why I made the decision to stop all treatment and come back into Spirit. I just knew my time on your side had to end.

I'm really sorry. I really must apologize to you for the drip. The veterinary never told me about your pain, maybe he didn't know that. Now, my mother and I feel so sorry to you. We couldn't understand your feelings about the drip and your pain. We believed medical treatment must have helped you. But it was our misunderstanding. We have to say truly sorry to you.

I know you did it because you loved me. No need to apologize.

Then, I often massaged you, was it good for you? You had pain, but even so you licked my face every morning when I go to school. I was really encouraged by it because school is very far and learning medical knowledge is very difficult to me. So, I would like to say thank you very much. But why did you lick my face, what kind of feelings did you have at that time?

I really loved your massages and it was "our" time. So yes, I licked you because I loved you and I was giving you "courage" to continue.

I believe that everyone has the mission in own life. If so, what was your mission in your life?

My job was to have a long life and to leave with dignity. During my lifetime, I had many jobs. I was important in the house and would let others know they had to respect me. I was a teacher and enjoyed all my students. If the dog was being a bully, I'd tell him he needed to be nice to everyone. I protected you when you were in a weak state of mind and doubting yourself. It was my great pleasure to take care of you.

If you have messages to family, would you tell us the messages?

For Yukiko: I'm sorry you don't have me as your friend. It's my wish that at some point, after you're done being so sad, you can find another cat to love and to keep you company. You can also teach her everything you learned from me. You have too much love to give and I wouldn't want to see you waste it.

For Father: You were so nice to me. I never expected a male energy to be able to love so fully and I appreciated every touch from your hands. Thank you for being my friend and for loving me so much.

For Mother: I know how much you're suffering because of me and I'm so sorry that I had to put you through that. But you know that the whole family relies on you and you need to take better care of your health to be able to be with them for many years to come. Thank you for all your attention and all your tears.

I loved you all so much. I hope you, and everyone else, can forgive me for leaving you. My spirit was calling me and I needed to do it. But please, know that I'm always here watching over you, loving you, guiding you, and protecting you every single day of your lives. I love all of you with all my heart, and this love will last forever. Just remember that love is eternal and I will be with you always.

Thank you so much. We are really encouraged by your message of love. We love you so much, too.

And I love all of you, too!

This conversation brought the family so much comfort, especially because they'd never been able to find Moe's body.

Communicating with lost pets is the type of communication where I have to do the best I can, for as long as I can, with whatever information lost pets are able to send me.

I wish there were some way I could be absolutely certain about when they're simply too weak to talk any more, or if they've already passed into Spirit, but it's just not always possible for me, or anybody, to know for sure.

If I receive no further communications or feelings from lost pets, then that's about as clear a sign as I can have that they're not of this earth anymore.

Both the client and I will have absolute certainty only if my client is able to find the body of a deceased pet, or if I can communicate with the pet in Spirit after an appropriate length of time.

If pets have *just* made their transition into Spirit, there's usually a period of adjustment they need to go through before they'll be ready to communicate with me from Spirit.

If you've ever lost a pet who has then died, you too may have searched for as long as you can, so you, my dear friends, need to reassure yourselves that you've also done the best you can.

After an appropriate amount of time has passed so that pets have become settled into Spirit (preferably about a month), you may also be able to have a warm and loving conversation with them again. I'm here for you whenever you're ready.

Franny

Barking dogs

Sometimes finding lost pets requires many hours or days of searching. Other times, though, finding a lost pet can happen very quickly as it did for Franny.

On a Sunday afternoon, a new client in New York e-mailed me with a request to help her find her missing 5-year-old cat Francine, who also answers to Fran or Franny.

She said, on the rare occasions Franny does go outside, she generally stays close to home, and she comes running immediately when called. She's never been missing before and she doesn't know much about being outside. She's not very curious or adventurous, and she usually likes people attention more than anything else, so it was very unusual for her to have wandered off.

They hadn't noticed she was missing until around 11:00 a.m. Each member of the family just assumed she was sleeping in someone else's bed, but when they realized she was missing, they began to search immediately and also to alert all their neighbors.

I wasn't able to check my e-mail on Sunday, so it was Monday morning before I saw it. Monday was going to be a very busy day, and I was ready to leave the house early, but I didn't want to leave without at least sending my client a quick e-mail.

I told her I'd already talked with Franny and she was alive and hiding somewhere close to home. For some reason, she was unable to leave the place where she was hiding. She didn't really know where she was. She just knew it was very dark in there, and she didn't know how to get out. I had the impression she might be in a garage or a shed nearby. She said she'd been trying to call out, but her voice was very soft.

By the time I returned home, I had several e-mails from my client asking for guidance. Among other things, she said, *"I'm wondering if maybe a dog scared her into a hiding place?"*

I replied to her e-mails right away saying:

> Now that you mention it, I do remember she said something this morning about hearing barking dogs, but at the time, that piece of information didn't seem all that relevant because it wasn't particularly distressing to her. The barking didn't cause her to go into the space she's now in.
>
> When I talked to her again just now, she says she still hears the dogs barking, but they're not close to her. The barking is more like background noise.

> She told me she crossed the street at first, and I didn't see her crossing back. It doesn't mean she didn't cross back, but she didn't send me any image showing that she did.
>
> I still maintain she's very close, so yes, look in all the nooks and crannies you can think of. I don't think anybody has seen her, even if she's in their yard.
>
> I told Franny you're looking for her and it's important for her to remain calm, but to meow loudly so you can hear her.
>
> Franny said she's in a dark place, even when it's daytime. She feels secure there, so she doesn't really want to come out.
>
> She's very scared, but I'm also telling her that as soon as it gets dark, she needs to try to make a run for her home if she can. I told her you'll be waiting for her.
>
> My client sent me another e-mail telling me they'd been looking all over the place, but they still couldn't find her. She asked me if Franny can hear her, and if maybe she'd fallen down and injured herself and that's why she couldn't be seen or heard.

I replied:

> Sometimes animals who are lost tell me they can't hear anybody calling them. They're so scared they no longer recognize their own name. It happens all the time. This is not unusual.
>
> The good thing is, she can still call out, so you may be able to hear her. That's why I'm telling her to continue to do that.
>
> I don't think Franny has fallen. She's not talking about being injured, she's just very scared. She didn't roll down a hill, and nothing fell on her.

FRANNY

That's all the information I have at this time. She is alive, so keep on looking.

Later on, the client thought about the option of bringing out her sister's dog, Reggie, to try to pick up Franny's scent.

This was my next e-mail:

As far as I can tell, she's under something, like underneath an elevated house, or in a small shed where things are piled up. It was a difficult place to get into, and there's no easy way out of there. It might even be something like a crawl space.

If you go out at dusk, which is the best time, make sure Reggie is wearing a reflective collar so you'll be able to see where he is, especially if he goes inside of something.

I'm telling Reggie that he'll be going out for a walk with his mom to help look for Franny and he would be a hero if he finds her. He'd also get lots of rewards and treats. Good luck!

I then went out to dinner with my husband, and during dinner I received the e-mail we were all hoping for:

We found her! She was under my neighbor's front porch with barking dogs inside the house.

Thank you so much for all your help!

Happily, this was a successful find in just a short amount of time. It was one of those cases where an animal was able to be fairly specific about where she was hiding, but she was a little too scared to think or reason her way out. Therefore, it was up to her owner to work with the information Franny provided. And her owner then came up with a very clever and effective way to help locate her.

Timmy

Meow loudly!

On another occasion when I was trying to locate a different cat, the search was also very quick.

When Jessica emailed me to say that her cat Timmy was lost, he'd already been gone for at least 15 hours.

She said she left through the open garage door to take the dogs for a walk. A few hours later they noticed the garage door was still open and Timmy was nowhere to be found. He'd never ventured outside his house alone and he'd never been lost before.

I started connecting with Timmy immediately and called Jessica right away.

I told her that Timmy was alive and well and hiding nearby. He was close to a fence (like a white picket fence) and was hiding under a bush. He was scared and didn't want to move. He'd been there all night long and was tired and thirsty.

I told him his humans were looking for him. All he had to do was stay put and meow loudly so they could hear him.

Jessica e-mailed me just four hours later:

> *I found Timmy!! You were right. He was about five houses down from me hiding under a large bush. I was searching that area and calling his name and he started meowing. Thank you so much!!! I am so happy.*

This was one of those times when a pet was able to tell me right away where he was, and his description was clear enough to guide his human to find him fairly quickly when we started working together.

Every once in awhile, finding a pet is so easy it feels as if I hardly have to do any work at all. It's just a matter of telling the human to look for the pet nearby, instead of having to search in an area of many miles.

Having a pet clearly describe a location, and knowing the animal is alive and close by, can make a huge difference in what a client needs to do to find a pet who has disappeared from home.

Helping to find lost pets is normally a fairly difficult part of my work except in cases like these, but it's always the happy endings that continue to make it so worthwhile.

Franklin

Let somebody see you

It was Friday, January 4th, 2019 when I found a voicemail message on my office phone asking for my help with a lost dog.

I receive many calls about lost dogs over the holidays, especially when there've been fireworks as there are on the 4th of July and New Year's, but as I listened to this voicemail, I realized this little dog was nowhere near fireworks.

FRANKLIN

Franklin had been found as a stray. He'd then been adopted by Tara and her husband Jeff from a Humane Society only a month before. He's an older dog, with a gray muzzle and a heart murmur, but it was love at first sight.

While Tara and Jeff went out of state for the New Year holiday, they left their dog in the care of Jeff's parents. When Jeff's dad opened the door to go outside on one occasion, Franklin slipped out, and off he went, running away from the house.

Tara and Jeff live in a downtown high rise, while Jeff's parents live an hour away in a small rural community in Royse City, Texas. There's lots of farmland but very few houses. That meant Franklin was now totally out of his element in unfamiliar territory where he wouldn't recognize the area or any of the scents.

He'd bolted out the door on December 30th and it was now January 4th. Tara and Jeff had returned to Texas as quickly as they could. Everyone had been searching constantly but without success. They then reached out to me, feeling as if I was probably their last hope.

I immediately connected with Franklin and wrote this e-mail to Tara:

> *You need to follow 1777 north. There are open fields on the right. Call him, although chances are he won't answer. Also, cross the road to where Hidden Creek Road ends and check there, too. There's a large tract of houses in that location.*
>
> *He tells me he ALWAYS flees. That's his thing. He's forever looking for his people, and this time he wasn't happy staying where he was, so he went looking for you. He wanted to find you because he thought you left him behind.*
>
> *I'm telling him you're looking for him and if he sees anyone, he should allow that person to see him so they can call you.*
>
> *Put some flyers in that neighborhood and talk with kids. They're quick to spot stray animals.*

> *Let me know about anything you find, especially any sightings.*

Tara told me in her e-mail reply that they were very worried. They'd been searching for him all along the empty fields with no success. She was concerned that he might have been hit by a car, or that someone had stolen him.

She'd arranged for hound dogs to follow his trail, but the scent ended in an abandoned house next to a large field. The search dogs couldn't pick up the scent after that.

It then rained relentlessly, with heavy downpours for two solid days, virtually bringing the search to a complete halt. Tara and Jeff did continue their efforts, but they didn't feel they could ask others to search during such terrible weather conditions.

She also mentioned the fields were so vast she wished she had something else to go on.

In my next e-mail to Tara, I said:

> *It appears Franklin is still out in the open. No one has picked him up, and he's afraid and running fast.*
>
> *I just want to remind you that I work with images and the images I get don't have a time stamp on them, so I don't know if the animal is still there when I receive the picture, or if this is an older image.*
>
> *What I can tell you is that Franklin tells me he passed a neighborhood and he wandered (or is wandering) around a large field, but it doesn't look to me as if it's the one you're in.*
>
> *I know it's a big area to look, but try going beyond the last neighborhood and looking for him there. He seems to be in a huge field where there are no houses.*
>
> *I also asked him if he still has his collar on and he said, "Yes."*
>
> *I'm repeating my request to him to let himself be seen by somebody, anybody.*

FRANKLIN

Any updates let me know.

I didn't hear anything further from Tara right away and I was almost afraid to ask. But then, a few days later I received this e-mail from her:

After many prayers we found him! I can hardly explain it all right now, as we are still in disbelief of this miracle! I believe, after you asked Franklin to be seen, for the first time in seven (the longest most heart aching) days, a family called with a sighting near their house on the cross streets you had referenced before. Literally, their address is on Hidden Creek Drive. So for the first time we had a sighting!

I didn't want to get my hopes up, but we headed to the area, just like you said, and of allllll the people searching through the fields, I was the one to see him, feet from me. He came straight to me and kissed me more all at once than he'd ever kissed me before combined!

I was so ready for him to run from me like I knew he'd run for days and days, but he came right to me, as if it were a movie scene. You'd just told me how scared he was, but I think, after seven days, he'd finally stopped running, stopped fleeing, let himself be seen, and then came directly to me. Thank you so much for all your help!

I wish all stories would have as happy an ending as this one did. Unfortunately they don't, but we must keep on trying, even if lost pets can't tell us exactly where they are.

They're so scared that most of the time they won't even respond to being called. They'll also often avoid being seen. If they're not able to find their own way home, then it's up to us to find them, even with the slightest of clues.

Tara and Jeff used all the clues I was able to give them during my many talks with Franklin, and their search ended in the happiest way!

Chloey

Free Will

The freedom to make choices about what we want to do and where we want to go is a very precious freedom for both people and animals.

When she moved into her new home, Chloey experienced that freedom in a way she'd never known it before, and she definitely enjoyed taking full advantage of it.

On the other hand, my own freedom had recently been curtailed when I'd unexpectedly been called on to spend a considerable amount of time in Argentina on behalf of an elderly relative who'd passed on.

CHLOEY

Finalizing her affairs was a daunting task that required being away from my own home, family, and pets for two whole months of tedious work, but at least there were moments when I could still continue my life's work of communicating with animals.

It was while I was in Argentina that I received an e-mail from a very good client who'd paid in advance for a consultation she hadn't yet used. She asked me now if she could use her credit toward a consultation for her parents' lost cat, and I said of course.

My automatic e-mail reply said it would be unlikely I'd be able to do any regular consultations during those two months, but when a dying pet or a lost pet needs help, that's an emergency, and I'm almost always able to respond to emergency cases.

Her parent's cat, Chloey, a beautiful short haired tabby, had been gone for three days already and they couldn't find her anywhere. While someone had spotted her not far from her home the first day, there'd been no other sightings since then.

She was microchipped, so if a stranger found her, she could easily be identified by a veterinarian or animal control officer using a microchip reader. But where was Chloey? How could I help?

In answer to the Lost Pet Questionnaire, my client's parents shared the following information with me in an e-mail message.

They'd recently moved into a community of attached single story homes about five miles from the second floor apartment where they used to live. Their new home had a small fenced yard and Chloey was constantly begging to go out.

For the first week or ten days, they continued to let her out because she enjoyed her freedom so much, and because she would usually stay in or near the yard. Of course, she'd sometimes climb over the fence, but she'd always come back after an hour or two.

Then . . . on Sunday night . . . she didn't come back. When they discovered she was missing, they started looking for her around 9:00 p.m.

Monday, they put up flyers and posted her general whereabouts on local websites. They also put Chloey's picture and information on the Pawboost Lost and Found website.

Three people came by and reported seeing her behind the houses across the street where there's a wooded area just beyond. There's also a pond not too far behind the houses where she'd been spotted on Sunday night.

Her family had been diligently searching everywhere, on foot and by car, both during the day and at night. Now it was my turn to see if I could help.

Chances of finding lost pets are sometimes slim, at best, if they can't tell me exactly where they're located, but what I *can* do is to provide them with the reassurance that everyone is looking for them.

I can also ask them to try to come home on their own. Additionally, I can take a look around where they are, through their eyes.

If they're in a populated area, sometimes the information I receive from them helps me give them, and their humans, better guidance, but if they're lost in a rural or wooded area, pets can send me very little information to work with at all because everything looks the same, and there are no clearly identifiable buildings, streets, or landmarks to use as guides.

Finding lost pets is such a challenge that I'm sometimes tempted not to continue that part of my work. Yet, when I hear about someone's need for help, my heart always wants to respond, and I do try, as I did in Chloey's case.

In my e-mail reply to her family, I told them that Chloey's pictures would not necessarily be in "real time." The pictures she was sending me could be from this morning, or they could be from yesterday.

Also, it's not always apparent from those pictures whether a pet is still alive or has already passed on. I hold on to the idea, though, that a missing pet is still alive until I get a different response from the pet, or until the family finds the pet and tells me otherwise.

Chloey did respond to me when I reached out to her. She told me she loves, loves, loves her new home because it gives her the freedom she so much enjoys. Being free to choose where to go, at will, is something that was missing in her life when she lived in a second story apartment.

No matter what was going to happen from here on out, she'd always be thankful to her humans for allowing her to enjoy the adventures she'd already had.

She said, *"This is the adventurous me I always had inside, but I was never able to experience it until now. I'm the luckiest girl to have such understanding humans to share my life with!"*

When I asked where she was, she replied that she was in the woods. I asked how she got there, and she said she crossed a street. Looking at the map, I believe it was High Point Greenway Trail.

I asked her why she went that way. In response, she told me that many things distracted her. She'd heard some noises that worried her. These were sounds she'd never heard before. She also said the air was moving differently, and there was a funny feeling of pressure she was unfamiliar with. None of the smells were familiar either.

It wasn't long before she didn't recognize where she was anymore. She was worried now, and she couldn't seem to get past her fear in order to find her way back home.

I told her that her humans were looking for her and calling to her. She responded that she didn't hear them.

It's not uncommon for animals who are lost to *not* recognize their humans' voices, even if they do hear them. Their fear keeps them from wanting to move or make a sound in case they're wrong about who's calling them. A cat might not meow even if her people were within a few feet of her.

That's why it's so important for us to search ever so diligently for lost pets, and not expect them to come to us, even when we're very close to their location.

One of the pictures she sent me was that she was high up. This is very unusual because normally when animals are afraid, they tend to hide under bushes, not climb trees. But just in case, I told her humans to look up as well as down.

I asked her for anything that would give us some clues about where she was. She said there was wind, she saw logs on the ground, lots of green, and tall trees. Birds were going crazy, and other animals were burrowing, running, or otherwise being concerned.

I was so sorry I couldn't pinpoint a direction for her humans to follow, but Chloey just didn't know where she was, and all of her descriptions were just too general.

I told her family I'd continue to ask her to try to go home, and I'd give her what guidance I could for at least the next two days. I was hopeful she'd come near some houses she could describe, or where someone might see her and then call her family. I asked her mom and dad to please let me know if they had any sightings so that I could give Chloey even better guidance.

The weather conditions surrounding Chloey's absence were very relevant in this case. It was North Carolina in September 2018, just before Hurricane Florence was about to hit the Carolinas with 90 mph winds. It was going to be one of the worst hurricanes in US history. So, yes, the smells were different, the birds were flying away overhead, there was already some rain, and animals everywhere were skittering, hiding, and burrowing. Chloey was right about everything she saw.

But what impressed me more than how right she was about what she saw was what she said about having free will, and being able to enjoy her life more than ever when she was able to freely roam and explore nature.

She wasn't complaining about the circumstances she now found herself in. She wasn't blaming anyone. She was never sorry for herself. She understood that it was because she had free will, and the heart of an adventurer, that she was now in this predicament. It was simply a consequence of her free will choice to roam freely.

We humans can learn a lot from Chloey's attitude. Our actions do have consequences, but we need to stop blaming others for the consequences of the decisions we ourselves make.

We're free to make mistakes because we do have free will, but we have to accept the responsibility for our choices, whether those choices turn out well, or they put us into difficult or even jeopardizing circumstances.

CHLOEY

On Thursday, I received an e-mail from Chloey's worried Mom and Dad asking if she'd seen large birds (Canadian Geese), other cats, or water. That information would help them know if they were looking in the right area.

I replied that she indeed had seen a flock of birds flying overhead. She showed me they seemed to be flying from her right toward her left, away from the water, and in a large swarm. There didn't seem to be any other cats around though.

On Friday morning, Chloey and I talked about the rain and the weather. She was still scared, but I continued to encourage her to try to find her way back home.

Then on Friday afternoon, I received an e-mail from her mom and dad with the news we'd all hoped to hear. Chloey *had* finally come home sometime on Friday morning!

The wind was blowing and it was beginning to rain. Chloey was looking bedraggled and she was rather lethargic, but that wasn't surprising considering what she'd been through for the last several days. She was just happy to be back in her cozy home with her loving family.

After spending so much time in the woods looking for her, her family was thrilled to have her safely back, and they were so grateful for my help.

Many people don't realize that I'm *very* invested in their search too, and they forget to let me know what the outcome is unless I reach out to ask them. When Chloey's Mom and Dad sent me an e-mail message before I even asked, I was ecstatic. Oh, such a good ending to my day!

Thunder Beans

A misunderstanding

Over many years, I've learned the importance of following certain protocols, but once in awhile, I shortcut the process and don't follow my own rules when it comes to finding lost pets. This was one of those occasions.

My scheduled work hours are from 9:00 a.m. until 4:00 p.m. California time, Monday through Friday, but in fact, I'm often at my computer both before and after those hours on many days.

Lost animals and other emergencies can happen at any time, so I often find myself working at odd hours, and on weekends and holidays. I do try to take off the week after Christmas as well as a week's vacation with family, but even then, emergencies still find me.

THUNDER BEANS

In September 2013, I was all set to go on a week's vacation. My voicemail said I was leaving and when I was coming back, and my e-mail had an automatic response set up as well. I was at the computer replying to the last of my clients when I received an e-mail with the subject: *Emergency*.

This particular client had e-mailed me earlier to request an appointment for consultations with four of her pets, so when I heard from her again, I opened her e-mail immediately.

Usually when I get an emergency request to help find a lost pet, the client fills out a questionnaire on my website, and they send me a picture of the pet, along with payment at the same time. This client didn't do that, and I didn't follow my own rule about receiving the questionnaire and payment up front in the case of a lost pet.

Her e-mail said:

> *I have an emergency question. Can you please tell Thunder Beans to come home where he can be safe and warm because there's going to be a thunder storm.*
>
> *Thunder Beans is a Bengal born last July. I have his mom and all his sisters. He's the man of the house, protector of the girls. He went out last night (never been out alone before). My daughter almost got him at 8:30 this morning, but he scratched free. He also jumped off the balcony to avoid getting caught. It's starting to rain. He's a very important family member. I talked to him and I know he heard me, and he's scared.*
>
> *As I'm getting scared, I'm having trouble grounding myself to continue sending any messages out to him. You can tell him there's a box with food in the carport and one on the porch. Please go into either box. If he yowls I can open the slider . . . tell him not to be scared. His sisters and mom are worried and want him home too. There are coyotes, osprey, cougars, and many other dangers. Thank you.*
>
> *PS - picture coming by phone. I hope you'll be able to find a spare minute to do this.*

YOUR PET CALLED

I went to work right away and e-mailed her saying:

> *I'm leaving on vacation right now and will be gone until September 30th, but I wanted to let you know that last night as I was closing my computer, I read your e-mail and I tried to send your little Bengal the information you requested. I did the same thing for a couple of hours that evening reminding him to go home. He was very scared, so I don't know if he complied.*

She responded:

> *Thank you so much. He did not come home. We haven't even seen him again. My 13-year-old daughter is sleeping outside waiting for him. I continue to holler throughout the day. Hope he's not lost and that he's just scared and close by. Putting up signs today!*

I was traveling by plane, but when I arrived at my destination, I e-mailed her back telling her that I'd spent most of the trip communicating with him, and telling him to go back home where he would find food in a box in the carport or on the porch. I told my client to be patient and to continue to look, that he was close to home, but too scared to move.

She responded again:

> *THANK YOU, THANK YOU. THANK YOU. If he's alive, I have great hope. I'll continue to try to send him loving messages to come home. Storm was delayed till tonight. You are amazing. I look forward to our call.*

Two days later, while still on vacation, I decided to check my e-mails again and found another one from my client about this lost kitty:

> *Thunder Beans was in the box (trap) this morning. :D Thank you. Hope you have an awesome vacation.*

Before Thunder Beans went missing, the client had originally made an appointment for me to talk with all four of her pets. However, she'd misunderstood about the charges. When I e-mailed her to clarify the cost, she told me she thought I could talk with all of her pets as long as she asked just 10 questions altogether. In fact, what she was actually requesting was four consultations. That's because each animal receives his or her own time, with however many questions the client needs to ask each one. What she hadn't understood is that the fee is per animal, not per question.

I also took that opportunity to mention that she hadn't yet paid for the emergency consultation to find her lost pet, and that her cat did come home and got into one of the boxes outside after I'd talked with him over several days.

She then e-mailed me saying she couldn't afford four individual consultations, and she didn't know that asking me to "tell" thunder Beans to come home was considered "locating" a lost animal.

As you may have already imagined, she canceled her request for the four consultations, and I never did receive payment for the lost pet services I provided on that occasion.

I understand that sometimes when I clarify payment information, my clients think the only thing that's important to me is money. That couldn't be farther from the truth.

If I cared only about money, then I would charge fees comparable to what other animal communicators charge, but I don't.

I want the help I can provide to be available, at a reasonable cost, to as many people as possible when they're in need. But at the same time, I don't want to feel that I'm being taken advantage of, so that's why I do request payment up front, especially when it comes to lost animals and other remote communications.

Nevertheless, I was very happy to know Thunder Beans made it home safely and is back with his loving family. His safety and well-being, and that of all lost pets, is what's always most important to me!

Chapter 16

Letting Go Is Hard to Do

Aiko

Difficult final moments

Many years ago, I received a call inviting me to attend an annual summer picnic. The call came from a member of a Shiba Inu Club who was responsible for lining up fun activities. Because they enjoyed having me there so much the first time, they've invited me to return again and again for over ten years now.

J was the one who called me all those many years ago, and now she was reaching out to me for a very special personal consultation. I welcomed the opportunity to help her, especially considering what she'd just experienced.

A week ago, it seemed the time had come for the vet to help her beloved Aiko, a female Shiba Inu, make her transition into Spirit.

Sometimes, after the final medication has been administered by a veterinarian, an animal's body will experience certain physical activity that can be very disturbing for a pet parent to see.

This happened in Aiko's case, and J was very troubled by what she thought Aiko had experienced in her final moments. Because her grief was so acute, J felt a desperate need to reach out to Aiko so she could hear directly from her.

This is what she said in her e-mail message:

Dear Dr. Monica,

Hello and how are you? We're in the process of setting the date for the annual Shiba picnic for this year, and I'll let you know as soon as possible once we select a date. I hope you'll be able to make it once again!

In the meantime, I'm in need of a consultation. We had to say goodbye to our beloved Aiko this past Saturday. Given the fact that she was 15 years old, I was somewhat prepared for what was coming, but my grief is immense.

There are some things about the way the end came that I'm struggling with a great deal, and I'm hoping you might be able to discover some answers for me, although I'm not sure if it's too soon for you to be able to talk with her.

I'm also hoping you'll be able to communicate some explanations to my other Shiba, Yoshi, who's terribly sad over the loss of his lifetime companion. I know our own sadness is causing him to empathize with us, and that may be a great cause of his distress, but he's definitely missing her, and I feel helpless to help him cope.

It was always my hope and plan that we'd be able to contact you for a consultation when we felt the end was near for either of our dogs, but unfortunately, things happened pretty quickly, just as Aiko had earlier said it would, so we didn't have that opportunity with her. She'd told us in a previous consultation with you that things would just suddenly happen, and she was right.

I feel the best way for you and me to talk will be via e-mail. I would be so very grateful! Thank you so much.

Blessings,

J

You may have noticed that J said "this past Saturday," and she also mentioned she thought it might be too soon for me to talk with Aiko.

I usually ask my clients to wait for 30 days before they contact their pets in Spirit. However, the gravity of the situation prompted me to make an exception, so I contacted Aiko a few days later.

J said in her e-mail:

I want her to know how much I love her, and that I'm so, so sorry for what happened at the end. I was trying to prevent her from being in pain and fear, but instead of it being a peaceful "falling asleep," it seemed as if she was very much in pain and/or afraid. This broke my heart into a million pieces. I don't understand what happened.

Did I make the wrong choice? Was she trying to tell me she wanted to stay and fight? Did I give up before she was ready?

I want to know if she forgives me for whatever fear or pain she might have had. I never wanted her to suffer in any way. My last memories of her on this earth are tearing me up inside.

YOUR PET CALLED

When I reached out to Aiko she responded with all the comfort her mom needed. She said:

> I'm so happy you wanted to talk with me again so soon. Things weren't right when I left, and I've had this need to explain everything that was happening to me during the last moments of my life.
>
> I can't tell you how important it is for me to say these things, so Mom, please pay attention to what I'm about to tell you.
>
> I was not myself. I'd lost my ability to think, to coordinate my thoughts, or to feel and act normally. I don't know exactly what you call it, but I believe my brain stopped getting enough air, so it wasn't operating normally.
>
> Now, I'm able to understand what was happening then because I can look back at what I was going through, and I can also understand the feelings you had at that time. I can see how you thought I was upset. But I was never upset with you for helping me make my transition. NEVER!
>
> My body just couldn't handle living any longer. I'm so lucky you were there with me, but now, I need to be able to trust in your ability to recognize that my soul was gone before my body started to react. It was gone. My mind and body were acting erratic because my soul was no longer present to guide them.
>
> So... do not dwell on what my body was doing. That wasn't me. Just know that my soul thanks you for helping me make my transition, for giving me a way to release my body.
>
> When the time came, you did exactly what I'd already told you before that you should do. I didn't want to linger, I needed to have you help me, and you did exactly what I needed to have you do. Please don't think I was telling you anything different because of what you observed.

AIKO

I'm so happy here! I don't think anyone can ever be happier. I haven't been here long enough to be able to explain everything, but I do know there's always a light surrounding me and giving me love and warmth. This light makes everything I do feel wonderful, as well as giving me hope and allowing all my senses to receive information and experience joy. There is nowhere better to be than here!

I can still see you every day, and I know how much you and your son have been thinking about me and missing me.

I've already visited with Yoshi and told him I wasn't coming back. Although he was very sad in the beginning when I didn't come back from the vet's, I tried to make him feel better by telling him he can be king of the house now, and it's ok for him to lie down in my favorite places if he wants to. I told him to stop looking for me, even though my scent is still there.

He understood me very well. Soon you'll see that he'll be acting normal again.

I've also tried repeatedly to visit with you, but I don't think I'm doing that kind of visiting very well yet. I'll continue to try though.

Please know that my love for all of you has grown so incredibly much. I know how much I was loved. I can feel it, and I sense the love coming from all of you, even now.

I was so very happy living with you and I know we'll see each other again when it's your turn to come to Spirit. But don't worry, it will be a long time in your years still.

Did I tell you how beautiful everything is here? Everything is different but at the same time you tend to remember everything and everyone you meet here. That's crazy, isn't it? But so true. I'm still getting used to that.

Other souls come in to see me and it takes me a little while, but I soon recognize them from before. We've all been here before, but we forget when we go to your side. I'm gradually remembering everything now and it's so beautiful!

Please don't miss me because I'm always here next to you.

I'm loved here, too, as much as you loved me there.

I send you all my love now and I'll continue to do it forever. You were, and will continue to be, my best friends.

J was so relieved to read what Aiko said. She wrote back to me right away saying:

> Oh, my goodness…I'm crying my eyes out as I read this, but this time they're tears of joy and happiness. Thank you SO much for conveying this message to us. It helps SO much to know that all is well and we did make the right decision at the right time for our precious Aiko. I knew in my heart, but at the very last, I had doubt and worry. You've given us so much comfort and peace.
>
> I was so surprised that she mentioned not only me, but my son being so sad. My youngest son and I have spent a lot of time crying together. He's extremely empathetic and sensitive and was so heartbroken. He has pictures of Aiko pinned up all over his room because he's afraid he'll forget her face. I'm glad to know she's been able to see how much we miss her and love her.
>
> It's so interesting that you had this conversation today. This morning, there was a period where our other Shiba, Yoshi, was lying down in another room. I walked in to find him looking extremely sad and even whimpering a little. I sat with him, petting him and talking to him, and he laid his head on my hand and sighed loudly. He felt so overwhelm-

ingly sad to me. I even said to him at the time, "I know it's hard to accept. I miss her too, but I love you, and everything will be ok."

This evening he's finally wanting to be in the same room as the family. This is a big deal since all week he's been skulking off alone, not wanting attention or to even be near us. I think he's found some peace and comfort, too.

I can't thank you enough for this. I'm so grateful!! I hope all is well with you and that we'll see you at the Shiba Picnic again this summer.

Blessings,

J

What Aiko's body experienced after the medication had been administered were some reflexes that were normal and natural. These reflexes are not a sign of pain. Instead, they're unconscious and involuntary responses.

Once J knew that what she'd observed had not caused any pain or distress for Aiko, her relief was immense.

Sometimes, when a pet leaves under apparently unusual or difficult circumstances, as Aiko did, a conversation such as the one I had with her can be just what a pet parent needs in order to more easily move through the grieving process into healing.

Paquito

His freedom means having to do the unthinkable

I have a very good client who's been rescuing birds in her native country of Argentina for the last 20 years. The birds are a species of doves that are abundant in the city. Sometimes they fall from trees and suffer a broken wing or a broken leg. She finds them, takes them home, and nurses them back to health. Many are then able to be released when they recover, but some of them can't fend for themselves so she adopts them.

One of her new doves, Paquito, had a broken beak. The upper part of his beak was perfect, but the lower part was gone. When she picked him up from the street, he was weak and very thin. She knew he already hadn't been able to eat for many days. All birds need both their upper and lower beaks to be able to pick up food or seeds from the ground. A broken lower beak would mean starvation and a slow and painful death.

Diana took him home and placed him in a large cage, but in order to feed him, she'd have to capture and hold him at least twice a day. She sent me an e-mail wanting to know if he'd accept living under those conditions.

She also wanted to know if he liked the food she was preparing every day especially for him. She'd mix white bread, lentils, split peas, oats, popcorn, apples, and lettuce into a firm dough. Then she'd dip little bits in water before placing each bite far enough toward his throat so he could swallow it easily.

After he'd been with her for awhile, she noticed his tongue had become very dry and was continually out of his mouth. Now he didn't have a lower beak or the use of his tongue.

When I connected with Paquito, he said he could no longer feel his tongue and it was very difficult for him to swallow. He told me he didn't object to his food, but he just hated to be handled. He'd retreat as far as he could into his cage so Diana couldn't reach him with her hands. He'd flap his wings and fly against the sides of the cage to prevent her from touching him. He was wild and he definitely wanted to stay that way.

I asked him how he injured himself. He explained that he'd crashed against a closed window with such force that his bottom beak became loose. Eventually he lost it altogether. He also told me that having freedom to fly around was the only thing that made him happy, and he was very depressed having to live in a cage all the time now.

I talked with Diana extensively. She told me she could never kill a creature, no matter how dire the circumstances, so we talked about other options.

Possibly someone with a 3D printer could offer their services to print a lower beak, and someone else could try to fit it for him. I inquired here in the United States while she inquired at the University of Veterinary Sciences where she lives. Nothing would work. The lower jaw was too far gone to attempt that type of procedure.

It took Diana awhile to call me back to request another consultation with Paquito. She was willing to do everything she could to help him survive, but she needed to know if *he* was willing to continue to fight for his life.

He wasn't. He told me this year had been so traumatic for him. He never got used to her touching him and feeding him and he wanted nothing more to do with that. If he didn't have his freedom, he'd rather die.

I had to translate Paquito's words and feelings for Diana, knowing he was asking her to do what she never thought she could.

She e-mailed me back saying:

> This is the hardest decision I've had to make in my 80 years, but I will have to do it. I understand that I only have two options: 1) grant him the freedom he so desires, knowing full well that he'd die of hunger, or 2) accept that I've done everything humanly possible for him but he'll never be happy. The decision is obvious and I need to be strong so that I can keep my energy up and not send him my sadness.

PAQUITO

Two days later I received the next e-mail from her:

> *I went to the vet yesterday and he confirmed that an implant would have little possibility of success, if any, so I did what I never wanted to do. The doctor administered the injection and I put him close to my heart while reciting a prayer. The medicine was taking effect. I told him God would grant him the opportunity to experience other lifetimes on this earth. I'm sure he left in peace.*
>
> *Monica, as you can imagine, my heart is bursting with thanks towards you and everything you do. God bless you and guide you always.*

I talked with Paquito in Spirit some time after I received her latest e-mail. He said many angels came to meet him and take him into the light. He's now free. He was happy and excited to have a perfect upper and lower beak, and to once again let his wings take him anywhere he wanted to fly. He thanked me for my translation and wanted to pass on his heartfelt thanks to Diana for listening to his plea and honoring it.

Zac

It's not time yet

I think one of the most heart-wrenching things I have to do is to ask pets if they're ready to leave this life. Sometimes they're just so old and frail they can hardly move anymore. Other times, they're very ill and their humans don't want them to suffer any longer.

Whatever the reason, it's never easy to ask pets if their time is up. Not for them, and not for their humans. But many times it's very helpful to know just what they're thinking and how they're feeling, and even more important, to find out if they have any special requests.

Often, hearing what their pets have to say, and finding out what they need, is welcome knowledge for the many clients who ask for my help when they don't know what to do, or when to do it. Regret is a terrible thing, so no one wants to act too soon or too late when it involves the life of a beloved pet.

Zac's story is a good example of "It's not time yet."

Recently, Leslie came to see me with Zac, a white German Shepherd/Lab mix. She'd adopted him when he was between two and four years old.

Leslie was concerned about him because she'd had him for 17 years. Yes, you're reading that right. *She'd* had him for 17 years, and the rescue estimated that he was already 2-4 years of age when she adopted him. For that reason, we have to assume that, at minimum, Zac was 19 years old.

When she called me and told me Zac's age, I thought I was going to be talking about end of life, which in my line of work is fairly common.

But that was not the case with Zac.

Yes, Zac was old and you could see it. He walked slowly, he paced quite a bit, and his head was tilted to the side because he'd had a stroke, maybe even more than one.

When I met him, we talked about his inability to relax, about how hard it was for him to remember things, about getting lost inside his own home, and about having small seizures.

I asked him if he thought it was time for him to go. "No," he said, "it's not."

Because he continued to have good days and bad days, Leslie came to see me two more times for a total of three visits. Each time, she wanted to be certain Zac was still ok with staying.

The last time he was here he told his mom, "I don't want to leave just yet. I'm still having joy! Yes, I know I have all these problems, and some days are harder than others, but I still recognize you and I still love to be petted. I love my food and I can go out and relieve myself whenever I need to. I want to stay around. It's not my time yet!"

Then Zac told his parents what to look for so they'd know when he felt his time was close to the end. Leslie and her husband remained tuned in to the signs.

The last few days before his passing, Leslie could tell that Zac was failing but he was still eating and walking around the yard that he loved. His legs were getting weaker and he was unsteady on them, but he would still follow Leslie around to check on her. He was always connected with what was going on in his home.

The day before his passing, Leslie could see that he didn't have the usual spark in his eyes and that his "bingo" just wasn't there. He just seemed different, more quiet. He knew his family was there, but it was as if he also seemed to be somewhere else . . . transitioning?

Leslie slept on the floor with him most of the night to check on him and give him comfort.

During the night, she logged into Facebook where she found a posting about a dog's passing. The posting said that it was better to be a week early rather than a day late. This was a thought that really hit home with her.

Then, to pass the night, she chose one of her favorite books to re-read called Racing in the Wind. She'd forgotten that it opened with the dog in the book being old and wishing he could tell his owner he was sad that his legs didn't work well, and that he really didn't want to eat, but he kept going to please his owner whom he loved so much.

Even though Zac had said he still enjoyed his food, his legs weren't working well at all, so that thought also hit home with Leslie. She felt she really needed to pay attention to both of these signs from the Facebook posting and the book.

In the morning, Zac got up and went outside to go to the bathroom, then he came in and laid on his bed. He never moved off of it again. He slept, while occasionally opening his eyes to see what was going on.

Leslie knew it was time to call their vet of 30 years. There was no second guessing, and there were no regrets.

Was it an easy decision? NO! It was hard, and she and her husband cried and cried as they held Zac and petted him. Friends he was close to also came over to be with him. Zac then passed peacefully with the help of their veterinarian.

Although his family misses him so much, they do have the comfort of knowing, from his communications with me, that Zac was right when he told them it was not time for him to leave any earlier. They also have peace of mind knowing they made the right decision for him at exactly the right time, just as he wished.

Wilfork

Even if you're not ready, it's time

Wilfork was an 8-year-old black lab who was terminally ill. As I connected with him, he asked me to choose a particular picture instead of the one I was ready to select. He said, "I'm nothing without Dad, and to use this picture would mean that this is the way I want Dad to remember me . . . always together, always happy!"

He then continued to say, "I'm proud of Dad for allowing himself to have the opportunity to hear directly from me, and for being brave and receptive to this new avenue of communication. I'm ready to tell him the truth. I won't hold back."

This was our conversation as I asked Wilfork the questions his dad had prepared . . .

Do you know how much we all love you?

I do, because I've been trying all my life to be a lovable being, to give love, and allow myself to receive love. I think that's the best thing I can say about myself. I *am* love. My life's mission is to be lovable.

I've tried to embody love so everyone who knows me and meets me can't do anything but love me. I do that in order to teach others that not all dogs are scary, not all black dogs are mean, not all big dogs are aggressive. We are, and can be, loving, gentle, and easy going, just like me.

Are you in severe pain or suffering?

I am. Usually I wouldn't even respond to this question because I have a lot of dignity, and because I'm very stoic. But it's obvious now, and I'm not going to lie. Yes, I'm in pain. Yes, it's been difficult. Yes, I'm suffering now.

Do you want us to keep fighting for you or put you to rest?

You've done so much already! I wouldn't know what else to ask you to do, so I won't. All I know is that nothing has worked and I can't hold on much longer.

Do you know that we want to keep fighting for you?

I know this, better than you think. And it's because I know you, Dad, that I haven't been able to make a decision to leave. I've been holding on to life with everything I can. I also know that I can't leave until you give me permission, or until you accept that leaving is best for me. I'm not going to get better, Dad. You need to know this.

Do you want us to let you go?

As difficult as this may be for you to hear, I think the time has come for us to part. My body can't take it much longer. I'm not hungry anymore. My mouth is hurting, my nose is hurting, my head is hurting. My body can no longer function the way I want it to. You can't keep going the way you're going, picking me up like a baby. It's just beneath my dignity. I can't handle this. It hurts me to think that I was once so vibrant and happy and could do everything, and now I can barely lift my head.

Do you know how sorry Dad is for not noticing the cancer earlier?

You shouldn't be sorry about that! I told you I'm stoic, and I didn't complain. No one wants a whining dog! It was my decision not to complain, so you shouldn't blame yourself for not seeing it sooner.

Is there anything we can do to make you more comfortable?

Unfortunately, nothing you can do makes me more comfortable. I do like having you there with me, touching me, telling me what a good dog I am, and was. I enjoy your love even when you don't have anything to say. Just the touch of your hand tells me everything.

Is there any place you want to go?

No, not anymore. I need to be home with you. I need to feel loved.

What can we give you that you want to eat?

This is the thing, Dad. I can no longer eat anything. Everything hurts too much. I can't bite into anything, I can't swallow, and my tummy doesn't feel like it's hungry at all. I'm no longer enjoying food . . . and that's saying something!

Do you know you've been the best dog to Dad and that I'm so thankful to have you in my life?

Yes, I know. And do you know you've been the best Dad for me? And do you know how thankful I've been to be able to share my life with the one human I was supposed to find? That's right. I knew you were mine since the first minute I laid my nose on you. I knew you were going to be my human and I knew I was here to find you, and I did. No one will take that away from me. I am, and have been, the happiest dog in the world.

Do you know that Dad doesn't want to let you go?

Yes, but the end is coming soon. If you can't help me, it will be up to me, but I'd really like to hear from you first that it's ok for me to go. I want so much to please you, even now. However, I do have one request . . . if I'm dying, whether with help or without, I want you to be next to me, touching me, loving me. It would be sad if I were to have to do it all on my own. That's all I want, that's all I need . . . to have you love me until we say goodbye.

The messages Wilfork had for his dad were difficult for him to hear, but having had this conversation did make it easier for his dad to honor Wilfork's wishes.

The stories in this chapter have all shown how important it can be to talk with pets when they're experiencing pain, or having a lot of discomfort toward the end of their lives. The pets themselves may be able to tell us when it's too soon, or when it will soon be too late.

And most importantly, they can tell us whether we can or can't do anything else to help them. Their guidance may be just what a pet parent needs to be able to make that very important final decision.

Thoughts About Letting Go

Being ready to release our pets when they need to leave is always so difficult to do, but looking at their leaving from a different perspective sometimes helps.

I recently heard it expressed this way during a show I saw on television. The words were spoken by the captain of a space ship during a mission in the distant future. He was speaking at a memorial service for two crew members when he said:

> *The body is a shell, a vessel, within which we carry our spirit. When that vessel shatters, our life continues, released from the constraints of terrestrial life, free to explore the vastness of the heavens and return to the stars from which our lives first sprang.*

Henry van Dyke also describes the continuity of life in a very comforting way in "A Parable of Immortality."

He writes:

> *I am standing upon the seashore. A ship at my side spreads her white sails to the morning breeze and starts for the blue ocean. She is an object of beauty and strength, and I stand and watch until at last she hangs like a speck of white cloud just where the sea and sky come down to mingle with each other. Then someone at my side says, "There! She's gone!"*

> *Gone where? Gone from my sight . . . that is all. She is just as large in mast and hull and spar as she was when she left my side, and just as able to bear her load of living freight to the place of destination. Her diminished size is in me, not in her. And just at the moment when someone at my side says, "There she goes!" there are other eyes watching her coming and other voices ready to take up the glad shout, "Here she comes!"*

It's so important to remember that our pets, and our human loved ones, are not just gone from our sight after they leave us. They're continuing on with their lives in a place that's filled with love and joy, and one that's so incredibly much more wonderful than anything they ever experienced while they were here on earth.

Once you've walked through the initial part of the grieving process, I hope that thoughts like these will then help you share their joy.

Chapter 17

COPING WITH GRIEF

Hana and Snow

Dreams do come true

When I'm communicating with a pet who's already in Spirit, it isn't necessary for the pet parents to be with me at the same time, but some people really do want to be present with me while I'm talking with their pet in Spirit. It's part of their healing process.

This was true for a family who'd lost their 12-year-old female German Shepherd named Hana in 2017.

When clients come in person to talk with their pets who've passed on, they're still in mourning. Their emotions are so intense that they're not likely to remember everything their pet has to say, or all the questions they want to ask their pet.

That's why I always ask my clients to prepare a list ahead of time with the questions they want to ask, or any comments they may want to make. This helps them have a much more satisfying conversation with their pet because they're able to remember all the important things that are in their minds and hearts, and they don't forget to ask some of the key questions for which they want answers.

During the consultation, I also ask them to take notes, or even better, to use their cell phones to record the session so they can review it again later. This family did record the session, and it was very helpful for them later on.

When the time came for their appointment, a man, his wife, a young boy and a young girl, both under the age of 14, arrived in my consultation room. The family members were inconsolable, and they needed something, anything, to help them go on living without their beloved Hana.

While everyone was visibly upset, they were all open and interested in what Hana wanted me to tell them.

It was a very good communication and they received answers to their many questions. But one thing Hana told them was more important than anything else she had to say.

She told her family that to heal from their grief, they needed to share their love again with another pet after an appropriate length of time.

She told them she also knew exactly the soul who was coming to be their companion, if only they would be open to having a new pet. Additionally, she said she would find a way to let them know when the time was right.

A few months later I received an e-mail, full of excitement, telling me about a new puppy, and about a dream the little girl had had. This is what the mom wrote:

Hi Dr. Monica,

I hope all is well. I just wanted to give you an update. We got the new puppy!!! Here's what happened:

After the consultation, we kept our eyes and ears open looking for a dog to adopt.

HANA AND SNOW

One day, Jessica had a dream . . .

She was in our front yard and it was covered with snow! Then she noticed there was a white dog in the yard with the tail curled up. She was thinking, "This is our dog now."

When Jessica told us about this dream, we thought it was just a dream . . . because there is no snow where we live in southern California.

A week later, I found an internet post from someone who was trying to find a home for a puppy. It said, "8-week-old white Siberian Husky puppy. She has blue eyes, and is white as snow."

At that time I didn't connect this puppy to Jessica's dream. We just fell in love with the puppy's cute pictures, so we decided to adopt her. When we picked her up, I asked the previous owner if they'd already picked out her name.

He said " Oh, we just called her Snow Ball." !!!

It was more than a coincidence!

We then named this puppy Yuki because it means "Snow" in Japanese.

We believe that Hana kept her word to let us know when it was time, and sent this image to Jessica in a dream with the key word "Snow!"

I'd like to thank you for communicating all of Hana's messages to us. That was such a big relief for my family.

Without your consultation, I wouldn't have known what to do at all after losing her.

Now we're doing our best to give Yuki a wonderful life as a new member of this family.

And I'm sure Hana sometimes guides and educates this little girl.

Thank you again. I wish you the best.

The RS Family

Above: Snow Ball/Yuki

Indeed, Hana did keep her word, and the family's grief healed quickly when they were once again sharing their love with another pet.

Coping With Extreme Grief

I have many clients who've lost their best animal friend, often quite unexpectedly. Some are so consumed with grief over their loss that they even think of committing suicide just so they can be with their beloved pet again.

They think that if they die, they'll go to Spirit and immediately be reunited with their loved ones, pet or human. But this is a false impression. It's just *not* true in the case of suicide.

I've been given answers, time and time again, explaining that those souls who choose suicide *will* go back into Spirit, but the area where they'll spend their time will not be the same area where their pets are. Therefore, they won't be seeing each other anytime soon. Someone who commits suicide has special lessons to learn before they're ready to join with others again.

On the other hand, if those who grieve deeply will walk through the normal grieving process, and then continue to live life fully again until their normal time comes to go back to Spirit, *then* they'll be reunited with those they've loved.

The following excerpt is from an actual consultation (person and pet names have been omitted to protect her privacy) where the person had lost a beloved pet, and was so grief stricken as to consider suicide. It will help to illustrate some key points.

Client: It's so very painful. I want you back so I can pet you, tickle you, cook for you, buy presents for you, walk you, sleep with you, watch our favorite TV series together. I don't know how to live without you.

> Pet: I'm sorry you're missing me so much, but you need to know I'm next to you at all times. Actually I haven't been able to leave your side at all.
>
> It's mostly because you're so sad that I need to be next to you all the time. This is my job. I need to give you strength and to make sure you understand that my essence, my soul, is still with you.
>
> I'm in front of you when you're walking to guide your every step. I walk behind you to protect you and to be there when you need an extra push. And most of the time I'm next to you so that I can still be your friend and keep you company when you're sad.
>
> I know we can't do the same things we did before, but I can still hear you. It doesn't matter if you say it out loud or if you're just thinking about me and telling me things through your heart. I hear you and I feel what you feel, always.

Do you want me to die so we can be reunited? Because I don't mind dying.

> What a silly thing to say, Mom. No, because if you take your own life, we wouldn't be together again. Only if you complete your life cycle, then I can promise you that we will see each other again, and we can plan to come back together in another lifetime. That is the only way.

Is there something you want me to do for you to make you feel better?

> The only thing that would make me feel better is to know that in the not too distant future, you can think about me and smile. Laugh at the things I used to do to make you laugh, and remember all the good things we did together.

When you see my T-shirts, I want you to smile. When you're out and about and you see a dog that reminds you of me, I want you to smile. Yes, smiling when you think about me, and about the love we shared, would be the only thing you can do for me to make me feel better. And even if I know it's too soon to ask you to do it now, I know you'll be able to do it in the future.

What's next for you? What will you do?

To be honest with you, I'm a little stuck at the moment. I can't do anything else other than being with you to comfort you all the time. Your sadness is too great, and because we're connected by our love, my job right now is to be next to you for support.

I can't go and do anything else. But when the time is right, and you start smiling again, I'll be able to continue with my lessons and my journey to be able to evolve a little more and plan for the future.

Will I see you again?

You can count on that. I'll be the first in line, even before any of your relatives, to come to the edge of the light and say hello to your soul when your time to come back into Spirit is the right time, but not before.

In fact, I'll be visiting you at your bedside to tell you when it's time to go and telling you that you need to follow me. That would be my most important job, and I'll be here for you.

Would you like me to continue with my life?

You just have to do that if you want to eventually be in the same place I am. Otherwise you'll go to another place to learn your lessons, and it will be a place where I can't go.

You still have to continue to live, and you still have to give of yourself to others who need you.

Each good deed you do brings you closer to me. So, if you love me, that's the path you have to take so we can see each other again.

Please Mommy, know that I love you with all of my being, and the fact that I'm in Spirit doesn't diminish the love I have for you. On the contrary, I understand now that our love is eternal, and I'll love you forever and ever.

As you can see, suicide is not the answer to extreme grief. But what can you do in such a case to go on living when all you want to do is die so you can be with your beloved pet once again?

It will take a major adjustment in your thinking. It may seem impossible at the moment, but you eventually have to stop focusing on what you no longer have, and start focusing on all the love you still have to give.

You have to lift your consciousness up, look upward with your spiritual eyes, and stop looking inward at all the sadness and loss.

Oh, it won't happen right away, because you do have to walk through the grieving process. But if, in each moment you're aware of the sad thoughts, you then begin to look upward and outward . . . even just a little bit at a time . . . you'll soon discover joy and happiness coming back into your life, just as your beloved pet, or other loved one, wants for you.

Those who've passed on are in a wonderful place. They're doing just fine. They want you to do just fine, too. You don't respect their memory by being sad. You respect their memory by learning to be happy, and by continuing to love again, even if it's only for one brief moment at a time.

But how exactly can you do that, especially when you feel so sad and depressed?

Let me share with you some of the things I do to lift my consciousness up to Spirit. Maybe you'll find some of these ideas will help you, too.

I find it necessary to start my day with thoughts that put me in the right frame of mind and continue to guide me throughout the day.

I usually start my day with a daily prayer that goes like this:

I open my eyes so that I may see all things with vision and clarity.

I open my ears so that I may hear the wisdom of my ancestors, and all the angels, saints, and sages of all time, space, age, and dimensions.

I open my mouth so that I may speak with love, peace, joy, wisdom, knowledge, compassion, forgiveness, and understanding.

I open my heart so that I may love and be loved.

I open my arms so that I may receive the bountiful gifts of Divine Spirit.

Blessings upon me and all whom I encounter. Blessed be this day.

These are the truly important things to pray for. But more often than not, we're busy asking God to help us accomplish what we *think* we want at any particular moment.

Consider, for example, the soccer games my husband watches regularly. Every single player, from *both* teams, goes out onto the field, makes the sign of the cross, kisses his fingers, looks up into the sky, and then proceeds to run to the center of the field to start the game. Every single one of them, on *both* teams, is asking for *their* team to win the match.

How can God possibly answer everyone's prayers on that occasion? He can't. One team has to lose. And many times players get hurt, too.

Instead of always asking for what we *think* we want, wouldn't it be more beneficial to ask for the things that are expressed in the prayer above?

We also ceaselessly ask God to take away bad things we don't want, as if we think He's the one who caused us to experience them in the first place.

It's as if we're continually trying to get God to change His mind and give us what we want.

But . . . Spirit (God) is *changeless*. The only thing *He* ever wants for us is *everything good*. It's *we* who have chosen to participate in what we call the experience of good and evil.

He doesn't send good to some and evil to others. So why are we asking Him to "change his mind" when all He ever wants for us... or gives us... is good because that's the very nature of Spirit.

I've also been told over and over again that we choose our own path and we can change it as we go along. That's because God has given us free will. Having free will means we have the choice to change anything we want at any time. We can make the right choice. Or... we can make the wrong choice. The bottom line is that *we* make that choice, not anyone else.

So as you walk through the process of grieving, start with baby steps, but make the right choices:

- Forgive yourself
- Live in the now
- Get up and do something, meet someone, walk, run, play, write, listen to music, play a musical instrument
- Honor the memory of your loved one with even brief moments of joy and happiness
- Talk with your loved one in Spirit, out loud, or in your mind and heart
- Meditate
- Lift your consciousness up to Spirit many times a day
- Visit a shelter, volunteer, offer to walk or spend time with the animals
- Be aware of signs from your loved one because they're always sending you clues to say they're still there around you
- Know that you will see them again
- Adopt again... because continuing to love is one of the greatest gifts you can give to honor your pet's memory

Expressing gratitude is another way to lift our consciousness up to Spirit. Think about the wonderful day you're about to have, or about the wonderful day you've just experienced.

COPING WITH EXTREME GRIEF

At night, just before I go to bed, I say a simple thank you to "God," "Spirit," "All That Is," or whatever you choose to call It. And sometimes, when I'm not too tired, I even enumerate all the things I'm thankful for, starting with the people and animals who are part of my family or whom I've been talking with that day.

Being grateful for the things I have has helped me see more and more of the wonderful things around me. That's right, because I enumerate them, I'm always finding more and more things I can be thankful for. Some people even like to keep a gratitude journal where they keep a written record of all the wonderful things that have happened in their lives for which they're grateful.

Because I try to lift my consciousness upward and to maintain a sense of gratitude, I can say that I live with a greater sense of happiness, joy, and satisfaction than many people do. And you can, too!

On the other hand, I do understand why people who've lost a loved one sometimes stop believing there's a God who will come to their rescue, after they've prayed so continuously for the wellbeing of the one who just died. They've become so disillusioned from trying, ineffectively, to bring God down into their lives that they stop believing.

The solution is not to bring God down into our lives, but to lift our eyes up to God.

Grieving, sometimes deeply, is a normal part of losing a loved one, human or pet. So, if you ever find yourself immersed in deep, deep grief over the loss of a loved one, be gentle with yourself. No one is holding you in that place of grief except you. Just know that grieving *will* come to an end, and that you *will* be able to go on with your life.

As soon as you can, begin to lift your thoughts upward, for even just a very brief moment at a time. Know that when you do, you bring happiness to those who have gone before you. They're in such a place of joy that they want you to experience it, too. Think of finding joy and happiness and love again, not just for you, but for them, as a way to honor their memory!

Chapter 18

ALL ABOUT ANIMAL COMMUNICATION

Picture Telepathy

People often ask, "How do you do what you do? How in the world is it possible for you to know what animals are saying, thinking, wanting, and feeling?"

To answer that question, let's first look at the way animals communicate. In addition to using sounds and body language, animals also communicate with each other telepathically. Pictures *are* their language.

They're also always trying to get their points across to their humans by sending images to them. However, for people who haven't learned to communicate with animals, their pictures usually have to be accompanied by some very clear body language in order to get them to pay attention and comprehend what they're saying!

This way of communication, using images, is not new. It's been around for eons. We humans were also able to communicate with each other in times past, even over great distances, using telepathic communication.

The problem is, ever since humans started using spoken languages, most of us have forgotten how to use the language of pictures. But . . . we're all still capable of speaking that language if only we'd consciously practice it.

Some people, who are very sensitively attuned to each other, still communicate certain thoughts telepathically to one another in their daily lives today. That's because telepathic communications are simply messages sent and received without the use of any spoken words.

You've no doubt read about one twin knowing what the other twin is feeling or doing, even when they're separated by some distance. They've just telepathically conveyed their feelings to each other very clearly without speaking a single word.

Maybe a parent will suddenly come wide awake in the middle of the night knowing with certainty that his or her child, even an adult child, is in danger. This sometimes happens when the child has been in an accident or has suddenly become very ill. The child's first thought, regardless of age, is to think about Mom or Dad, even when they're at a great distance from each other, and their thoughts are telepathically delivered.

The point to understand is that telepathic communications still take place today between humans, between animals, and between animals and humans.

The name I've given to this type of communication is *Picture Telepathy*.

But how does it work, especially between animals and humans?

When a pet is "talking" to me, I'm receiving the pictures they're sending me. It's a bit like looking at snapshots in a photo album or watching a video.

I see what looks like individual photos or movie clips. The movie clips, which are always filled with some action, last for two or three seconds. Then, it's as if they rewind and repeat themselves until the pet is satisfied that I've understood what he or she is trying to tell me.

Whether I'm seeing a colorful single photo or a movie clip, those pictures are providing me with information that includes sights, sounds, colors, tastes, scents, and even feelings, emotions, expectations, needs, and wishes. I can experience all of these images in my own body so that I'm able to identify them and explain them to a pet parent.

In return, I send pictures to pets to ask questions, give them reassurance, provide guidance, explain what's happening in their lives when they don't understand (about medical problems, travel plans, why people are doing certain things, and so forth), or whatever it is that will help them.

We simply carry on a conversation by sending pictures back and forth to each other. I then translate the pictures into words so that they make sense to the animal's human companion.

PICTURE TELEPATHY

As you can see, I'm very visual, but other animal communicators who are more auditory will simply "hear" the same information.

Even for those of us who are visual, many times, once the flow of animal communication has started and the animals feel comfortable, they'll use an even more accurate and faster way of communicating. At this point, by telepathy, they may seem to be sending actual words, and even sentences, to convey their thoughts and feelings.

Most people want to know when I first recognized that I could communicate with animals. They also want to know much more about what I experience when I'm talking with them, as well as how I'm able to translate their pictures. I'll answer all of those questions for you in the next article.

Some Frequently Asked Questions and Answers

When did I first notice I had the ability to communicate with animals using picture telepathy?

For me, receiving pictures from animals came very naturally. My first experience communicating with animals happened when I was eight years old during a visit to a farm. The animals' comments and answers to my questions came to me so naturally that I thought they were talking, when in fact, my mind was simply translating their images into words.

Many people told me I was crazy when I said I knew what animals were saying, so for many years, I ignored my gift because I didn't want to be the object of their ridicule. But fortunately, when I was just a little older, others encouraged me to nurture my gift, and it soon became my life's work.

What kind of information do you receive from animals?

Often when I start a conversation with an animal, I don't know when the picture they're sending me was taken, or when a certain event happened, but I do know it was an important event in that animal's life.

The pictures come in accompanied by feelings and emotions. I may suddenly be cold or even shivering. I may feel really stressed and want to move around, or I'll sense that I have a fear of heights, or I have a fear of other animals.

SOME FREQUENTLY ASKED QUESTIONS AND ANSWERS

I may momentarily experience other physical sensations as well. I'll cough because an animal is trying to tell me something is wrong with his throat, or I'll burp because he's telling me a certain food doesn't agree with his stomach, or I'll suddenly develop a headache or some other physical pain I didn't have before I started our conversation.

I'm *not* a veterinarian so I can never make a diagnosis, but I can feel a pet's pain in my body. I can then translate what I'm feeling, where it hurts, and how intense the pain is. These translations have often helped veterinarians and chiropractors move forward in the right direction when they're trying to treat an animal.

How easily am I able to translate what animals tell me?

Every animal is different, just as humans are different. Some communicate very well, while others hardly send enough of a picture to be able to understand what they want to say. Over the years, I've been able to quickly assess who's going to communicate easily, and who's going to pose more of a challenge.

Most of the time, a pet's pictures are clear enough for me to be able to give a direct translation. However, there are those times when I have to draw on my own personal life experience in order to translate what the pet is trying to tell me.

When I translate the information a pet has shared with me, I might say "he or she is saying . . . , or your pet is showing me . . . , or these are his or her words."

At other times when pets show me only images, or simply let me experience their feelings or energy, I then have to use my own words, life experiences, and vocabulary to describe those images and feelings.

But always, I'll be sure that you understand the difference between what your pet is actually saying, and what I'm having to describe using my own words and experiences.

For example, not long ago, a client asked her dog to tell me something about his previous home. Yes, it was a test question, and I do get a lot of those.

The pet's picture showed me houses that were right next to each other as if there were no backyards. Because I didn't know how to describe exactly what I was seeing, I had to draw from my own past experience.

I recalled a trip I took once to Henderson, Nevada. What I noticed more than anything else was that the houses were close together and all white.

Based on the pet's picture, and using my own past experience, I gave the client the best translation I could, telling her I was seeing what appeared to be many white houses with no yards. She then told me they used to live in a complex of 297 apartments, all painted white!

In another example, a dog was asked by her owner why she wouldn't allow her to touch her paws. Again, I had to use my own feelings and life experiences in order to arrive at a good translation.

When I reached out to the dog with her mom's question, instead of telling me she was just sensitive about having her paws touched, as most dogs would have done, she sent me a feeling.

As it traveled through me, my mind associated the pet's feeling with the feeling I get when I go to the nail salon for a pedicure. They use an instrument that scrapes the soles of your feet and I can't stand that sensation. It makes me so uncomfortable that I'm always either pulling my feet away or telling the person to stop all together.

When I shared this analogy with my client, she understood my explanation immediately, telling me she also feels exactly the same way.

And now, she understood what her dog might be feeling whenever she tried to touch her pet's paws. Her dog didn't like that sensation.

In the above example, there was only one sensation for me to experience. Other times, though, I'll experience a whole myriad of sensations or emotions that come in all at once.

I can feel what the pets are feeling, I can smell the food they're eating, or I can hear something they're hearing. All of these feelings that I receive, combined with the pictures they're sending, make it easier for me to translate what they want you to know.

SOME FREQUENTLY ASKED QUESTIONS AND ANSWERS

Speaking of hearing, I'm not only talking about things that make loud noises. Sometimes people sounds can also be extremely annoying to animals.

One time, a cat who'd gone missing told me he left on purpose because the people in his home were arguing and he didn't want to be around that kind of energy any longer.

My client confided to me that her brother, who was staying with her, came home drunk one night and they'd had a big argument. In the morning the cat was gone. I never asked, but I had the feeling this most recent incident was not the first time.

My client wanted me to tell her cat she was sorry and this wouldn't happen again because she'd already told her brother to move out. She promised to do better, to love her cat more, and to put his needs first.

Her cat wouldn't hear of it. He absolutely didn't want to go back home, so he became the neighborhood cat. I subsequently talked with him for six months. He was always in the neighborhood, and he regularly visited every single house in the cul-de-sac, but he never went back to his own home.

The answers to the questions in this article have shown you some of the techniques I have to use to translate animal's pictures when their meaning isn't all that clear. They also show how much sensory information animals can provide to help with those translations.

Now that you've become more familiar with some of the elements of picture telepathy, and you better understand how animals and I communicate with each other, in the next article, we'll explore some of the even more unique ways in which they send pictures to me.

Puzzles, Images, and PTSD Reactions

Sometimes, when animals have many things to tell me, they start sending me pictures one after the other in rapid succession. In these cases, it's very difficult to translate the entirety of each picture, so I have to do a fast and broad translation. Or, I can ask them specific questions. When I do, they usually slow down, concentrate on one thing at a time, and give me enough information so that I'm able to provide a more in-depth translation of each picture.

Other times when they want to send me a lot of information, it looks as if my inner TV screen has up to nine to twelve squares on it, and each square has a picture from the pet. That's when I say it's like having to put a **puzzle** together because I have to figure out which picture comes first, and in what order the rest of them follow. Those instances are challenging, but fortunately I love puzzles!

Then there are those times when an animal is trying to convey a complex concept and I'll see two pictures, side by side, sometimes with what seems to be conflicting information.

When I see a **split picture** like this, it often means animals are asking for something they used to get, but are not currently receiving. Maybe there'll be a favorite treat in the picture on the left, and no treat in the picture on the right. Maybe they've enjoyed a hike in the past, and would like to go again.

PUZZLES, IMAGES, AND PTSD REACTIONS

The picture on the left will show the pet walking on a trail, while the picture on the right will show the pet lying on the sofa feeling totally bored.

To come up with an accurate translation for split pictures, it occasionally requires some input from the client. Usually, when I describe both pictures, a client knows exactly what the pet is talking about, and he or she can help complete the translation accurately.

Other times, I might think I'm seeing a split picture at first, but it's so complicated that I have difficulty making any sense of it. Even when I try to ask the same question several times, the new answers still don't make any sense. That's when I realize I may be talking with a pet whose brain isn't functioning normally.

In these cases, I often perceive more of a sense that something is different, **unusual**, or just plain wrong.

This was true for Kismet in the story about her 180 first dates with Dad.

I knew something in her pictures was off. She was sending me images, but they were not the usual type of images I receive from pets.

In one of her pictures, she asked me who the man was who was sitting in front of me. It seemed as if, at that moment, she didn't recognize her own dad.

Her other picture showed her looking at her dad, but she had a queasy feeling in her gut and she definitely wanted to move away from him. She also had a questioning look on her face.

At first, I couldn't find the words to express what she was showing me. Then I put it all together. She truly didn't know who her dad was *at that moment*! And possibly she was mixing him up with someone else.

These pictures, along with the many others she sent me during our consultation, helped me understand that she was suffering from a neurological problem caused by prior abuse before she was adopted by her new family.

This condition was causing her to experience short term memory loss. Every morning, she couldn't recognize her dad, but later in the day she seemed to know and really love him. Fortunately, with a lot of love, patience, and time, her condition eventually began to improve.

Sometimes I recognize that pets have neurological problems when they can't, or won't, answer any of my questions. Instead, they say something inappropriate, or it's as if they're in a mental fog and don't understand what communication is.

Other times, I encounter animals with ADHD. They're so hyper their images are **scattered** all over the place in such a way that I don't have enough time to respond to each picture. I ask them to slow down so we can talk back and forth, but they just can't.

These animals usually appear outwardly very calm during the consultation, and you wouldn't know, just by looking at them, that there's anything wrong with them, or that there's such intense activity going on in their brains, but the images they're sending tell me the true story.

I've also had the opportunity to talk to several dogs who suffer from **PTSD**, often because something happened at the hands of a human. Many times loud noises such as fireworks also generate this type of response again and again. In these cases, the pictures and feelings I'm receiving show me that the pet feels sick to his stomach so that all he wants to do is curl up in a ball and hide.

Sometimes these conditions can be reversed through desensitizing an animal over many days or months, but first it's important to know what's causing the problem. That's where animal communication can help.

I mentioned above that there are times when I need some additional input from a pet parent in order to complete a translation. We'll explore more about that in the next article.

When Pet Parents Help to Complete the Translation

Marley, Puppet, and Runaway

People often think every picture animals send me is crystal clear, or that I'm easily able to describe every single picture and feeling I receive. As you've already discovered in previous articles, this isn't always true.

Many pictures are clear and direct. Others, not so much.

Even when some pictures are a little less clear, I'm usually able to translate those images using the right words. I can do this if the pictures make me remember an event or feeling I've had before, or if they make me remember something I went through that I can relate to, especially something as uncomfortable as pain.

But I've learned over many years that some pictures are just too vague for me to translate completely without having at least some additional information.

Because many people are skeptical, I don't like to ask questions while I'm translating their animal's pictures and feelings. That way they can be sure I'm not just repeating something they've already told me.

Occasionally, though, I do need some help from my clients to complete a translation. This is particularly true if I'm not privy to some essential information that's necessary in order to complete the explanation of a pet's picture.

These are just a few examples of that type of consultation...

Marley

Rick and Stella came to see me with Marley and her sister Sasha. Marley is a mixed breed rescue, part Golden, part Spitz, and part Lab. She's now about eight years old and has adapted very well to her new family. She watches them intently as she tries to understand them and read their intentions.

The minute she came into my consultation room she remembered me from years before and was very happy to be here because she knew she was going to be able to express her feelings.

We were almost finished when Dad asked Marley, "Why did you act so strangely the other night? You were supposed to get on the bed, but instead you ran down the hall and went straight to the kitchen. You sat down and you just looked at me. What were you trying to say?"

It was hard for me to get a clear picture from Marley, so I told Dad the best way I could translate it was, "Did you forget something?"

Dad then told me he always goes into the kitchen every night to set up the coffee pot for the next morning, but he'd forgotten to do that. Marley then ran into the kitchen to remind him.

That was exactly the information I needed to complete the translation of the picture Marley had sent me . . . and we all a good laugh!

Puppet

The first thing Puppet talked about was her sister, Pirate. She said Pirate smelled strange and that smell made Puppet worry that something was very wrong.

Mom explained that Pirate was at home recovering from surgery to remove a growth that was possibly cancerous. She also said Puppet had been smelling her like crazy.

Another thing Puppet told us was that she was missing the ice cream she enjoyed so much. It had been a long time since she'd had some.

Mom then told me that Auntie used to make ice cream just for the dogs, but hadn't done so for a long time. Auntie then promised to make some for them today.

Those two pictures were quite clear, but another picture was much less so. Puppet showed me her open back door. She was looking at the screen door, but not moving, just looking at it with a puzzled look on her face. I had to tell her mom I wasn't sure how to translate that picture, but when I described it to her, I said it looked to me as if Puppet was saying, "What's wrong with this screen?"

Mom started laughing along with Auntie. The screen they have is a magnetic one that consists of two separate pieces of mesh screen held together in the center with small magnets.

She said that very often Puppet stands at the back door without moving. She doesn't like to push through the screen using her head. Other times, she'll push her head through the screen, only to stand there with her head on the outside and her body still on the inside.

It was their clarification that helped to complete the translation. The description of Puppet, with her body on both sides of the screen, is an image I won't soon forget!

Runaway – An Example of Split Images

I talked with a little Pomeranian named Runaway who was now in Spirit. She sent me a split image. On one side was a baby with a lock of hair being cut. On the other side, I saw a picture of Runaway with a hand holding a pair of scissors cutting her hair.

I told the human I wasn't sure what this double image meant. The best translation I could think of was that someone had cut the dog's hair and then put it in a locket. That thought came to me because I'd done the same thing when my children were little.

The human turned to me with a smile and confirmed, "Yes! I did that. Her lock of hair is sitting next to her ashes right now."

As you can see from these examples, not every picture a pet sends me lends itself to a clear and immediate translation. What I can translate from the less clear pictures is usually quite accurate, but just not complete.

However, when the translation becomes a team effort, and a pet parent provides the connecting information, then we all know clearly what the pet is trying to say. Sometimes the message is touching, and other times it gives everyone a good laugh!

Conveying Difficult Information

Not all communications are warm and fuzzy. I have to be ready for whatever a pet tells me, but I never want to have to say something that would hurt the client's feelings.

Sometimes that makes it difficult to find the right words to translate an animal's pictures, but I do have to be honest about what animals are showing me, even if the message may be difficult for their humans to hear.

One day I was doing an interview for a local radio station in Argentina that also used internet radio. Listeners could send in pictures of their pets and ask questions in real time.

The DJ selected the animals for me to communicate with. His first pick was a dog who had died suddenly. The humans were upset and asking what happened to him.

When I connected with this dog, he told me in no uncertain terms that his death could have been prevented. In fact, this was one of the few times when I actually "heard" a voice saying just that.

That's right. I actually heard the words. I usually just see pictures. It's very rare for me to "hear" anything. The only times this has happened are when animals have been very adamant about what they needed to have me understand.

All I could do in this case was state exactly what the pet had said.

There was a moment of silence on the other end of the line and then a sob. The woman explained that both she and her husband had been at work all day long. When they got home, they were both so totally exhausted that they decided to wait until the next day to take the dog to the vet, even though the dog was showing some obvious signs of pain. Sadly, the dog passed on during the night.

The clients then said the dog was right. His death could have been prevented if only they'd gone to see the vet that evening.

During a consultation with a different client under totally different circumstances, I had to convey another sad message.

I talked with a female Newfoundland who was 14 years old. She could no longer move her back legs and she was spending almost the whole day on the patio all by herself.

This is the most important part of what she had to say:

I'm very sad because nobody loves me anymore. My mom adored me when I was young but now, she doesn't even come out to talk to me. It hurts to believe she thinks I don't need her anymore, just when I need her twice as much as before.

It's difficult to live without being able to move my body, and it's worse because I can't be next to my humans. That's why I'm very, very sad.

Mom, I still need to feel that I'm part of the family, but instead, I feel like a statue you look at every once in a while. You don't come out to see me, touch me, or talk to me unless it's absolutely necessary.

It's difficult for me to see how much you've changed over time. Why did you stop loving me? I gave you everything!

I need you to look at me. I need you to treat me like a living being who feels, who loves, and who needs your tenderness and your understanding.

CONVEYING DIFFICULT INFORMATION

> I've been thinking about dying for a number of days now because the truth is I don't experience happiness anymore.
>
> It's become more and more difficult not being able to share my life and my days with my family.
>
> When someone is not happy as I'm not happy now, it's time to say goodbye.
>
> I'm not opposed to having help to be able to go back to Spirit. My body is useless and I have no hope of a cure. My heart is broken.

My heart was broken, too. It was difficult to feel what this wonderful dog was feeling, and to have to share this sad message with the clients. But it was the information they needed to hear in order to make that important final and loving decision for their pet.

The husband, with whom I was having the consultation, told me his wife had had this dog since she was a teenager. She just couldn't cope with the fact that her dog was dying, so she was unable to bring herself to go out to the patio to see her except on very rare occasions. The feeding, petting, and cleaning were all left up to him.

He was certain the time had come, but he first wanted to know how their dog felt, so he contacted me. After our conversation, he and his wife took their beloved Newfie to the vet where she was helped to peacefully make her transition into Spirit.

When a pet is talking to me about something as sensitive as the end of life, it becomes a special moment for the pet, the client, and for me.

Even though I've been conveying difficult information for a very long time, and I do know how to center myself, there are times when I become emotional as well.

So during a consultation, don't worry if you need to express your feelings, because sometimes the only thing left to do is just cry. Cry hard, cry long, but then do as your pet requests. It's the best gift you can give them.

The Do's and Don'ts of a Consultation

How much or how little should you tell me ahead of time?

For my usual communications with animals, I only want to know the most basic pieces of information before we have a conversation: name, age, sex, breed, how long the pet has been with you, location (if remote), and a very *general* idea of what you want to talk about.

When I say *general*, I mean exactly that. You might tell me you want to talk about behavioral problems, health concerns, interactions with other animals, loss of another pet in the family, or end-of-life wishes. Or, you might say you just want to check in with your pet to see how he or she is doing, and if your pet has any special needs or wishes.

You'll also want to provide me with a list of the questions, comments, and concerns you want your pet to talk about, but please, express them only in *general* terms. We can talk about the specifics after I've heard what your pet has to say.

Why is it so important for you to give me so little information up front?

Both you and I want to be sure the information I'm receiving is coming directly from your pet and is not influenced by something you've already told me.

THE DO'S AND DON'TS OF A CONSULTATION

I don't want to know specific details ahead of time because I want our communication to be clear, and free from any pre-existing thoughts you may have given me.

After I tell you what your pet has told me, then I very much enjoy learning about anything specific you want to share with me, especially if it confirms what your pet has already talked about.

For that reason, your questions should not reveal any specific details, especially about a behavioral problem or a health challenge. This way, both you and I can be certain that any information I receive is truly coming from your pet.

What NOT to do

To illustrate what NOT to do, consider what happened with one of my clients.

Her dog had died and she wanted me to connect with her in Spirit. She was concerned that they'd made the decision to euthanize her too soon. Daisy hadn't been eating and she was repeatedly vomiting even after undergoing many, many tests and treatments. However, the doctors had never been able to pinpoint a definite reason for her illness. My client's hope was that her dog could give her some insight from Spirit about why she'd been so sick and whether or not there was anything else they could have done to help her.

That information alone was all I should have been given ahead of time, but in her e-mail to me, this client gave me ten whole paragraphs of *minutely detailed* descriptions of *every* event and *every* result (or lack of result) of *every* vet visit, hospitalization, test, and treatment the dog underwent for an entire month or more.

I now had such a complete account in front of me that, even if I were to receive some information directly from Daisy, the client would have no way of knowing whether I'd actually received the information from the pet or whether I was telling her something she'd already told me.

So at the risk of repeating myself . . . less information is always better to start with.

When would more information actually be needed?

There are those times when I do need more information before I connect with a pet, but when that happens in the case of a remote consultation, I'll e-mail you back to tell you specifically what I need, depending on the situation we're dealing with.

I do sometimes need specific information in order to have an effective communication, but I still will not ask you for information that will reveal anything I shouldn't know ahead of time.

HERE ARE SOME GOOD EXAMPLES:

When a pet died unexpectedly or too young

In the past, I didn't ask any questions ahead of time when I was doing this kind of communication, but lately I feel that I get a much better response if I at least know when a pet died, and from what . . . an accident, a brief illness, a prolonged illness, or a genetic condition they were born with.

Because every animal is different, I never know what kind of information I'll be getting from them. For that reason, it's sometimes important for me to know just a little bit more up front so I can ask the right questions, especially if the pet is not very forthcoming.

For example, the questions I need to ask if a pet dies in an accident are very different from the questions I need to ask if a pet dies as the result of an illness or a genetic condition.

In the case of an accident, the feelings the pet sends me will be very recent. In the case of an illness or genetic condition, I may be receiving feelings from the pet that happened over a shorter or longer period of time.

Also, depending on the reason for the pet's death, it may be important to ask questions about their life's mission, and even about the possibility that they may want to reincarnate.

THE DO'S AND DON'TS OF A CONSULTATION

So, if I know just a little something ahead of time about the cause of death, it will help me put the whole picture together more quickly and accurately. However, please, let me be the one to ask for just the information that would be helpful for me to have ahead of time.

When you need to ask questions that could be about people or animals

Another time I'll need more information is when you need to ask questions about people or animals whom I don't know.

Your questions initially may be something like this:

- How do you feel about Sasha, Donna, Eric, and Joe?
- Are you happy living with Amma and Acha?
- Would you rather spend time with Linda or Phil?
- Are you OK when Brian is walking you?

In the cases above, I need to know:

- Do the names belong to a human or an animal?
- Is that human or animal living with your pet, or not?
- If not, are they neighbors, playmates, or other?
- Most important, would your pet recognize that name?

When I need to clearly identify people so the pet knows with certainty whom you're talking about

Animals talk about their owners and describe them in various ways. I've been told:

- They're my humans
- They're my roomates
- He/She's my partner

- She's my Mom
- He's my Dad
- He's my playmate
- He's my boss
- She's Mommy
- He's Plan B (as in the story by that name)

When you formulate a question you want me to ask your pet, you need to be very specific about names you use. You may call yourself Mom or Dad, but when you call, talk to, or refer to your husband, wife, or significant other, you might not use that term at all. Instead, you might use proper names. I need to know that, because otherwise your pet may not be able to recognize the person I'm talking about.

When you want to give your pets a choice

In another type of situation, you may want to give your pets a choice, for example, identifying which dog waker they like best. I would then need to know the difference between one dog walker and another so I can send the pet clear pictures. For example, one has blond hair and the other one has short black hair.

Always remember that I'm asking the question by sending an image, and if my image is not specific, then I may not receive the right answer.

When someone asks for the impossible

Because I am able to communicate with animals, people sometimes think I can see specific things even if they don't give me any information ahead of time, or give me any questions to ask at all.

For instance, they're *hoping* their pet will describe the other two pets in the family, and then describe how he gets along with each of them, but they don't want to tell me that this is what they want to know. They think I'll just automatically pick up that information.

If an animal's relationship with other animals in the family is something the pet actually wants to talk about himself, he might give me that information when I ask if he has anything he wants to say first.

But, if that's not important to him to talk about on his own, then I need to know what the question is that the humans want to have answered so I can pose that question to their pet. Otherwise, they may not receive any answer to what they want to know at all. I can't translate what I don't see, and if it's not important to your pet, then he won't tell me about it.

An animal living on earth may have no problem showing me who the other members of the family are, and how he gets along with them, but not many animals in Spirit are able to describe the breed or sex of other pets. Instead, they may describe another animal's energy as being more demure or more macho, even if it doesn't match the other animal's actual gender.

For them, many times a pet is a pet, a dog is a dog, and a cat is just a cat. It's a little like trying to ask a two year old about his Asian friend or his Spanish friend. All he sees is a friend with a name. That's it. He can't see any difference in the color of his skin or the shape of his eyes. It's just his friend. The same is true for our animals.

Lost Pets

When a client requests a consultation to help locate a lost pet, there are many things I need to know ahead of time. All of those questions are listed on my website so that a client requesting that kind of help will know exactly what information to provide right away. You'll also find many of those questions in the stories in the chapter about Lost Pets.

You're invited to visit my website where you can learn much more at **www.petcommunicator.com.**

Now that you understand some of the dos and don'ts about animal communication, let's also take a look at the kinds of pet pictures that work and don't work. I'll explain more about that in the next article.

Pictures

The good, the bad, and the useless

Pictures are the main thing I use to be able to communicate remotely with animals. Clients are welcome to send me as many as they like.

The pictures need to be very recent ones. I feel what the animal feels, so if an animal is sick today, but I receive a picture from a year or more ago when the pet was healthy, it's very difficult for me to feel what the pet is feeling today.

At least one picture needs to clearly show the eyes, and at least one needs to show the whole body. I meet the animal by seeing the eyes first. Doing that helps me connect with them. The full body gives me an idea about how big they are, and many times it helps me assess personality traits.

It's always best to have a picture of the animal all by itself. If clients submit pictures of themselves with their pet, or pictures of the pet with other animals or people, I then have to crop those pictures so there will be no distractions.

If a client sends me several pictures, I review all of them and then select the one that makes it the easiest to connect with the pet, but sometimes a pet will tell me I should choose a different picture instead. The reasons vary.

One pet told me she just didn't look her best in the picture I'd chosen, while another told me to use the one where he was out in the field. He liked that one best because it showed how much he enjoyed nature.

PICTURES

There's one exception to needing a recent picture. If an animal has passed into Spirit, a picture when the pet was at his or her best is then preferable. After animals make their transitions, they never show me their tired or sick bodies. Instead, they'll show me the best of them when they were younger, happier, and healthier.

As you can see, pictures are very important to me for communicating remotely with animals on earth or in Spirit, so I'm going to share with you some examples of pictures that are very helpful, and some that couldn't be used at all. You'll easily be able to see the difference.

Pictures that are NOT helpful:

Yula, an 18-year-old gray cat, hiding under the sofa

Needless to say, I can't ascertain anything from this picture, other than the fact that she likes to hide there.

Hudson wearing a hunting hat, plus a beret

When I first saw this picture, it was confusing. I thought Hudson had long ears when, in fact, he has pointed ones. Because they were covered by the hunting hat that happens to be the same color as his fur, I didn't have a true picture of who this dog is.

PICTURES

Luna sitting on a bed

Not only is she too far away from the camera, but she may even be facing away from it. Her fur is so dark that it's impossible to see her eyes at all, even if she were facing the camera.

Mary

If you study this picture carefully, you can see that her mouth is open (to the right) and the tip of her tongue is the normal pink color. But there are all sorts of problems with this picture. The shade lines are distracting, the background is very cluttered, and because the picture has been taken from above, it doesn't clearly show the pet's eyes. Only one eye is visible, and from an odd angle at that.

Additionally when I first saw this picture, I thought she was bleeding from her mouth, but the red color I thought I was seeing was actually another pink part of her tongue.

The white color on her mouth was the result of a large patch of very bright sunlight shining directly on her. The interruption of a shade line through the bright white, allowed another part of her pink tongue to show through as red, which made it look at first as if there was blood coming out of her mouth. Most confusing.

PICTURES

Ms. Blue

I'm sure that Ms. Blue enjoys looking through the window at twilight, but, once again, this picture isn't useful for communicating with her at all because it's so dark and it doesn't clearly show her eyes.

Irish

This is Irish with her Mom. At the time this picture was taken, she was still at the breeders and was just 5 weeks old, but I was trying to establish communication with her when she was already 2 years old and was now a full grown Curly Coated Retriever who weighed 75 pounds!

PICTURES

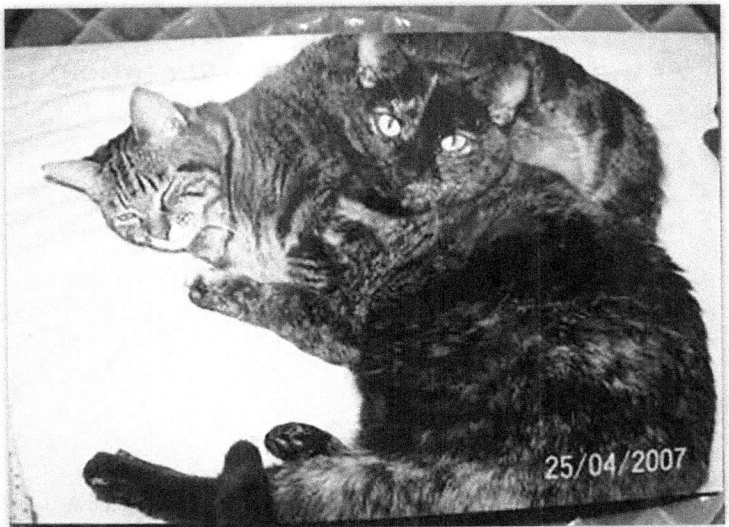
Two sisters

Beautiful picture, right? The only problem: it was date stamped 2007 and I was doing the consultation in 2018!

I could fill an entire album with pictures like these, but these examples will show you what NOT to submit for your consultation with a pet.

Now, here are some samples of pictures that really help with effective communications:

Angel, 1 ½-year-old male

This is an excellent view of his eyes and a very good view of his body. Eventually, though, I cropped this picture to remove everything in the background. That way I was able to concentrate just on his face.

PICTURES

Cadence, 4-year-old female

The look on her face was caused by stress, which is the very reason we needed to talk. Fortunately, the clients were able to capture a picture of her at the exact moment she was expressing her concerns.

Martina, 8-year-old female

I can clearly see her eyes and her whole body, which helped me have a good connection with her to find out why she was so sick. Even though it looks as if she was playing with her ball, the client explained that even when they tried to engage her in play, she would just stand there and look at the ball without running after it.

PICTURES

Rocky, 11-year-old male

This is a good full body picture showing his eyes. He was so very sick that he passed on just a few days after this picture was taken.

Asian, 2-year-old male

This is an example of an acceptable picture because I can see his eyes and full body. However, I did have to crop this picture so I wouldn't be distracted by his brother, as well as by the dining table in the background.

PICTURES

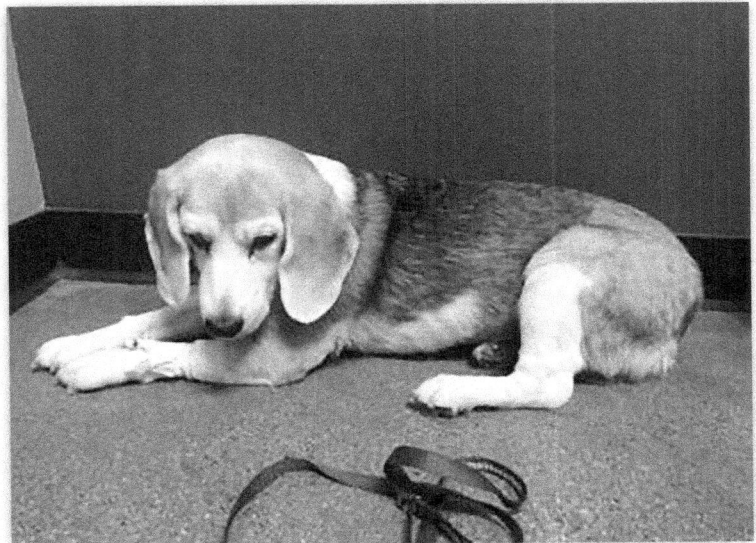

Cali, 11-year-old female

Even though I can't clearly see her eyes, this is an acceptable picture taken when she was very, very sick. When I first saw this picture I thought for sure she was going to pass very soon.

However, during our communication, she said there was a bigger story behind what was happening to her. The client did a lot of research and then found an acupuncturist who was able to help her recover from acute pancreatitis. She's now made a complete recovery.

Kiwi, 4 1/2-month-old female Senegal parrot

Birds can't usually be photographed clearly showing both eyes because their eyes are so far apart, but this picture is close to being perfect, even though I can see only one of her eyes. It's also helpful that the background is light and clear.

I really appreciate the fact that the clients actually opened the cage to take this picture instead of sending me one taken of Kiwi inside the cage with the cage wires showing in front of her.

PICTURES

Luna, 9-year-old female now in Spirit

Perfect! This picture was taken in the place she loved most when she was looking her best. She actually told me to use this one instead any of the many others her mom had sent me.

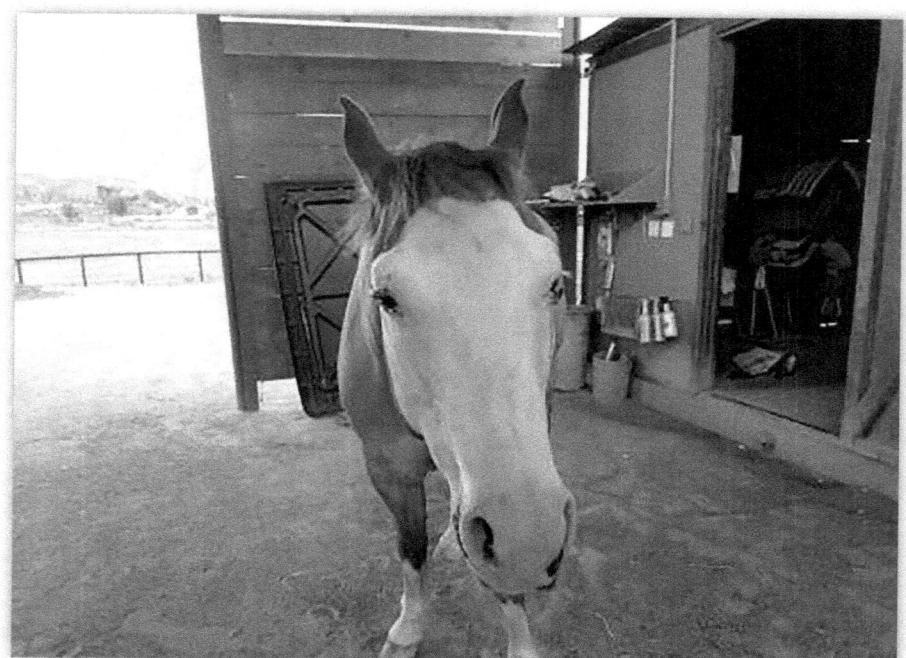

Pancho, 23-year-old male horse

This picture is very good because, even though horses have eyes that are far apart, my clients managed to get both eyes into the picture and still have it be a reasonably close-up view. They also sent me another picture of his full body, so between the two pictures, I had everything I needed to establish a good connection with him.

PICTURES

Pupito, 7-year-old male rabbit, now in Spirit

It took me a moment to realize that Pupito, the white bunny, was sitting next to a statue of a brown bunny. Once that became clear to me, then this was a very effective picture to use.

Being able to see a pet's eyes and full body is so important that I wanted to be sure you understand some of the finer details about picture taking.

Remember, the eyes are the windows of the soul, and for me, seeing them is indispensable for knowing how pets feel. The better the pictures you take, the better the information I'll be able to give you.

What About Skeptics?

I'm one, too!

It's not at all unusual for me to encounter skeptics in my line of work. Some people will say something to me very directly right away, and some won't, but it's still pretty obvious how they feel at first.

I don't mind skeptics at all because if I were in their shoes I'd be one of the biggest skeptics around until I experienced something that convinced me otherwise.

Those who directly tell me they're skeptical are easy to work with. Those who don't say anything usually test me by asking special questions. If their pet answers correctly, that helps them to overcome their skeptical feelings.

They want to ask things such as: what's your favorite color ball, or what's your favorite outing, or do you remember what happened two years ago when we went to such and such a place?

The answers to these questions are the kind of validations people are looking for because they want to be sure I'm really communicating with their pet and not just making things up. I definitely understand.

Sometimes their skepticism does make me a little anxious, though. It's a bit like taking a test every single time.

Remember when you went to school? Studying on your terms was better than having to take a test on a particular subject, wasn't it?

Grading was the worst. You had to prove to yourself and to your teacher and parents that you had indeed studied, and the grade said it all. To me, it's often the same when I feel I have to meet the expectations of a skeptical client.

Nonetheless, throughout my career, I've been able to turn many skeptics around when their pet has had me tell them something I couldn't possibly have known on my own. That in itself is a very satisfying accomplishment.

One of my favorite sayings is: *You can fool all the people some of the time, and some of the people all the time, but you can't fool all the people all the time.*

Over the years I've successfully spoken with thousands of animals and their humans, so if I were a fraud, I would never have had the opportunity to continue my work for over three decades.

But it's not always the client who's the skeptic. Sometimes during a communication, *I* even end up being skeptical at first about what a pet is showing me.

Yet, when I reach the end of a consultation, all the pieces usually fall into place. I can report what the pet shows me, even if it doesn't seem logical to me, but only the pet parent can actually give the correct meaning to the translation I provide, as you'll see in some of the following accounts.

For example, during my conversation with Molly Lisa who was in Spirit, I couldn't understand why she was telling me she'd already seen her mother in Spirit, when in fact, I was talking to her mother right here on the earth plane. I almost didn't mention what Molly had shown me because I couldn't quite believe it myself.

Fortunately, I did mention it, much to the delight of my client. As it turned out, it wasn't her mother Molly saw after all. It was her mother's sister who'd passed on before Molly died.

It was such a joy for her mom to know that her sister was taking care of her beloved dog now. And I was so pleased to know, with certainty, that I'd translated Molly's picture accurately.

There was another instance when I was taken aback by the pictures I was receiving. This dog told me he was in Spirit with his human mother who loved him dearly. He also sent me an image of many people sitting in a semicircle around a fireplace. One of them had a piece of paper in his hand and was reading out loud.

Because I could see the women dressed in dark colors, it seemed as if everyone was in mourning, but my human mind couldn't understand someone mourning that way for a dog.

I translated this picture as best as I could for the gentleman who was sitting in front of me. I told him I thought his dog was talking about a gathering of some kind, or a wake. I said the family was together and someone was reading from a piece of paper.

The client started to cry. He said his mother had passed away, and then their dog also passed away within just a few days. The whole family had gotten together and were listening to the reading of a poem that one of the children had written for both Grandma and their dog.

Of course, this was a validation that both his mom's spirit and their dog's spirit were right there with them when they were all together listening to the reading of the poem. And, with this man's explanation, in spite of my initial skeptical response, the pictures the dog sent me now made perfect sense.

Another example took place about a year ago with a client who'd lost her dog suddenly.

I try to refrain from making any religious translations because I don't know, and I never ask anyone, about their religious affiliation. So when her pet told me, "I'm sitting at the foot of the Mother," I wasn't exactly skeptical, but I was somewhat reluctant to translate the image I was seeing. The picture was of a woman wearing a long dress, standing with her arms outstretched toward the dog. The dog was simply sitting down next to her.

When I explained to the client what I saw, she sobbed quietly. Then she told me she'd wondered if her dog was alone on the other side, and she'd been praying to the Blessed Mother to keep her safe. When her dog's message showed her that her prayers had been answered, she was very happy indeed. Those were tears of joy.

Even if you felt highly skeptical, or even just a little bit skeptical at first, about animal communication, I truly hope the stories and articles in this book have now helped to minimize at least some of those feelings for you.

How You Can Communicate More Effectively with Your Own Pets

All animals attempt to communicate telepathically with images they hope their humans will comprehend.

They also understand our pictures, even when we don't think we're trying to communicate with them. How can they do this? They do so simply by reading the mental pictures that always accompany our thoughts.

Yes, we're creating images all the time. We just don't realize it. But think about it. Any time you even entertain a thought about doing something with your pet, your mind forms an image. You're thinking, "We should go for a walk in the park as soon as I finish what I'm doing right now," or, "It's time to get ready to leave for our appointment with the vet."

A picture of each of those events forms in your mind. Even if you're not paying any attention to it, your pet reads that picture and understands perfectly. That's why your dog will excitedly be right next to you, ready to have his leash put on, even before you're ready to go for a walk, or your cat will run and hide under the bed because the last thing she wants to do is go to the vet, and she knows, beyond a shadow of a doubt, that's where you plan to take her because she's picked up your mental image.

Even though telepathic communication is actually a natural ability for humans, and we're all born with it, learning how to send and receive these telepathic messages accurately and clearly, without putting our own human feelings, ideas, thoughts, and beliefs into them, is a skill that does require some time, practice, and awareness to develop.

It does require first quieting the mind . . . something we humans don't easily do. To really know what your pet is trying to tell you, you do need to temporarily stop producing thoughts of your own so you're able to receive thoughts from someone else. If you don't quiet your mind, it's almost like trying to make a phone call when the line is already busy.

The easiest way to achieve a clear mind is to practice meditation for ten minutes each day.

Many of us think of meditation as spending time sitting on the floor, with legs crossed, humming along. But you can also be in a meditative state when you're watching the ocean, or going for a walk in the forest, or simply sitting in your backyard, looking up at the sky and watching the clouds glide by.

You can also be in that state when you're sitting in a chair getting ready to talk with your pet ahead of time. Meditation is simply a time when you reconnect with your innermost self without thinking about your life. It's a time for simply "being."

Learning to do this does take practice, but as a preparation for being able to send and receive pictures to and from your pet, it will be so worth it.

You'll find an abundance of helpful information about *Picture Telepathy* and how you, too, can learn to communicate with your pets in my second and third books *Pets Have Feelings Too! and For Pet's Sake, Do Something! Book One*.

Not only that, but I've just recently developed an online course of instruction so that you can learn how to communicate with your pets without even having to travel to attend a seminar or workshop.

The online courses for beginners, intermediate, and advanced students are available for you to take whenever it's convenient for you. I can be available to answer questions and give you support as you practice. More information is available on my website at www.petcommunicator.com.

If only you'll learn how to use the language of pictures, you'll also be able to communicate effectively with your own pets. It's very rewarding!

Communicating with Pets in Spirit

In the previous article, you learned that the best way to connect with your pets is to be in a meditative state when you try to start a conversation with them. This is true whether your pet is currently living with you, or has already made his or her transition into Spirit.

The questions to ask a pet in Spirit, though, are usually different from the questions someone might ask when a pet is still alive. That's partly because pets who are already in Spirit now have different interests than they had when they were living with their human families.

The questions for a pet in Spirit might include:

- How are you?
- Where are you?
- Are you well?
- Did you meet someone you knew on the other side?
- What are you doing?
- Have you made new friends?
- What was your life's purpose when you were with us?
- Can you still see us and know what we're doing?

- Is your energy still around us?
- Are you sending us any signs we should watch for?
- Do you know when we think about you, and do you know when we send you our love?

Another way to connect with pets in Spirit is to send them a message just before you fall asleep. That's when your own spiritual energy quickens and you're better able to send and receive information.

Dreams are yet another way to connect with your pets in Spirit. Some dreams about pets seem to contain clear messages, while those dreams that are mainly symbolic may simply provide you with clues about what your pet wants you to know.

Your pet may even appear to you in a dream about the future and what you may need to be watching for. This is especially true if a pet wants to come back to be with you again, or wants to send you a new companion to love.

If your pet wants to return to you, she may not present herself, in the dream, with the same body she used when she was with you before. Instead, she may appear to have a different body, which may be the one she'll use when she comes back.

If your pet wants to send you a new companion to love, she may provide you with clues about where to look, as well as what to look for in a new pet.

However, when you're dreaming, you'll know beyond a shadow of a doubt that this is your pet in Spirit coming to give you a message.

It would be wonderful if you, too, can learn to communicate with your own pets, but if you, or someone you know, needs help to connect with a beloved pet on earth or in Spirit, please don't hesitate to ask me to be their translator. It would be my honor and my privilege to do so.

Contact information for Dr. Monica Diedrich:

- **Phone:** (714) 772-2207 (does not accept text messages)
- **Email:** drmonica@petcommunicator.com
- **MSN Messenger:** drmonicadiedrich
- **Skype:** drmonicadiedrich1
- **Facebook chat:** Dra Monica Dulman Diedrich
- **Mailing Address:** Upon request.

Epilogue
My Vision for the Future

In 1999, when I was completing my first book, I wrote what I envisioned for the future of animals. This is what I said 20 years ago:

I believe the future will see a lot of changes for the better concerning our animal friends as more and more of us treat them as part of the family.

In my vision for the future, animals will no longer be used for medical research, clothing, or recycled as food.

Stricter legislation will make dognapping and cruelty cases criminal offenses. I recall the news story in which a man in Northern California threw a woman's fluffy little lapdog into traffic following a minor traffic incident, and was sentenced to three years in prison. While the crime stemmed from road rage and was appalling, I was pleased that the legal system also saw it that way, although nothing could bring the little dog back.

We will see regulations on spaying and neutering across the country. When you purchase or rescue an animal, it will need to be sterilized prior to going home with you, as some shelters are doing right now, specifically in California, where such a law passed at the beginning of the new millennium. Hopefully, this will avoid the millions of animals a year that are euthanized now because they can't find a home.

Special licenses will be issued for breeders, who will operate under strict supervision in order to eradicate puppy mills.

EPILOGUE

All pets will need to be licensed, whether dog, cat, rabbit, iguana, bird, or horse. All will need some kind of identification that can't be removed, whether a microchip or retina identification, or whatever new technology we can come up with.

Humans will no longer be referred to as "owners," but rather as guardians or companions of our pets. Animals will stop being property and start having some rights.

Education for humans on how to care for pets will become just as important as education for child care.

Day-care will be available where you leave your dogs while you go to work, so that they are not left home alone. And work places will be more "dog friendly." This will reduce the number of animals needing medicine for separation anxiety and other behaviors related to boredom like excessive barking, chewing and digging.

Dog walkers and pet sitters will be trained in proper animal care and CPR, and special classes will be available through high school courses and adult education classes.

Enclosed parks, and special stretches of beaches will be safe havens for those humans who like to take their animal companions on outings.

Seat belts will eventually become mandatory for pets. Otherwise a carrier will be required. No more riding in the back of pick-up trucks or jumping out of open windows!

Pets will be allowed in all sidewalk cafes and restaurants with outside patios as they are right now in parts of Europe.

People will know they have to pick up after their animals or otherwise they will be fined.

Pet health insurance will be as common as it is for humans.

For a nominal fee, euthanasia will be available when an animal is suffering from an incurable disease.

We will see more pet cemeteries and more cremations done for pets. We will see more memorials, religious or otherwise, where we can celebrate their lives and mourn openly.

Cruelty for sport or pleasure, such as dog and bullfights and foxhunting will be unthinkable and prohibited by law, with penalties as severe as for cruelty to humans.

Finally, more dogs will work in all areas of life, whether medical assistance, therapy, search and rescue, and sniffing for termites, drugs or drug money.

We will learn from our animals to commune with nature, to work with all our senses, to smell the wind, hear the water, taste the rain, feel the moon and see the spirits.

We will be certain, no matter what our religious belief, that there is no heaven if our animal friends are not there with us.

In the meantime, let us continue to give them a place in our homes and in our hearts. Let us continue to try to improve our communication skills and maybe one day we will be able to speak to them just as our ancestors did.

We've already made great strides since I wrote that vision for the future 20 years ago. I know we have more to do, but everything I talked about has now become more of a reality, particularly in the United States, and every single point I made then has improved by a large percentage.

I continue to believe that we can achieve all of the above and more, all over the world.

I also believe we'll form associations where all animal communicators can share their gifts and pave the way for those who are coming behind us.

Animal communicators, medical empaths, and other healers will all bridge the gap between the needs of our animals and new or existing medical technology.

Communicating with animals so we can understand their needs is essential to fully integrating them into our society.

And pets, whose human companions learn to communicate with them, will no doubt lead longer, fuller, happier lives.

These are my wishes for all of our pets.

Acknowledgments

It takes a village . . . and when it comes to this book, that couldn't be more true.

I wanted to share with readers more heartwarming and inspiring stories that so many pets have told me since I wrote my last book.

These pets are not mine, so I needed to have many pet parents read, approve, and agree to let me publish what I wrote about their pets and our communications.

Every account really happened, and the names have not been changed except in a couple of stories where the pet parents made a special request that I do so.

I'm deeply indebted to their willingness to share their stories . . . some funny, some inspiring, some heartwarming, some sad, and all true.

But simply compiling their stories is only the beginning of the work that's required to bring a book like this to completion.

The stories need to be written with a certain flow so the reader can not only follow them easily, but also be able to immerse themselves in the story as well. So many items need to be checked and cross-checked, and so many questions arise that need to be answered. Then there are the technicalities of grammar, word choices, sentence structure, and so forth that all need to be finessed.

I could not have done all of this without the help of my ghostwriter/editor Colleen Fox. She's been with me since my second book, and now with my sixth book, we've once again traveled this road together.

In the process, we've become friends and we speak with one voice. She's able to intuit the true meaning of what I want to say, even when my own words don't come close.

I owe her my legacy, and I know I would not have been able to do it without her. This book is as much hers as it is mine.

I also owe a debt of gratitude to my publication editor, Yolanda Hernandez. She took the manuscript and, with great professionalism and enthusiasm, created readable formats for both the e-book and the print book versions.

My thanks go out to all of you for making this book possible. My hope is that it will inspire readers to realize that communication *is* going on between humans and animals if only we will listen to what our animals are trying to tell us.

Love and light,

Dr. Monica

Author's Note

Thank you for reading my sixth book! Why have I written another one?

After I wrote my first book in 2001, my clients wanted me to ask their pets even more questions about their health, their souls, reincarnation, and life after death, so my files grew with more and more information each year.

In response to my clients' many requests, I then wrote another book about my conversations with animals, followed by a series of three books that address how to communicate with your pets, and how to use homeopathic and other alternative remedies to help them heal.

When the fifth book was published in 2010, I thought I was finished writing, but recently I couldn't shake the feeling that there was so much more I wanted to share with you.

Then one morning, after a wonderful communication session the day before, I woke up knowing it was time to write again. The sixth book was born that day.

Even if a book doesn't become a best seller, writing it does give me a sense of accomplishment, as well as a sense of knowing that the knowledge I've gained has been shared with as many people as possible.

To help me reach an even wider audience, and to let me know if this material was beneficial, I want to ask you a favor. If you found this book interesting, and maybe even helpful, would you please take a moment to write a review so that others may also be encouraged to read it?

Reviews are very important to authors, and to the success of their books. They help to rank our books a little higher than those books that have no reviews at all. They tell other readers that a book is worth buying, and what's even more important, worth reading.

So whether you're purchasing a book on Amazon, Google, eBay, iTunes or elsewhere, please do leave your comments for me and for others.

I look forward to reading each of your reviews and I'll take to heart all the information you offer. Thank you so very much!

About the Author

Monica Diedrich knew she could hear animals speak ever since she was eight years old. Since 1990, communicating with animals has been her life's work. Improving the quality of their lives, and the lives of their human companions, is her passion.

She holds the degree of Doctor of Metaphysics and is an ordained minister. Studying Eastern traditions helped her better understand the natural interconnection between humans and animals. It also showed her how important it is to be certain that healing takes place at all three levels—physically, emotionally, and spiritually.

In addition to providing private consultations, and 15 minute individual introductory consultations for groups, Dr. Monica presents seminars and teaches classes. She's also written six books about her conversations with animals, how to help animals heal, and about the art of animal communication. She's often been a guest on various radio shows, and is a regular contributor to several TV shows.

Her first book has been translated into Spanish, Japanese, and Croatian, and all of her other books have been translated into Spanish. All of her books are award winners.

Among the honors they're received:

What Animals Tell Me

- The 2003 Nonfiction Award, Farmer's Market Online, "Direct from the Author Book Award," First Place

- The 2001 National Self-Published Book Awards from Writer's Digest, Certificate of Merit

Pets Have Feelings, Too!

- Listed on USABookNews.com for five months

- An award winning finalist in the Animals/Pets:General category of the USA BookNews Best Books 2006 National Awards

For Pet's Sake, Do Something! Book One - How to Communicate with Your Pets and Help Them Heal

- Listed on USABookNews.com for five months

- 2009 Silver Recipient, Mom's Choice Awards, Self-Improvement category

- Award Winning Finalist in the Animals/Pets:Health category of the National Best Books 2007 Awards

For Pet's Sake, Do Something! Book Two - How to Heal Your Sick, Overfed and Bored Pets with Nutrition, Supplements, Herbs and Exercise

- Listed on USABookNews.com for five months

- 2009 Silver Recipient, Mom's Choice Awards, Self-Improvement category

- Award Winning Finalist in the Animals/Pets: Health Category of the National Best Books 2007 Awards

ABOUT THE AUTHOR

- Won the Bronze Finalist award in the Pet's Category in ForeWord Magazine's 2007 Book of the Year Award; this award was presented in a ceremony held during the 2008 BookExpo America event in Los Angeles, California

For Pet's Sake, Do Something! Book Three – How to Heal Your Pets Using Alternative and Complementary Therapies

- 2009 Silver Recipient, Mom's Choice Awards, Self-Improvement category

Although she's originally a native of Argentina, Monica has lived in Southern California for over 40 years, with her husband, and children, both human and pet.

You can learn much more about her work on her website:

www.petcommunicator.com

Or contact her at:

drmonica@petcommunicator.com.

www.ingramcontent.com/pod-product-compliance
Lightning Source LLC
Chambersburg PA
CBHW060908300426
44112CB00011B/1384